Credit Mastery: Developing Aged Corporations
Build Multiple Companies With High Dollar Credit Lines

Credit Mastery: Developing Aged Corporations

Welcome to ISG3 Credit Mastery: Developing Aged Corporations:

How to Build Your Own Aged Corporation with Credit.
Build $1,000,000 credit lines in 7 months!

Keep These Quotes in Mind as You Begin
and Continue To Complete Building Business Credit

"Mental Ownership Always Comes Before Physical Ownership"
See Your Dream of $1,000,000 or More in Credit at Your Fingertips

"The Journey of a 1,000 Miles Starts with a Single Step"
Each page and section completed is another step to $1,000,000

"How Do You Eat An Elephant? One Bite At A Time"
Have patience and follow the rules and the results will show

"Quality is Long Remembered - After Price Is Forgotten"
This quote simply speaks for itself

"What is the Purpose? What it the Intention? What Is The Action I Need Take Now? "
If the Purpose and the Intention are in alignment, then move into the Action of Success!

At ISG3, we are committed to giving you the tools, tips and best practices for growing your small or midsize business. Our team of experts compiled this workbook from our years of business consulting and coaching various business and equally diverse owners into an easy-to-use format for success.

Visit our website www.isg3.com for information on how to use this workbook and guide for maximum effect.

This publication has been updated with current information from the previous 2015-2022 printing of the Aged Corporations with Credit Developer's Manual Series.

Credit Mastery Developing Aged Corporations – Sixth Printing Feb 2024 – Updated Version

SPECIAL SEMINAR TICKET COUPON WITH THIS BOOK!
Page 232

Credit Mastery: Developing Aged Corporations

Terms and Conditions:

Copyright 2015-2024 ISG3, LLC. All Rights Reserved. No part of this book / eBook may be altered in any form whatsoever, electronic or mechanical- including photocopying, recording, or by any informational storage or retrieval system without express written, dated, and signed permission from ISG, the author.

Disclaimer and Legal Notices: This report is for informational purposes only and the author, his agents, heirs, and assignee's do not accept any responsibilities for any liabilities, actual or alleged, resulting from the use of this information. This report is not "professional advice." The author encourages the reader to seek advice from a professional where any reasonably prudent person would do so. While every reasonable attempt has been made to verify the information contained in this book / eBook, the author and his affiliates cannot assume any responsibility for errors, inaccuracies or omissions, including omissions in transmission or reproduction. Any references to people, events, organizations, or business entities are for educational and illustrative purposes only, and no intent to falsely characterize, recommend, disparage, or injure is intended or should be so construed. Any results stated or implied are consistent with general results, but this means results can and will vary. The author, author's agent(s), and assign(s), make no promises or guarantees, stated or implied. Individual results will vary and this work is supplied strictly on an "at your own risk" basis. This content is only an expression of organization development components recommended to certain conditions and thereby is not lawful, bookkeeping nor economical advice. Please seek advice from with a CPA, Lawyer, Financial Adviser in these concerns. The contents of this e-book/ document/ publication are for informational or entertainment purposes only. Before engaging in any action, you should consult a CPA or Attorney for accounting and legal advice. Author, Publisher and distributors are not responsible for any profits, losses or debts incurred or accrued using the information presented within. We are not related to any credit reporting agency or lenders and give no endorsements either, the mention of FICO, DNB, Dunn & Bradstreet Trademarks are used in reference only.

This publication is strictly for use by initial purchaser and is not for redistribution or duplication in any form. (Continued on Page 233).

Copyright © 2015 – 2024 ISG3,LLC.
All rights reserved.

ISBN-13: 978-1505876314
ISBN-10: 1505876311

First Printing -	Jan 1, 2015 Copyright ©2015 ISG3,LLC.
Second Printing -	Jan 2016 Copyright ©2016 ISG3,LLC.
Third Printing -	May 2017 Copyright ©2017 ISG3,LLC.
Fourth Printing -	Jan 2018 Copyright ©2018 ISG3,LLC.
Fifth Printing –	Sept 25, 2021 Copyright ©2021 ISG3,LLC.
Sixth Printing –	Feb 1, 2024 Copyright ©2024 ISG3,LLC.Sixth

Credit Mastery™ is a registered trademark of ISG3, LLC
Suggested Retail Price: $297 US

Credit Mastery: Developing Aged Corporations

CONTENTS

Getting Started	1
Legal Entities	3
South Dakota	9
Wyoming Companies	10
New Mexico Companies	15
Colorado Companies	18
Montana Companies	24
Aged Corporation Acquisition Methods	28
Beginning the Credit Building System	32
Online Business Bank Accounts	34
Golden Rules for Business Credit Building	35
Credit Reporting Agencies for Business	44
Credit Vendors – Funding Sources – Updated 2024	44
If Loan is Not Funded	63
Credit Building Plan to $1,000,000	67
Business Plan	69
Corporate Guarantees	71
Mergers and Acquisitions – Multiplying Credit	79
TradeMarks and ServiceMarks for Funding	84
Company Information	88
Credit Submission and Usage by the Month – Updated 2024	91
Company Business Plan	123
Extended Resources for Credit – Funding Sources	159
SBA and SBIC Lenders	161
National Funding Sources	173
Credit Unions Listings	194
Second Chance Bank Accounts	198
Forms - Banking Resolutions	207
Buy Sell Agreement for Corporations with Credit	213
ISG3 Products and Services	234

Credit Mastery: Developing Aged Corporations

Getting Started

This Workbook and Guide focuses on certain key aspects of business credit development and therefore is not an all-encompassing panacea for everything involved in operating a business. With over 36 years combined experience in coaching, consulting and subcontract management we have seen the most common mistakes made by new business owners. These mistakes tend to be the aspects that most new owners tend to overlook such as the proper business structure, business plan that is a working model, marketing plan, sales plan, credit building plan and finally keeping business records that validate the business as a legal entity.

We are also including the ability to conduct multiple companies at once as a massive credit building machine.

Please keep in mind that this is the workbook used in our seminars and is thereby formatted accordingly. It does not contain the extended explanations of each entry as that is given during the seminar. If you purchased this book without attending our seminar, please visit our website for more details on seminar dates and locations www.isg3.com as we go into massive detail on everything discussed within this book along with the most advanced methods of building business credit.

Some of the material may seem to repeat again and again because it does keep in mind that we need to make clear certain points. The sections where legal entities are discussed are very repetitive as there are differences from state to state.

First decide on a Business Structure that is appropriate for your business credit building model and then we will begin the process of acquiring one for pennies on the dollar. Keep in mind that every legal entity can be converted into another form with a filing fee, however you may wish to consult with your CPA prior to a conversion due to taxable considerations.

Next is taking care of the domiciling and, legal addresses as in a virtual or executive office suite, appointment of officers, setting up telephone lines and business voice mail.

Preparing Your Business Structure from the very first pages in this book.
To make sure your business is properly setup to begin the initial Business Credit Development. First and foremost is to decide on the type of legal entity you will be building business credit on. The next consideration is the actual name of your business. Even if you are already incorporated or have been in business for a while, it is important that you check to see if your business name conflicts with other established businesses, or if it could potentially cause Trademark infringement lawsuit.

Dun and Bradstreet and Experian Business Name Search
Check to see if any businesses with the same or very similar names are listed with Dun and Bradstreet (D&B). Your business name should not already be used with the credit reporting agencies, otherwise you will always have to explain "There is another business with the same name and not ours." This is an exercise in futility that is guaranteed to waste valuable time and perpetual frustration.

Trademark Search – (Also attend the Credit Mastery™ seminar on how to use Trademarks)
Check with the U.S. Trademark Office and the Secretary of State's websites to make sure that your business name will not cause a Trademark infringement. This search is a little complicated and time consuming,

Credit Mastery: Developing Aged Corporations

however you want to do it right from the beginning. Pay special attention to all the instructions on each respective website to get accurate results.

Domain Search -
You need to verify that the domain URL (website address) for your business name is not currently being used if possible. You should purchase your business name URL (domain name) if it is available as a ".com" and immediately because every business needs a website today as much as business cards were required 50 years ago!

Home Based Business Opportunity

Building Aged Corporations with Credit Lines is a great Home-Based Business for those who wish to make large amounts of money per sale. The process is so easy to work from home that you rarely must travel out or your house to conduct business thanks to the internet. Aged Corporations with credit lines generally sell for 25% of the lines of credit available plus $1,000 per year in age of the company itself.

We suggest starting with three to six companies in the beginning and culture them to $50,000 to $100,000 then offer for sale. It is an easy sale using an online escrow company like safefunds.com or escrow.com. You can use our services for selling these as we have hundreds of buyers always waiting for an aged corporation with usable credit lines. ISG3 charges 10% of the sales price only, not from the line of credit.

Is The Future for Obtaining Business Loans Still Possible with the Current Economy and Lending Trends of 2024?

Yes, it is possible to obtain business loans with the post mortgage and credit card industries debacles. There will always be the demand for capital and sources of funds, however the stipulations by the lenders are getting tougher. Keep in mind however, that the banks cannot survive on ATM and overdraft fees (even though they will try). Banks survive on Long Term, Low Risk Loans and Mortgages! Notice <u>LOW RISK</u>! Now more than ever, but there is a solution to organizing your business to demonstrate low risk by using a few easy and low-cost methods.

Yes, every business can benefit from having a well-rounded and strategically developed business credit profile. This really has become a science in the past few years due to the information age and the ability of the internet to access databases and records in milliseconds. You just can't show a business registered at your home residence and expect to get $100,000 in credit lines ... unless you use the property and give a personal guarantee! Personal Guarantee? NOT! That's just one of the reasons you made your company a registered legal standalone entity and pay higher taxes!

Many companies get credit from local vendors and fail to get it reported and some have not gotten registered with any agencies at all.

If you fail to plan your credit development, you will certainly add a red flag to the credit reporting agencies and lenders. The best resource available today is ISG3 and their continual monitoring and credit building systems. They spend thousands of dollars a year in strategies to help new or existing companies develop a great profile.

After the mortgage industry tanked, by lending to everyone thanks to their underwriting practices, made the lending system tighten up after all the loan defaults and bank failures. One important note is that real estate goes in cycles and we should be prepared for another eminent failure as big as the 2009-2011 period.

Look, your profile at the credit reporting agencies is not only about your credit ability, it's also a reflection of your company history. Many Government Agencies and Large Corporations will not give a contract to a company that does not have a sufficient credit score. The reason is that they equate payment history to a company's ability to deliver a product or service in a timely manner. So, a company that has a history of paying its obligations on time or a few days early reflects organization, planning and a professional commitment to its obligations. They credit lines do not have to be large to make this strategy effective, but the bigger the better.

Probably at this point to give you more details and inside information from bankers and professionals who develop aged corporations and shelf corporations with credit is to follow the link to ISG3' website. It will be worth the effort and give you a deeper understanding of the methods that succeed in business credit building.

Legal Entities

Let's examine the types of legal entities that are available for use as a business and the pros and cons associated with each. Once you decide which one is best for your situation, we will begin the process of acquisition or conversion from one type to another. Use the LLC or C-Corporation Business Startup Workbook and Guide for each entity you own to keep your monthly company records legal.

Sole Proprietorship

The simplest form of business in which a sole owner and his business are not legally distinct entities; the owner is personally liable for all business debts! Sole Proprietorship's may or may not be required to file formation documents with the Secretary of State's office in the state they are doing business. However, in some states such as Nevada requires a State or Local Business License or filing a Notice of Exemption before conducting business.

So why not just form an LLC and eliminate liabilities as the record keeping, costs and taxation are almost identical!

General Partnership

A partnership in which there are no limited partners, and each partner has managerial power and untitled liability for partnership debts. Highly Not Recommended, Too Much Risk! Only recommended for Business-to-Business arrangements where both businesses are either Corporation's or LLC's and then we would recommend a Limited Partnership.

Limited Partnership

The limited partnership has limited and general partners. The general partners manage the business and are individually liable for the debts of the partnership. The limited partners are limited in the amount they can lose, by the amount of money they invested in the partnership. Only recommended for Business-to-Business arrangements where both businesses are either Corporation's or LLC's.

S-Corporation

Acceptable, but not our first choice. Limited Credit!

Credit Mastery: Developing Aged Corporations

A corporation that is eligible and does elect to be taxed under the Sub-Chapter S of the Internal Revenue Code. A corporation's status as an S-corporation is governed by the Internal Revenue Code, not by State law.

Basically, shareholders pay tax on the corporation's income by reporting their pro rate shares of pass-through items on their own individual income tax returns. This Invites Audits!

Low Potential for building business credit!

Also, if using your residence address it looks like Ma & Pa working off the kitchen table for some get rich network multilevel opportunity!

C-Corporation – YES!

A corporation is an organization authorized by state law, to act as a legal entity distinct from its owners. A corporation has its own name, and has its own powers to achieve legal purposes, and therefore, is a separate legal entity.

Higher (33% plus) Taxation on profits along with paying personal income tax is the disadvantage to this structure, however a competent CPA can do wonders to reduce adverse taxation by creative accounting or multiple legal entities. *Mean you have to pay a CPA*

Keep in mind that a C-Corporation is the easiest to build company credit with as the credit reporting agencies tend to rank them higher.

Benefits of a Corporation

Are you paying too much in taxes and putting your personal assets at risk by not having the correct business structure? Many business owners start their business as a sole proprietorship because it's the easiest structure to form. However, it can be one of the worst to operate your business with.

The benefits of a C-Corporation:

Limit personal liability of officers and owners.
Protection of personal assets from the business.
Protection of corporate assets from the owners and officers.
Build a separate business credit profile.
Easier to raise capital.
Easier to solicit investors.
Corporate Image.
Lower risk of IRS audit.

Important Note: The C-Corporation can be converted into an LLC within most states and allow the same for an LLC to convert to a C-Corporation or vice versa. These conversions are mostly done for more favorable taxation with minimal costs. The conversion is usually limited to the state filing fees, your attorney fees if you do not do it yourself online and modifying your bookkeeping with your accountant. With these conversions, the IRS must be notified, and proper forms completed. See samples forms in appendix area.

Limited Liability Company (LLC) – Absolutely!

The LLC is a hybrid between a corporation and a limited partnership. LLC's provide protection from personal liability, just as corporations do, and yet LLCs receive the tax treatment of limited partnerships, or a C corporation, whichever the members of the LLC desire. Direct pass through of profit and losses. - NO DOUBLE TAXATION! Use the LLC or C-Corporation Business Startup Workbook and Guide for each entity you own to keep your monthly company records legal.

LLC - WHY FORM AN LLC?

BMW of North America, Microsoft Network, Chrysler-Fiat, FOX Interactive Television or NFL Productions are all very familiar names that have one thing in common. They are all LLC's!

The many benefits of an LLC are:

1) **LEGAL & ASSET PROTECTION -** The LLC has a major distinct advantage being those laws governing LLC's do not allow a lawsuit to be filed against a member of the LLC for the liabilities of the LLC, whereas the main officers of a corporation are routinely named as defendants in a lawsuit filed against the corporation. Therefore, the LLC member's personal assets are safe unless he/she has personally guaranteed a debt. In many states, Lawsuit and Judgment recovery is through a process called COPE's that completely differs from corporate judgment and recovery.

2) "Pass Through" of profits and losses:

All the profits and losses of the LLC are taxed on the member's personal income tax returns. Meaning if you are a single member of an LLC, you will report the profit or loss of your LLC in your form 1040. As such, an LLC offers the benefits of a regular corporation without separate taxation. As with a partnership or a Sub-S corporation an LLC is a Tax Pass through entity.

What this means is: LLCs by default do not pay taxes. All income and losses pass-through to you as a member.

So, if you have losses in your LLC, you can claim it against your personal income on your individual 1040. It is great for a startup business.

3) Ability to easily change to another form of entity:

It's easy to change your LLC to another form of legal entity. For example, you can change it to a C-Corporation. If you are starting a company, it may be beneficial to start a company as an LLC and write off the initial losses from your personal income and change to a C-Corp when the company becomes profitable.

4) Flexibility while allocating profits or loss:

This is a major benefit of an LLC. Unlike a Sub-chapter, S Corporation where you are restricted as to how profit and loss are distributed among the owners and the type of losses can be pass-through to the owners, the members of an LLC can allocate ownership, profits and loss among the members anyway they like. In case of a C-Corporation, the profits and loss of the corporation cannot be allocated among the shareholders.

5) Business Asset protection:

==LLC held assets cannot be seized by a member's creditor.== Even if the creditor gets a judgment against a member, ==the creditor cannot get to the property owned by the LLC.== The creditor has what is known as charging order remedy. Under which, if the creditor gets a judgment against a member of the LLC, the creditor is only permitted to collect any actual cash distributions that are made by the company to the member. Therefore, if no distributions are made to the member, there is nothing to collect.

Preferred Method: Manager-Managed LLC (MemLLC) – An LLC that provides for one or more designated managers to have management rights, and with the members having no management rights. With a Member Managed LLC, the members are in a role very similar to limited partners.

Not Recommended - Member-Managed LLC (MgrLLC) – An LLC that allows the members to have management rights, very similar in operation to a general partnership, but with some degree of limited liability for the members.

Not Recommended - Single-Member LLC (SMLLC) – An LLC with only one member, who is normally the manager also, formed in a jurisdiction that allows a single member. Because they are relatively untested, the liability protections of SMLLCs are mostly theoretical, but should be like that of a sole-shareholder corporation.

LLC's and Charging Order Protected Entity's (or commonly referred to as COPE's). Visit our website for a listing of current COPE's friendly states.

Entities that control the solutions of a lender of a proprietor to a "charging order" that allows the lender to withdrawals created in regard of that possession, but do not allow—at least initially—the lender to take full possession.

From a resource security viewpoint, the advantages are obvious: The lender has no immediate remedy of getting at the resources in the enterprise, even though the lender maintains a verdict against one of the entrepreneurs.

Creditors' Remedies: A lender must have gotten through the following processes when looking to acquire resources from a COPE:

1. Obtain a judgment.

2. Charge the interest.

3. Foreclose the charging order.

4. Appoint a receiver.

5. Partition the entity.

Each phase and its part in defending the resources of the LLC from the lender is mentioned in detail below.

First, the lender must acquire a verdict, since the charging order is only available to "judgment creditors". After acquiring a verdict, the lender must acquire a charging order. The charging order is against the debtor's economical privileges to submission from the enterprise. A restricted associate or member in an LLC does not own stocks of inventory as in an organization. Partners own a package of privileges as described by the entity's managing contract, such as certain economical privileges to submission. However, associates do not own an immediate attention in the resources of the enterprise.

The lender may also take or acquire a forcible task of the debtor's right to submission from the relationship. That is, the relationship must pay the lender instead of the person until the verdict is fulfilled.

Federal Laws and Regulations

1. Federal Income Taxes of course is the most common among both entrepreneurs and the companies that they might run. Taxes are imposed on the income that is generated by the business or its owners depending on the type of entity the business is.

Corporations known as "C" corporations pay tax on the net income that they generate while "S" corporations generally do not pay a tax on the earnings of the company but passes the income and its liability on to the shareholders of the company.

Partnerships, Limited Liability Companies and sole proprietors pay the income tax from the business operations at the individual level. General information regarding federal income taxes is available at the IRS.

2. Federal Employment Taxes are taxes imposed on both employees and employers. Social Security, Medicare and Federal Unemployment taxes are imposed on the earnings of the employees of a business and are collected by the employer and paid to the US Treasury through the Internal Revenue Service. Information on employment taxes and their collection procedures are also available at the IRS. As employer businesses need to register their business with the Internal Revenue Service by filing form SS-4. Employers are also required to verify the employability of their workforce by getting proof from the employee with form I-9.

3. Other Federal Taxes and Regulations are too numerous to cover in their entirety. There are excise taxes on manufactured items including – sporting goods, firearms, alcohol, tobacco, fuel, tires and more. The federal government regulates civil rights issues, worker safety, consume r protection, labor standards and environmental protection just to name a few. Almost everything that a business does is regulated to some extent by the laws of the land. You, as an entrepreneur should educate yourself about the regulations that affect your business. Most industries have associations that represent them, and they should have information about the laws affecting their industry. Estate and Gift taxes might be imposed on business transfers and our inheritance.

Watch for Employment Laws and their Definitions (for example below is Florida's)
Employment - Any service done by an employee for the employer.
Employee - A person who is subject to the will and control of the employer as to what
must be done and how it is done.
Casual Labor - Work that is not during the employer's regular trade or business
and which is occasional, incidental, or irregular. Do not confuse casual labor with
temporary or part-time employment. A corporation cannot have casual labor, as covered

in the Internal Revenue Code.

Independent Contractor - A person not subject to the will and control of the employer. The employer does not control or direct the manner or method of job performance. The general public is aware that the person is an independent contractor.

Officers of a Corporation - Any officer of a corporation performing services for the corporation is an employee of the corporation during tenure of office, even when no compensation is received for such services. Compensation, other than dividends upon shares of stock and board of director fees, is presumed to be payment for services performed.

Limited Liability Company (LLC) – A limited liability company is treated the same as it is classified for federal income tax purposes. A person performing services for an LLC, treated as a corporation for federal income tax purposes, is an employee. A person, other than a partner or exempt employee of a partnership, performing services for an LLC treated as a partnership for federal income tax purposes, is an employee. A person, other than the sole proprietor or an exempt employee of a sole proprietorship, performing services for an LLC, treated as a sole proprietorship for federal income tax purposes, is an employee. A single member LLC may be treated as a corporation or a sole proprietorship for federal income tax purposes.

S Corporation - Salaries paid to corporate officers are considered wages. All or part of the distribution of income paid to corporate officers who are active in the business and are performing services for the business can be considered wages.

Employee Leasing Company - An employee leasing company is an employing unit that has a valid and active license under Chapter 468, Florida Statutes. (F.S.).

Salesperson - Any individual paid solely by commission under your direction and control is an employee. The law provides exemption for insurance agents, real estate agents, and barbers who are paid solely by commission. If they are paid by salary only or salary and commission, both are taxable and subject to unemployment tax. There is no federal unemployment tax exemption for barbers paid solely by commission.

Business Trusts are covered at the Credit Mastery Serminar

South Dakota Companies

A recent trend over the past few years has been a growth of high-income individuals, trusts and their companies domiciling in South Dakota with its updated business incentives.

Billionaires, major banks, credit card companies and business trusts are now using South Dakota in their overall plans to mitigate liabilities and excessive taxes.

South Dakota Has Tax Incentives!!!
When you form a new company in South Dakota then you will be able to benefit from the South Dakota's business tax incentives such as:
– No corporate income tax
– No personal property tax
– No personal income tax
– No inheritance tax
– No business inventory tax

There are several other forms of tax credits and incentives such as motor vehicles will not be subjected to state and local sales tax.

South Dakota Governor's Office of Economic Development has instituted the following programs:
– Revolving Economic Development & Initiative (REDI) Fund
– Economic Development Finance Authority (EDFA)
– South Dakota WORKS Program
– South Dakota Microloan Express
– South Dakota Jobs Grant Program
– Reinvestment Payment Program
– Proof of Concept Fund
– Dakota Seeds Program
– SBA 504 Programs

The initial filing fee is $150 plus your registered agent fee. Annual renewals are only $50 plus your registered agent fee and done online.

Application for Registration of Trademark/Servicemark	$125
Renewal of Mark Registration	$125
Assignment of Mark Registration	$125
Reinstatement Domestic (plus delinquent reports and fees)	$150 + fees

Application for Reinstatement: A Tax Clearance Certificate from the Department of Revenue MUST be received by the Secretary of State Business Office before the Application for Reinstatement can be processed. Please request the certificate at:
https://dorresources.sd.gov/f/2026, and they will forward the certificate.

Articles of Merger	$60
Statement of Dissociation	$10

Business Trust Fees
Certificate of Trust	$125

Certificate of Amendment	$125
Certificate of Cancellation	$125
Certificate of Merger or Consolidation	$125
UCC-1 or EFS-1 (one debtor name)	$20
UCC-3 or EFS-3 (one debtor name)	$20
Terminations	FREE
County Recording Fee (additional fee for UCC-1 & UCC-3)	$30 per document
DBA (Fictitious) Business Name Registration	$10
Amendment to DBA (Fictitious) Business Name Registration	$10
Renewal of DBA (Fictitious) Business Name Registration	$10
Cancellation of DBA (Fictitious) Business Name Registration	FREE

Down side, LLC's have a limited lifetime.
Foreign company registration fees are high:
In South Dakota it is called an Application for Certificate of Authority
Filed Electronically online $750
             Filed via Paper (includes paper filing fee) $765

Wyoming Companies

Wyoming ranks #1 for the best state tax climate according to The Tax Foundation who ranks the tax climates of states on 113 different variables. Those variables are placed into five major categories including corporate tax, individual income tax, sales tax, unemployment tax, and property tax. Online Filing is now available in Wyoming!

Wyoming businesses, however, are not solely subject to state taxes, but are also responsible to follow federal, state, and local regulations, file and report income to federal and state taxing authorities and report other financial and non-financial information to agencies at all levels of government.

Wyoming LLC's are the Best! (in our opinion) – Wyoming was the very first state in the USA to legalize the formation of the Limited Liability Company!

Wyoming is a COPE's friendly state for LLC's = Greater personal asset protection. Here is the latest law regarding charging order protection (or COPE's). You will note that it is to the point and ever so in our favor. It does not leave any room for legal interpretation:

"On application by a judgment creditor of a member or transferee, a court may enter a charging order against the transferable interest of the judgment debtor for the unsatisfied amount of the judgment. A charging order requires the limited liability company to pay over to the person to which the charging order was issued any distribution that would otherwise be paid to the judgment debtor."

"This section provides the exclusive remedy by which a person seeking to enforce a judgment against a judgment debtor, including any judgment debtor who may be the sole member, dissociated member or transferee, may, in the capacity of the judgment creditor, satisfy the judgment from the judgment debtor's transferable interest or from the assets of the limited liability company. Other remedies, including foreclosure on the judgment debtor's limited liability interest and a court order for directions, accounts and inquiries that the judgment debtor might have made are not available to the judgment creditor attempting to satisfy a judgment out of the judgment debtor's interest in the limited liability company and may not be ordered by the court."

Wyoming Domestic Asset Protection Trust

In order to avoid having income frozen inside the LLC as a result of a charging order, if someone goes that far. A Wyoming LLC can be owned by a Domestic Asset Protection Trust (DAPT) and thereby a trustee may make discretionary distributions to the debtor's family and perhaps even directly to the debtor. Twelve states now offer various forms of DAPT, including Wyoming.

However, significant potential benefit may be realized in terms of leverage against creditors, if ever needed. There is the chance a home state court would apply that state's law rather than Wyoming law, even with minimal home state contacts, but asset protection planning can work for solvent but prudent families and businesses who want to put up additional barriers, legally and in good faith, between their assets and potential future creditors. These additional barriers—set up in good faith, well in advance—frequently result in a better settlement.

The following is provided to assist you with those regulations and taxing authorities that enforce their compliance.

If your company will have offices in or does business with other countries, you should comply with that country's laws and regulations, however, that is beyond this short synopsis and we cannot hope to list or explain all the laws and regulations that may affect your business for your country, state or local community that may have their own unique laws.

Wyoming State Laws and Regulations

1. State Income Taxes – The state of Wyoming does not levy a personal or corporate income tax. Wyoming does not impose a tax on intangible assets such as bank accounts, stocks, or bonds, either. In addition, Wyoming does not assess any tax on retirement income earned and received from another state.

Further, there is no legislative plan to implement any of these types of taxes according to the Department of Revenue and Taxation.

2. State Employment Taxes are taxes imposed on the employers of the states for unemployment insurance, workers safety and compensation. Information about these taxes and their filing requirements can be found at the Wyoming Department of Employment's website. Employers are required to report newly hired employees.

3. Other State Taxes and Regulations, again are too numerous to list, yet most of the information regarding taxes are found at the Wyoming Department of Revenue.

The Wyoming Department of Revenue handles most of the taxes of the state including excise taxes (sales, use, lodging and cigarette tax), mineral production and severance taxes property taxes and estate taxes.

The Liquor Division serves a dual purpose of being the exclusive wholesaler of alcoholic beverages in the state and also the exclusive authority to license malt beverage wholesalers and industry representatives. They also certify local licensing authorities.

Other state agencies have regulations and fees related to the operations of various types of businesses and industries. A valuable resource to the state is the Wyoming Business Council's Business Permit Program. Business permitting and agency regulations at the state level can be overwhelming and sometimes confusing. A call to (307) 777-2843 will get you help understanding the processes and where to go. Visit the Wyoming Business Council Business Permitting page.

Local Government
Local government may regulate or permit certain types of businesses in a community. Licensing information is usually available at the city or county clerks' offices.

Businesses that are regulated at the local level usually include building contractors, daycare's, restaurants (health inspection), and businesses are subject to local zoning rules and regulations as well.

Wyoming Corporations, Wyoming Shelf Corporations, Wyoming LLC, Wyoming Aged Corporation: A key benefit of doing business in Wyoming is not having to pay corporate or personal income taxes.

Besides allowing business owners to enjoy higher earnings, the lack of an individual income tax contributes to a lower cost of labor in the state.

Wyoming has ranked #1 for business-friendly taxation on Tax Foundation's State Business Tax Climate Index every year, 2003-2020!

Wyoming - Wyoming's favorable tax laws:
- No individual or corporate income tax
- No capital gains tax on trust income
- No state gift tax
- No state estate tax
- No intangible taxes
- Low property tax
- 75 bps premium tax

Wyoming's favorable modern trust laws include:
Dynasty Trust: A 1,000-year duration on trusts (Rule Against Perpetuity)
Purpose Trust Statute: A trust that is created for a purpose rather than for a specific beneficiary.
Decanting and Reformation/Modification
Beneficiary Quiet
Strong and Private LLC Laws

Self-Settled Domestic Asset Protection Trust (DAPT) Statute:
One of only 17 states that provides Self-Settled DAPTs which allow the grantor to be a permissible discretionary beneficiary.
Trust Protector Company/Special Purpose Entities (SPEs)
Works with qualified trustee and houses the trust protector, the investment and/or distribution committees or advisors of a directed trust.
Wyoming does not require the mandatory registration of investment-advisers even if an adviser is not registered with the SEC.

Taxes in Wyoming — What Taxes?

No corporate state income tax
No personal state income tax
No inventory tax

Sales and use tax base rate of 4% with 2% county optional tax

Sales and use tax exemption on equipment used directly and predominantly in the manufacturing process, for manufactures in the 31-33 NAICS Classifications. Looking for small business tax incentives? Wyoming does not have tax incentives because Wyoming already has very low taxes. According to the Wyoming Taxpayers Association, Wyoming's personal tax burden is the second lowest in the nation.

Wyoming's major yearly personal taxes are about 4 percent of income, while the regional average ranges from 7 percent to 9 percent. The national average varies from 8 percent to 10 percent, depending on income level.

So Who really pays taxes in Wyoming?

Wyoming's largest source of revenue is mineral extraction with the second being the tourism industry. This means citizens and businesses have one of the lowest tax burdens in the country.
In 2002, Mining and Extraction contributed $4.49 billion to Wyoming Gross State Product or 26.74% of all private industry in Wyoming. Mineral Production is taxed as property tax, although it is in fact a severance tax based on market value of the natural resource being severed. Wyoming taxes minerals at 100% of value, unlike "other" property taxes, which are taxed at rates between 9.5 and 11.5%. In the end, because of higher valuations than other lands and higher tax rates, mineral production ends up paying 94.4% of all "property taxes" paid to the State of Wyoming.

In 2003, Tourism contributed $87.6 million to state and local tax receipts, with money coming from state and local sales tax, local sales, lodging tax and gasoline.

Wyoming's property taxes are low compared to most other states. The state assesses agricultural lands at 9.5% of agricultural value; residential and commercial at 9.5% of fair market value; industrial at 11.5% of fair market value; and minerals at 100% of fair market value. To calculate residential and commercial taxes, use the following equation: (Fair Market Value x 95%) x Local Mill Levy Rate = Property Tax.

For-profit corporations, limited liability corporations, limited partnerships and registered limited liability partnerships do pay an annual license tax/franchise fee to the Wyoming Secretary of State. This fee is based on a company's assets located and employed in Wyoming. Non-profit corporations pay a flat fee of $25.

Note: Wyoming Secretary of State Office is not completely Internet friendly yet for filing or making changes in records.

Most of the filings are done manually so expect 2 – 3 weeks processing time or pay expedite fees or local attorney for faster service.

State of Wyoming Funding Sources:
Wyoming Innovations Network
Dedicated to fostering an environment that creates an atmosphere for technical and monetary growth. Develops a local, national and international voice for Wyoming's technology sector and entrepreneur community. Evolves to maintain a thriving diversified
economy. Wyoming Innovations Network at www.VentureWest.org

Wyoming Business Council (WBC) Loan Programs
For more information on the loan programs, contact Portfolio/Loan Program Manager 307.777.2845 or visit the website. Wyoming Business Council www.Wyoming Business. org

Workforce Development Training Funds
The Wyoming Workforce Development Training Funds were created to assist small business with training needs.
Department of Workforce Services www.wyomingworkforce.org/how/wdtfp.aspx

The Wyoming SBIR/STTR Initiative Small Business Innovative Research (SBIR) and Small Business Technology Transfer. WSSI is to assist all qualified Wyoming small businesses and individuals in accessing the funding opportunities provided by the Small Business Innovative Research (SBIR) and Small Business Technology Transfer (STTR) Programs; $2 billion annually!
WSSI www.uwadmnweb.uwyo.edu/SBIR/

Wyoming Women's Business Center
The Wyoming Women's Business Center offers Wyoming's current and prospective women business owners the business assistance they need, including access to business counseling, training, technical assistance and networking opportunities. Wyoming Women's Business Center   www.WyomingWomen.org

– **States not currently requiring 501(C)(3) non-profit registration: Arizona, Idaho, Indiana, Iowa, Montana, Nebraska, South Dakota, Texas, Vermont, Wyoming.**

New Mexico Companies

If you are considering starting a business in New Mexico, you will need to decide how you want to organize your business. The decision involves many different factors, including questions of legal liability, tax considerations, and operational factors. It is a good idea to consult with professionals in making this decision. Many of the registration and licensing requirements imposed by State and local governments are determined by the type of entity that you select. The following is a brief summary of some of those requirements and the agencies that you should contact.

Sole Proprietorship

A sole proprietorship is not a separate entity. The owner of the business and the business itself are one and the same, and there is no need to file a document to create a sole proprietorship. The General Tax and Licensing Requirements discussed above will usually be applicable to a sole proprietorship.

Partnerships

A partnership is an association of two or more persons who carry on a business for profit as co-owners. There are various types of partnerships. As with a sole proprietorship, the General Tax and Licensing Requirements may be applicable.

General Partnerships

Although it s a good idea to have a written agreement, a general partnership can be formed orally or in writing. There is no requirement that a general partnership file an agreement or certificate before it can exist. However, the partnership may file a certificate of registration with the New Mexico Secretary of State, under the New Mexico Uniform Partnership Act.
Limited Partnerships

A limited partnership provides some protection from liabilities of the partnership for limited partners.
The partnership must have at least one general partner who is not protected from the liabilities of the partnership, and at least one limited partner. A limited partnership is formed by filing a Certificate of Limited Partnership with the New Mexico Secretary of State, in compliance with the Uniform Limited Partnership Act.

Limited Liability Partnerships. Partnerships (general or limited), who comply with certain insurance requirements, and file a registration statement with the New Mexico Secretary of State, may obtain some protection from liabilities.

Corporations - C-Corp or S-Corp

Corporations are legal entities separate from the owners. Corporations provide the owners (referred to as shareholders) with some protection from liabilities incurred by the business. A corporation is created (formed), by filing articles of incorporation. New Mexico corporations are formed by filing articles of incorporation with the New Mexico Public Regulation Commission-Corporations Bureau. Certain special purpose organizations may be required to comply with other laws before they may file articles of incorporation. For example, organizers of banks formed under State law are required to obtain permission from the Director of the Financial Institutions Division of the Regulation and Licensing Department, prior to filing articles of incorporation with the Public Regulation Commission.

Similar requirements apply to trust companies and other special purpose corporations. Many people mistakenly believe that S-corporations under Federal tax law are formed differently from other corporations under State law. A corporation's status as an S-corporation is governed by the Internal Revenue Code, not by State law.

Professional Corporations
Professionals such as lawyers, doctors, accountants, engineers, and other licensed professions may incorporate under the New Mexico Professional Corporations Act. Unlike business corporations, a professional corporation may only be incorporated by a person licensed to conduct the profession for which the corporation is organized. The corporation is organized by filing articles of incorporation with the New Mexico Public Regulation Commission-Corporations Bureau.

Limited Liability Companies
Limited liability companies (LLC's), are a relatively new type of entity. They are sometimes mistakenly referred to as limited liability corporations. The New Mexico
Limited Liability Company Act was adopted in 1993.

LLC's provide the owners with protection from liabilities that is similar to corporations. LLC's are formed by filing articles of organization with the New Mexico Public Regulation Commission- Corporations Bureau. The owners have some flexibility in deciding how an LLC will be taxed, and professional assistance is generally advisable.

Non-Profit Corporations

To qualify as a nonprofit corporation, no part of the income or profit may be distributable to its members, directors or officers. The corporation is formed by filing articles of incorporation with the New Mexico Public Regulation Commission- Corporations Bureau. In addition, charitable corporations that solicit funds may be required to register and file reports with the New Mexico Attorney General's Office under the Charitable Solicitations Act.

Foreign corporations - Businesses Organized in Other States

Businesses that have been organized in other states may be required to register and qualify to do business in New Mexico. Foreign corporations and limited liability companies should contact the New Mexico Public Regulation Commission-Corporations Bureau. Foreign partnerships should contact the New Mexico Secretary of State.

Tradename (D.B.A.) and Trademark Issues
The State of New Mexico does not require that a business register its use of a tradename (sometimes referred to as a fictitious name, doing business as or d.b.a.).

The use of a tradename that is different from the legal name of the business can have legal implications that should be discussed with your attorney. If the business has a unique tradename or mark that distinguishes it from other businesses, the business may want to register the mark with the New Mexico Secretary of State.

New Mexico's trademark and service mark registration law is designed to mirror federal trademark protection. It should be noted that the Secretary of State and the New Mexico Public Regulation Commission-Corporations Bureau, you maintain separate databases, and registration with one of these State offices may not prevent someone else from registering the same name with the other State office.

Other Applicable New Mexico Laws
Depending upon the nature of the business, and its intended activities, other State or local laws could affect your business. For example, if your business intends to raise capital by issuing securities, you may be required to comply with the New Mexico Securities Act, which is administered by the Securities Division of the New Mexico Regulation and Licensing Department. The definition of "securities" is broad and includes stock, limited liability company membership interests, limited partnership interests, notes, and investment contracts. Solicitation of capital in violation of the Securities Act, could subject a promoter to civil and criminal liability under State and Federal law.

If your business will have more than a few owners, or owners who are not going to be directly involved in the operation of the business, you should determine whether you are required to register or file a claim of exemption with the Securities Division of the New Mexico Regulation and Licensing Department.

Insurance companies, credit unions, escrow companies, trust companies and other types of businesses may also be required to comply with registration requirements and other applicable State laws. Most professions, and many other business activities, such as construction activities and businesses that serve alcohol, are also regulated by State law, and require compliance with licensing requirements. Most of the occupation licensing laws are regulated by the New Mexico Regulation and Licensing Department.
Local governments may also have special permit requirements for certain businesses.

Businesses that serve food or drink may be required to obtain permits by the municipal or county government where the business is located.

General Tax and Licensing Requirements in New Mexico

In New Mexico most businesses must register with the New Mexico Taxation and Revenue Department, and may be required to report and pay gross receipts tax and state income tax withholding on employee wages, as well as income tax on taxable income of the business. If the business has employees, it will be required to register with the New Mexico Department of Labor, and will probably be required to pay State Unemployment Taxes. In addition, if the business is required to provide Workers Compensation coverage, the business will be required to file quarterly reports with the New Mexico
Taxation and Revenue Department.

Most businesses will also be required to obtain an occupation license from the municipality or county where its office(s) is located. Property used in the business must be assessed for property taxes by the County Assessor's office in the county where the property is located.

Credit Mastery: Developing Aged Corporations

Colorado Companies

The Colorado Advantage:

First Advantage: Colorado Corporations can keep within the Articles and Bylaws the ownership of stock shares / members along with the names of corporate officers /directors. This creates a certain level of privacy as this information does not have to be recorded at the state level. The only requirement is that a Colorado corporation must have a registered agent and that agent can be the corporation itself with a physical Colorado address.

Second Advantage: Online Filings and Changes for a minimal fee and done instantly – No Expedited Services like Nevada charging $1,000 for limited changes in an hour.
Third Advantage: Colorado is ranked usually in the top ten for places to do business and live. The state also has many resources for business development and expansion.

Disadvantage: Property purchases within the state can be taxable and all other interstate transactions are taxable. This applies to aircraft purchases also. So domicile your primary holding company here and your sales division in a tax friendly state of Wyoming!

C-Corporation or S-Corporation
If your business is a corporation located or "doing business" in Colorado, it is subject to state and federal corporate income taxes. In general, a corporation will be considered to be "doing business" when it has employees or business property in Colorado. If you will be filing as an S-Corporation, your business income will be taxed as a partnership and will be exempt from corporate income taxes, although a corporate income tax return must still be filed.

Working corporate officers are still treated as employees, even in an S-Corporation, and must be paid a reasonable wage that is subject to all payroll taxes. At the end of your corporation's fiscal year, you must figure its net taxable income or net loss.

To do this, you subtract the operating expenses and "allowable deductions" from the gross income. The laws governing federal tax rates, allowable deductions and losses change frequently. Annually, you should obtain from the IRS a summary of the current applicable federal tax laws. IRS Publication #542, "Corporations," is a useful guide in determining your federal tax liability.

Every corporation, including S-Corporations, "doing business" in Colorado or deriving income from Colorado sources must file a corporate income tax return with Colorado. Colorado taxable income is determined by adding and/or subtracting various adjustments to your federal taxable income. If your corporation is "doing business" in Colorado as well as other states, you must apportion to Colorado the share of your income derived from sources within Colorado.

There are two methods that may be used to determine state corporate income tax. If you expect your federal tax liability to be $500 or more and/or your state tax liability to be $5,000 or more, you are now required to file and pay estimated taxes during the year.

Use Form 1120W, "Estimated Tax for Corporations," to figure federal estimated taxes due. The state form for making estimated tax returns is the 112 EP. Report your federal corporate income annually on Form 1120, "U.S. Corporation Income Tax Return," or Form 1120S," U.S. Income Tax Return for an S-Corporation and on your corporate state tax on Form 0112.

A corporation that owes more than $500 (and no estimated tax payments equal to the smaller of current year's or prior year's taxes) in federal income tax or $5,000 in state income tax may be subject to penalties and interest. If you receive dividends from your corporation you must report them as income on your personal income tax return and pay the appropriate income taxes.

Partnerships & Limited Liability Companies

If your business is a general partnership, limited partnership, limited liability company, limited liability partnership, limited liability limited partnership or a limited partnership association, you must file state and federal partnership income tax returns. The partnership business is not required to pay income tax.

The state and federal partnership income tax returns are used to report your business' income and expenses, changes in your balance sheet and how the partners share profits and losses. First, complete your federal return of income, Form 1065, "U.S. Return of Partnership Income" or Form 1120S, "U.S. Income Tax Return for an S Corporation." You will need this information to complete your Colorado return, Form 0106. your partner in the partnership is then responsible for his/her own income and self-employment taxes as an individual.

If you expect to owe the IRS more than $1000 in individual federal taxes, you must make federal estimated tax payments using Form 1040-ES (Estimated Taxes for Individuals). If you expect to owe Colorado more than $1,000 in individual state taxes, you must pay state estimated tax payments. Estimated payments are made using the Colorado Form 104-EP. If you and your spouse run your business together and share in the profits, your business may be considered a partnership. You should record your respective shares of partnership income or loss separately for self-employment taxes. Doing this will usually not increase your total tax, but will give your spouse credit for social security earnings on which retirement benefits are is a useful guide regarding partnership filing requirements and the allocation of income to the partners.

Self-Employment Taxes

If you are a sole proprietor, a partner in any form of partnership or a member in a limited liability company, you must file your own estimated self-employment taxes. When you work for others as an employee, your employer withholds your taxes from your paycheck. As an employee, your employer pays half of your social security taxes and you pay half. When you are self-employed, you must pay the entire amount. Estimated taxes are normally paid quarterly on actual income. If you do not have taxable income, you do not have to pay estimated taxes.

If you expect to owe the IRS more than $1,000 in federal taxes, you must make federal estimated tax payments using Form 1040-ES.

The IRS prints a number of useful publications regarding your income tax rights and responsibilities including Publication #334, "Tax Guide for Small Business," Publication #05, "Tax Withholding and Estimated Tax," Publication #533, "Self-Employment Tax" and Publication #587, "Business Use of Your Home."

Contact the IRS directly at 1-800-829-1040 for these publications and any additional information on calculating your taxable income and federal tax payments. Colorado income tax is a flat 4.63% of your adjusted federal taxable income. If you expect to owe Colorado more than $1,000 in state taxes, you must pay state estimated tax payments. Estimated payments are made using the Colorado Form 104-EP.

Property Tax
Property taxes are assessed on any real and/or personal property (land, buildings, furniture, equipment, etc.), which directly or indirectly produce income within your business.
The County Assessor determines the value of property using a market, cost or income approach. Property taxes are assessed on a percentage of actual value. To determine your property tax bill, multiply the assessed value by the local tax rate. The county assessor will mail a declaration schedule for property taxes after January 1.

Taxes must be paid by April 15 unless an extension has been obtained. The County Treasurer is responsible for mailing and collecting the actual property tax bill. Agricultural and natural resources are treated somewhat differently. You should contact your local county assessor regarding property taxes, personal and real estate, whenever you start a new business.

When You Are an Employee...

Your employer must withhold and submit to the IRS your federal income tax withheld and your portion of Social Security (FICA) and Medicare taxes withheld. Your employer is also responsible for paying state and federal unemployment taxes (SUTA and FUTA).

FOR YOUR INFORMATION
Businesses with more than $200,000 of annual employment tax obligations and $50,000 in Colorado State withholding have been required to make electronic payments since July 1, 1999.

All businesses may be required to use the electronic system sometime in the future. For more information on EFTPS (Electronic Federal Tax Payment System), call the IRS at 1-800-555-4477 or 1-800- 945-8400.
• For more information on federal taxes, contact the Internal Revenue Service at 1-800-829-1040 or visit their website at www.irs.gov.
• For more information on Colorado income taxes, contact the Colorado Department of Revenue at (303) 238-FAST or (303) 238-SERV.
• Property taxes are due on Real Estate and Personal Business Property.
• The Internal Revenue Service's Small Business Tax Education Program. (STEP) is a cooperative program with Small Business Development Centers and other local organizations to provide business tax education to the small business owner. Check into the IRS Small Business Tax Education Program in your area.
COLORADO ENTERPRISE ZONES

An Enterprise Zone is defined as an economically lagging area of Colorado in which special tax incentives are offered to businesses that expand or locate in the zone.

More information can be found in FYI General 6 "General Information about Colorado Enterprise Zones" available from the Department of Revenue at www.taxcolorado.com or by calling (303) 238-7378. The purpose of the tax incentives is to encourage economic development in the zone.

Credit Mastery: Developing Aged Corporations

There are ten tax credits or exemptions which may be taken by businesses located within a zone, including:

1. The Investment Tax Credit for businesses located in a Colorado Enterprise Zone. A 3.0% tax credit is available for equipment used solely and exclusively in a designated enterprise zone. Request FYI Income 11 for more information.

2. New Business Facility Job Tax Credit is available for new or expanding businesses located in an enterprise zone that create new jobs. A $500 tax credit against state income taxes is available for your employee. Request FYI Income 10 for more information.

3. New Business Facility Job Tax Credit for Agricultural Processing is available for new business facility employees for businesses which add value to agricultural commodities through manufacturing or processing. Request FYI Income 10 for more information.

Businesses located in an enterprise zone in a county that has been designated as an Enhanced Rural Enterprise Zone can qualify for an additional credit of $2,000 per new job (for a total credit of $2,500 per new job), and an additional credit of $500 per new agricultural processing job (for a total credit of $3,500 per new job).

4. New Business Facility Job Tax Credit for Employer Health Insurance is also available for your new business facility employee who is insured under a qualifying employer-sponsored health insurance program. Request FYI Income 10 for more information.

5. Research and Development Tax Credit for R&D carried on in an enterprise zone. Request FYI Income 22 for more information.

6. Tax Credit for Private Contributions to Enterprise Zone Administrators may be taken by any taxpayer who makes monetary or in-kind contributions to an enterprise zone administrator for the purpose of implementing the economic development plan of the zone. Request FYI Income 23 for more information.

7. Tax Credits are available for the Rehabilitation of Vacant Commercial Buildings located in an enterprise zone. Request FYI Income 24 for more information about this credit.

8. Job Training Credit will help employers who carry out a qualified job training program for their enterprise zone employees Businesses may claim an income tax credit of 10 percent of their eligible training costs. Request FYI Income 31 for more information about this credit.

9. State Sales and Use Tax Exemption for Manufacturing and Mining Equipment used in an enterprise zone. This exemption is for equipment used directly in the manufacturing or mining process (including gas and oil). It applies to sales and use tax and state-collected local taxes. Request FYI Sales 10 for more information on manufacturing equipment. Request FYI Sales 69 for more information on the mining equipment exemption.

10.Local Government Tax Incentives may be negotiated by any city or county within an enterprise zone with individual taxpayers who have qualifying new business facilities:(a) an incentive payment or property tax credit equal to or not more than the amount of the increase in property tax liability over pre-enterprise zone levels; and (b) a refund of local sales taxes on purchases of equipment, machinery, machine tools, or supplies used in the taxpayer's business in the enterprise zone. FYI's can be found on the Department of Revenue's website, www.taxcolorado.state.co.us

Colorado Business Registration, Form CR100
This is a multipurpose form used to open state sales and use tax accounts, and establish state withholding and unemployment insurance accounts.

Trade Name Registration
Is done online with the Secretary of State www.sos.state.co.us. This is used by general partnerships and sole proprietors who only need to register their trade name.

City Sales Tax Applications
These are required for city sales tax licenses or business registration. For city forms, contact the appropriate city clerk.

Secretary of State forms
To obtain any forms that must be files with the Secretary of State please contact the Secretary of State at (303) 894-2200, www.sos.state.co.us or your SBDC Small Business Hot-line at (303) 592-5920 for assistance.

Colorado Manufacturing Revenue Bond Program

Colorado Manufacturing Revenue Bond Program provides favorable tax-exempt Private Activity Bond financing to small manufacturers in Colorado. The program helps finance real estate, machinery, and equipment associated with expansion projects specific to manufacturers. Borrowers must meet all eligibility thresholds and federal tax code requirements.

Deputy Director and Business Finance Division Director
1625 Broadway, Suite 2700
Denver, Colorado 80202
(T) 303-892-3840
(F) 303-892-3848
Local Government Property Tax Incentives (Business Incentive Agreements)

The Colorado Urban and Rural Enterprise Zone Act and House Bill 02-1399 enable local governments, at their discretion, to provide property tax credits or incentive payments ('Business Incentive Agreements' or 'BIA's') based on the amount of increased property taxes for qualifying new business activity in their jurisdictions. The key provisions of these laws are summarized below: House Bill 02-1399 (formerly SB 94-182)

WHAT LOCAL GOVERNMENTS:
Municipalities, Counties, Special Districts*. At local government's option. (30-11-123, 31-15-903, 32-1-1702, C.R.S.)

ENTERPRISE ZONES:
Municipalities, Counties, Special Districts*. At local government's option. (39-30-107.5, C.R.S.)
GEOGRAPHICAL RESTRICTIONS:
None (Statewide).

TAXPAYER ELIGIBILITY:
Negotiated on case-by-case basis with taxpayers who establish a new business facility or expand an existing facility which qualifies as a new business facility, as defined in C.R.S. 39-22-508.2

AMOUNT OF INCENTIVE PAYMENT OR PROPERTY TAX CREDIT:
Up to 50 percent of the jurisdiction's levy on taxable personal property, used in connection with operation of the new or expanded business facility for current property tax year.

Up to the increment in real and personal property tax levy in current year above levy on same property in year prior to year in which enterprise zone was designated.

DURATION OF INCENTIVE PAYMENT OR PROPERTY TAX CREDIT:
Up to 10 years Local discretion, provided state enterprise zone statute remains in effect.

APPROVALS AND NOTICE REQUIRED:
Local governing board/council approval. Notify any other municipality/county in which facility is located of incentive agreement. Local governing board/council approval.
*Special districts may not enter into agreements unless the company also entered into an agreement with a municipality or county.
SCHOOL DISTRICTS: The General Assembly repealed the former authority of school districts to negotiate business incentive agreements, effective May 22, 2003. Agreements in place prior to that date continue in effect. (S.B. 03-248; 22-32-110 (ff)(III) and (gg)(III), C.R.S.)
Colorado Venture Capital Authority (VCA)

The Colorado General Assembly in 2004 passed legislation that established a Colorado Venture Capital Authority (VCA). The VCA was allocated $50 million in premium tax credits, which it subsequently sold to insurance companies. In 2005, the VCA selected a fund manager (High Country Venture, LLC) and established its first fund of approximately $25 million (Colorado Fund I), and in 2010 established a second fund of approximately $25 million (Colorado Fund II) which is also managed by High Country Venture, LLC. These funds make seed and early stage capital investments in businesses.

High Country Venture is independently operated and generally makes funding decisions. State approval is limited to ensuring that businesses receiving funding meet minimum specified requirements. The minimum and maximum investment size generally ranges from $250,000 - $3.375 million.

Investment Mission and Philosophy Mission:
To invest in the most promising and innovative early stage Colorado companies, help build them into strong, profitable businesses, and to capture that value creation through strategic financial decisions.

Investment Philosophy and Macroeconomic Analysis:
Advances in information technology, telecommunications, alternative energy and biotechnology will substantially drive significant changes in productivity. These are all areas in which Colorado can excel.

A new paradigm is developing in the biotechnology and pharmaceutical industry, whereby innovation is largely being supplied by younger, more focused biotechnology companies, commercialization and distribution is largely being supplied by mature, large pharmaceutical firms, and drug development is being shared by both. Information Technology and the Internet will continue to expand and will generate significant cash after large-scale investment. Those firms with simple, scalable business models and a high value proposition will benefit the most.

Credit Mastery: Developing Aged Corporations

Montana Companies

The reason for including Montana in our companies list is that this state has not had the volume of business registrations of other states like Delaware or Nevada, therefore it has less credit failures and associated business failure addresses. With states that have high density filings may limit in many cases establishing high credit lines you desire.

Small businesses are critical to the economic vitality and stability of the Montana economy. Their Secretary of State's Office is there to assist as you launch your new business venture but not for legal nor accounting advice.

Every Montana citizen or business is impacted by administrative rules. Administrative rules are agency regulations, standards or statements of applicability that implement, interpret, or set law or policy. An agency can also adopt administrative rules that describe the organization, procedures or practice requirements of the agency. Agencies are given rule making authority through the legislative process.

– **States not currently requiring 501(C)3 non-profit registration:** Arizona, Idaho, Indiana, Iowa, **Montana**, Nebraska, South Dakota, Texas, Vermont, Wyoming.

Business Names:
A Montana registered business name must be sufficiently distinctive from another registered business name so that it does not cause confusion in an absolute or linguistic sense.

Business names that contain key words that are different and do not copy a business name already on record are "distinguishable." For example, "Bill's Carpentry" is distinguishable from "Bill's Builders."

Geographic and numeric designations, phonetic similarities, and abbreviations of words (other than business identifiers) will make business names "distinguishable." For example, "Two for One Shoe Club" is distinguishable from "241 Shoe Club."

The following conditions WILL NOT make a business name distinguishable on the Secretary of State's records:

The use of punctuation marks or special characters, for example: "R/D Construction" is not distinguishable from "R D Construction", "R And D Construction" or "R & D Construction";

the use of articles "a," "an," "and," "&," or "the," for example: "The Painted Pony" and "Painted Pony" are not distinguishable;

the use of business name identifiers or their abbreviations, for example: "ABC Inc.," "ABC Co.," and "ABC Corp." are not distinguishable;

the substitution of an Arabic numeral for a word, for example: "2" and "Two" are not distinguishable;

the substitution of a lower case letter for a capital letter, for example: "d" and "D" are not distinguishable;

the use of plurals, possessives, or tense, for example: plurals--"Fine Line Inc." and "Fine Lines Inc." are not distinguishable; possessives--"Employee Services" and "Employees' Services" are not distinguishable; and tense--"Swim, Inc.", "Swimming Inc." and "Swims Inc" and "Swam Inc" are not distinguishable; and the use of internet domain suffixes, for example: .com,.org, and .net are not distinguishable. You can get forms and information from the Business Services Division, (406) 444-3665.

ALL INFORMATION IS PUBLIC IN MONTANA!
All information provided, including names and addresses of the principals of the entity, will be made available on the Secretary of State's web site or upon request.

Note: You can have a nominee company form the company and be it's officers or managing member!

The Montana Constitution guarantees citizens both a right to know and a right to privacy. When it comes to public records, these guarantees sometimes seem to conflict.

Article 2, Section 9 of the state constitution states: "No person shall be deprived of the right to examine documents. of state government and its subdivisions, except in cases in which the demand of individual privacy clearly exceeds the merits of public disclosure." State law further gives citizens the right to inspect and copy public records.

Article 2, Section 10 of the constitution states: "The right of individual privacy is essential to the well-being of a free society and shall not be infringed without the showing of a compelling state interest."

So which is more important? The right to privacy or the right to know?

Sometimes you can provide a citizen with information he or she seeks without allowing him or her to look at confidential portions of records. You can do this by reading a record yourself and giving the person information verbally or by photocopying the record and blocking out confidential portions.

In an attempt to balance these two rights, Montana courts have created a body of case law that may provide some guidance. If you are unsure whether a document is confidential or accessible to the public, consult your attorney.

MONTANA LEGAL AND ACCOUNTING IMPLICATIONS
There are important legal and accounting implications with respect to this entity's actions. Suitable legal and accounting advice should be secured before submission. The Secretary of State's office suggests that
such advice be sought prior to filling out forms to be sure that you understand the terms and procedures.
Montana is 6.75% to 7% corporate/business income tax.

MONTANA FORM PROCESSING TIME
Please be advised that the Business Services Division of the Montana Secretary of State will process your business documents within 10 working days of receipt.
• During this period if it is determined that your document does not meet statutory requirements, a letter outlining the deficiencies will be returned to the original submitter.
• If the document is complete and correct, the document will be filed and a letter certifying the filing of the document will be returned to the original submitter.
• If you wish a "FILED STAMPED" copy of the document to be returned with the certification letter (at no

additional fee), it will be necessary for you to submit the original and a copy of the document.

MONTANA Express Handling
• You may request 24 hour priority handling of your document by simply marking the "24 hour priority handling" box and include an additional $20.00 with your handling fee.
• You may request 1 hour expedite handling of your document by marking the "1 hour priority handling" box and include an additional $100.00 with your filing fee.

Simple Filing for Montana Company Formation (Montana Does Offer Online Filing!)

– Look how simple this is:
Executed by the undersigned person for the purpose of forming a Montana corporation (35-1-216, MCA). If the document is hand written, please print legibly or the application may be denied.

1. Select 1 corporate type and complete as requested. Please note: The business name must contain the word "corporation", "incorporated", "company", or "limited" or an abbreviation (35-1-308, MCA). If a professional corporation the business name must contain the words "professional corporation" or an abbreviation (35-4-206, MCA).
o General For Profit Corporation and the corporate name is:
_____
o Professional Corporation and the corporate name is: _____
o Close Corporation which will operate o with directors or o without directors and its corporate name is:
_____
o Professional Close Corporation which will operate o with directors or o without directors and its business name is: _____

2. The name and address of its registered office/agent in Montana:
Appointment of the Registered Agent is confirmation of the agent's consent.
Registered Agent: _____
Street Address (required): _____
Mailing Address (if different from street address):_____
City: _____ State: MT Zip Code: _____
Signature of Registered Agent: _____

3. The number of shares of Capital Stock which the Corporation has the authority to issue is (can not be left blank or "zero"): _____. Such Capital Stock shall have no par value.

4. The name and business mailing address of the incorporator is as follows:
Name: _____
Business Mailing Address:_____
City:_____ State_____ Zip Code_____

5. I, HEREBY SWEAR AND AFFIRM, under penalty of law, that the facts contained in this document are true.
Signature of Incorporator _____ Date _____

Daytime Contact:
Phone _____
Email _____

Aged and Shelf Corporations – How to Obtain Them At A Discount!

The following methods will help you avoid a costly $1,000 per year cost for a shelf company or 3 to 10 times the annual net revenues or gross sales of an existing company depending on the evaluation basis.

Method 1: Contact Local CPA's and ask them if they know of any companies for sale or that are closing without a ton of debt but with a clean credit file – Yes, they are out there! The great news is that you will get tax returns with them and buy them cheap. Keep the CPA on retainer for these companies and let the CPA know this in the beginning. This is a great way to get an aged corporation or LLC with full records and many times with a D&B Number that has a credit profile!

If you find a company with moderate debt and can service the debt great! This alternative strategy is to float the company's debt until you can finance out of it, use it as a parent entity to spawn new subsidiaries utilizing the parent company as a guarantor. This can be difficult if your finance plan has not been constructed to service this in the beginning. Debt with a new owner many times can be renegotiated as the creditor is looking for their exit from a bankruptcy that will yield nothing. If this company with debt has asset you may consider stripping the company and selling these to neutralize the existing debt after being negotiated down.

Method 2: Business Brokers – tell them you are looking to take over a company and are willing to strip out property, equipment, customer base and debt. These four items can be sold off to competitors in many cases and debt can be sold by the CPA should they have a client in need of a deduction or a loss write-off. This can sometimes relieve a business owner by selling or keeping their property or equipment and you take the structure and credit / tax history. Many time you will want to give the seller a non-compete agreement.

Method 3: The Little Know Secret To Getting an Aged Corporation for Pennies on the Dollar!

The Dissolved and Delinquent Business Reinstatement Method!

This is where you bring an existing company back into good standing with the state by paying back fees and taxes. This is a very easy process, but one must observe rules or risk a heap of trouble.   This is easily done in many states and especially Florida, Colorado, Wyoming, Texas, Nevada and New Mexico.

First go to the Secretary of State website and do a company search for a company formed 3 years earlier. You will have to enter part of a company name and for this example we will use the word "Holding". The search may result in 1 to 100 companies like "XYZ Holding, Inc".

Some States ask for dates, so enter dates that are 2 years or older into these areas. Colorado for example only allows you to view under 450 records so you may have to keep adjusting dates accordingly. For our example "holding" we had to narrow the dates to around 6 months as there were thousands of records of companies with the word "holding" within it.

Check the status of the company and look for those who are dissolved, voluntarily or administratively dissolved (or similar wording as each state has its own verbiage) will be our first choice and then those not in good standing or delinquent in paying annual fees and annual filings.

Now pick and name and look at its records and then do a free search on Dunn and Bradstreet to see if it appears. If it does then you may wish to purchase a full report or go straight to the contact letter.

Then go to DNB or Experian Business, Equifax Business and do a company search this sometimes gives more information about past legal issues of a business.

Print out everything on this company for your records and further research.

Now we will contact the names within the filing information in-order to contact the previous officers of the company which are most likely the shareholders, owner or member of that business entity. Call, email or snail mail the contact names and tell them you are interested in purchasing their company and wish to know if it still has a bank account, EIN, Resale Number, D&B Number, any outstanding debt or obligations and any known or possible lawsuits. If the company meets your criteria and you can find a mutually acceptable purchase amount, then complete the transaction. It is recommended that if the company is registered with Dunn and Bradstreet try to keep the business address the same as the original filing with D&B. This also goes for the officers of the company. (We have these forms and agreements available on the ISG3.com). Make a reasonable offer to buy the company for $100 to $500.

MAKE SURE YOU GET PERMISSION FROM A PREVIOUS MEMBER, SHAREHOLDER, OR PREFERABLY A FORMER OFFICER OF THE COMPANY!!! REINSTATEMENT WITHOUT PREVIOUS RELATIONSHIP IS ILLEGAL IN MOST STATES- SEE SECRETARY OF STATES WEBSITE FOR THEIR REQUIREMENTS.

Many times, a sale can be arranged and make sure to get all the old tax returns, banking records, Dunn's Number and the Federal EIN Tax Number.

Florida, Arizona, Colorado, Minnesota and New Mexico are great states for these resurrections. Florida many times has the EIN listed on their website and the companies Dunn & Bradstreet DNB# or CCS Federal Supplier Number.

Unfortunately, Nevada is too expensive for reinstatement's due to the annual business license cost, for example a 3yr old Nevada company will cost around $1,800 with penalties and reinstatement fees.

Use the letter on the following page for reinstatement offer to past owner/officer

Credit Mastery: Developing Aged Corporations

Offer to Purchase Company Name for Reinstatement

RE: _____ company name

   registered in the state of _____

Dear _____

I have found the company name _____ , you have filed or been an officer with in the state of _____ has been dissolved (or inactive) and is the name that we wish to conduct business under.

Before doing so I am requesting any information from you as to the state of the business before its change in status, from active, such as: does the company have any outstanding debts or taxes due? If so can you give me specific details such as amounts and dates? If you have a EIN and / or D & B DUNS Number that would be great bonus.

I would like to also purchase this from you for the amount of $_____ if you find this to be a fair offer.

Please contact me by phone at _____ or email _____ as I wish to do this as soon as possible.

Best regards,

_____

your contact address

(you can send a buy - sell agreement (in form section) for this purchase via email to the prospective seller following this inquiry / offer letter.)

The Credit Building System - Part 1

As we instruct everyone at our seminars – if you have a problem or do not agree with a particular strategy that is presented – don't proceed with it as there are options given within this system.

Our presentation of this material is based upon the understanding that you are building business credit for the right reasons and used for the specific purpose that is designated in your business planning and operating a legal business. Make sure all your debts are planned so you can service your debt! After Enron and Bernie Made-Off corporate officers are held responsible for taxes and debt if the company is not run properly.

We use multiple companies within the strategy to get to $1,000,000 in credit as the fastest possible way. This does have an overall higher cost; however, it is offset with unlimited options! You can use the extra companies as a fail-safe mechanism should one of the other companies fail, you can use them as guarantors of loans for another company or yourself and can also be sold for a profit! Should you wish to sell a company with credit that you have developed please call us at 720-443-3317 and usually we can have it sold and the transaction completed in 7 business days if it has over $50,000 of usable credit and manageable outstanding debt to income.

Within this system, you will do business between these companies and report these transactions, move money in payments of these transactions, deliver a product or service, declare the debt via UCC-1 Filings along with giving this information to the credit reporting agencies.

This is not uncommon as major brand name companies do business within their own system! A key point is that each company is properly formed and domiciled in a particular state with different officers / members/ shareholders even if they are nominees.

Financials for Lenders

When building business credit and seeking loans you must have documented financials 98% of the time.

The trouble for most small businesses is that they want $500,000 to $1,000,000 in credit but can only show annual cash flow of $100,000 or less. With this poor cash flow and matched against DnB Industry Norms ™ a company will never get a loan due to the lack of ability to repay.

There is a solution however, financials can be done in a creative fashion as long as all taxes are paid and actual products and services are rendered with money moved in payment. The bonus to this plan is reported credit.

Credit Mastery: Developing Aged Corporations

Initial Credit Building Setup for Each Company

We will start the initial business credit building from $0 for a Start-up or an existing business by using a minimum of three (3) companies - with best results using six to ten.

Make certain you have the following for each company:

1. Choose a company organization structure either C-Corp or LLC - Incorporate and have the Articles of Organization/Incorporation - Complete the Minutes of First Meeting! Using 2.5 to 3-year-old companies are best suited to our needs to develop credit faster, but not necessary (see section on Aged and Shelf Corporations).

Make sure these companies have different Directors and Officers! Use a nominee service if necessary. You do not want your name showing on all of them at the credit reporting agencies or in a corporate search by a lender.

Don't worry about opening the bank accounts as you will do a banking resolution for each company that is not seen by the state or credit reporting agencies – only check systems that appoints you as the company financial contact.

2. EACH COMPANY MUST HAVE IT'S OWN INDIVIDUAL OFFICE ADDRESS AND NOT JUST A DIFFERENT SUITE NUMBER! NO RESIDENTIAL ADDRESSES! Virtual Offices or shared office spaces will restrict your ability to gain credit. The reason is that all the banks, credit reporting agencies and data providers know exactly how many square feet is in an address and with the number of employees that can be contained in that space. They can be had for around $125 - $200 per month in large office buildings and these do not have to be in your town or city. Have the mail forwarded. A word of caution when having a virtual office reporting your monthly payments, if the credit reporting agencies find you only spend $125 per month you probably don't have any employees! Its best if they do but as an answering service.

3. Obtain a Federal EIN for each company– Form SS4 – Can be done on-line at www.irs.gov

3. Create a Website for each company or better yet purchase an aged domain name! All reporting agencies verify these! Make sure the website content encompasses everything about the company in detail with at least 25 web-pages. Also have a contact page with addresses, telephone numbers and email contact(s). Make sure website and your company name is visible in the Google, MSN and Yahoo search engines. Create a Facebook and Twitter page and next Purchase 5000 back-links to your web-page, 1000 likes on Facebook, 1,000 twitter followers from vendors on Fiverr.com. This is important nowadays as the credit reporting agencies are looking at a company from its social media presence to validate its existence.

4. Telephone communications and 411. There are several ways to obtain a local telephone number: 1) go to local telephone company and have a hard line forwarded to another phone 2) Get a local Skype Number and Subscription for $60 per year! 3) we also recommend getting an 800 number with an auto attendant and five department mailboxes (sales, accounting, customer service, etc). Another solution is to make an Asterisk PBX with voice-mail and auto attendant – this is Linux based and can use multiple Skype trunks and multiple companies, plus it can even forward call to you cell and announce the caller! Google Asterisk PBX for free install download. Then a listing with Verizon Super Pages or Yellow Pages in your area for each company. If

the reporting agency cannot find your company with directory assistance – you company is not real to them.

5. Apply for D&B (Self Monitor or credit builder program*) – Purchase the monthly plan for each company if you are looking for DnB credit reporting (price changes all the time as D&B is a marketing company).

This allows your company to report trade lines every quarter between your companies with their appropriate plan. This is a key step to getting to $500,000 in reported credit lines fast!

4. Enter your company information in the appropriate section for credit submissions and approvals, complete the business information section, bank information, EIN Approval, State and Local Business Licenses (if required). We also suggest our companion workbooks for LLC's or C-Corporation's for record keeping and business development.

5. For maximum dollar volume usage with credit accounts we suggest using friends and relatives to do their purchases on your credit accounts. When they need to purchase anything and put it on one of your credit accounts and have them pay you cash at the time of purchase! This gives you far more purchasing power using their funds.

6. Another option that we use is to purchase and resell items at a 10 to 25% discount. Stick to iPads, iPhones and high-end gaming laptops as they have a high resell value if the box is unopened.

7. Always update your calendars with dates or credit applications and approvals, charges and payments.

NOTE 1: Being too frugal with the credit reporting agency is self-defeating! They are the happiest when selling their services and reward their customers with top service (if you can read between the lines on this statement, you will understand what to do).

NOTE 2: *D&B changes their credit building/monitoring program names on a regular basis for marketing purposes, but the programs are essentially the same. Make sure you take the plan that allows you to report 25 trade-lines per quarter as we will be using this reporting.

Online Bank Accounts

These are great Small Business Bank Accounts you can get online with simplified applications:

NBKC Bank	https://www.nbkc.com/business
NOVO	https://www.banknovo.com/
Hatch	https://www.hatchcard.com/
Lending Club	https://gobank.lendingclub.com/
Mercury Bank	https://mercury.com/
NorthOne Bank	https://get.northone.com/

Merchant Accounts to take charges between your companies:
Stax https://fattmerchant.com/ merchant account
Clover https://www.clover.com/ merchant account
Helcim https://www.helcim.com/ merchant account
Payment Cloud https://paymentcloudinc.com/

Credit Mastery: Developing Aged Corporations

Golden Rules for Business Credit Building

Do You Know and Follow: The Golden Rule of Business?

Credit is Golden!

In Business - Those with the Gold Make the Rules!

Gold (Credit) Gives Timing + Options = Power

Follow All Steps Completely in Order and Without Alteration!

DO NOT RUSH THE PROCESS
- DO NOT RUSH THE PROCESS
and **DO NOT RUSH THE PROCESS!**
USE NAV.com for your credit reports

ALWAYS USE YOUR EIN - NEVER USE YOUR SSN

Call in Applications and Wait for Response!

Be Careful About Online Applications during the earlier section! A Digital Signature and text in the Terms and Conditions could very well make you personally liable and personally guarantee the debt!

Download an application whenever possible and mail in, this avoids a personal guarantee that is automatically included with online applications. If you must, call the vendor and have them mail you an application.

If they refer you to their website, just tell them that you do not feel the internet is secure and do not wish to send vital information in this format unless you can download the application to print and mail in. Plus, you want to add the credit application signature as per our instructions.

Attach as much ancillary documentation as possible to your hand-written credit applications. Add as many credit references as possible along with UCC-1 filings to the credit application submission. This makes the data entry person create more entries to validate (not all credit issuers will validate these additional credit references). Never use online credit applications, unless you wish to agree fully to their terms and conditions that you digitally sign upon submission.

Write down all application dates, communications and approval dates in the credit calendar section your month.

It costs money, time and energy to make money and the same is true about building business credit!

The business must spend money on purchases from reporting vendors to create credit trade lines!

The cost to build business credit is in the range of 10-25% of credit lines developed.

Credit Mastery: Developing Aged Corporations

Avoid applying for the same type of credit accounts in one month (fuel cards, credit cards, office supply, etc)
Do not exceed 6 applications every 30 days!

Be Careful About Online Applications during the earlier section! A Digital Signature and text in the Terms and Conditions could very well make you personally liable and personally guarantee the debt!

Download an applications whenever possible and mail in or email.

If you must, call the vendor and do application over the phone.

If they refer you to their website just tell them that you do not feel the internet is secure and do not wish to send vital information in this format unless you can download the application to print and mail in. Plus, you want to add the credit application signature as per our instructions.

Write down all application dates, communications and approval dates in the credit calendar section each month.

It costs money, time and energy to make money and the same is true about building business credit!

The business must spend money on purchases from reporting vendors to create credit trade lines!

The cost to build business credit is in the range of 10-25% of credit lines developed.

Avoid applying for the same type of credit accounts in one month (fuel cards, credit cards, office supply, etc.)

Do not exceed 6 applications every 30 days!

        Credit Application Signature
        Above Signature Line Write:
        For and on Behalf of _____ (Company Name)
        Without Prejudice UCC-1-207 / 1-308

        _____
        Applicant Signature

This is a contract modifier / disclaimer and allows you to strike items within contract. The Other Party Agrees to These Changes if they Countersign the Contract (the acceptance). You can look this up on Google as Universal Credit Code or UCC-1-308 and read the text regarding this internationally accepted code and its use.

Credit Mastery: Developing Aged Corporations by ISG3

Credit Building Plan per Company

First is Preparing Your Business Structure from the very first pages in this book.
To make sure your business is properly setup to begin the initial Business Credit Development. First and foremost is to decide on the type of legal entity you will be building business credit on. The next consideration is the actual name of your business. Even if you are already incorporated or have been in business for a while, it is important that you check to see if your business name conflicts with other established businesses or if it could potentially cause Trademark infringement.

Dun and Bradstreet and Experian Business Name Search – Check to see if any businesses with the same or very similar names are listed with Dun and Bradstreet (D&B). Your business name should not already be used with the credit reporting agencies, otherwise you will always have to explain "There is another business with the same name and not ours." This is an exercise in futility that is guaranteed to waste valuable time and perpetual frustration.

Trademark Search
Check with the U.S. Trademark Office and the Secretary of State's websites to make sure that your business name will not cause a Trademark infringement. This search is a little complicated and time consuming, however you want to do it right from the beginning. Pay special attention to all the instructions on each respective website to get accurate results.

Domain Search
You need to verify that the domain URL (website address) for your business name is not currently being used if possible. You should purchase your business name URL (domain name) if it is available as a ".com" and immediately because every business needs a website today as much as business cards were required 50 years ago!

Web Site Listed in Search Engines and Directories
You need to list and validate your business with the online directories to check if your business is listed and make sure the information is correct. We suggest free listings with: Google Local, Superpages.com, LinkedIn, Facebook, Twitter, DMOZ.org and Merchant Circle. Superpages will help establish a 411 listing later with your business telephone number used with the credit reporting agencies.

Important Note:

Websites and Trademarks/Service Marks can be valued and thereby used as collateral!!! - See Credit Mastery Seminar for detailed applications.

Business Credit Reporting Agencies

Dun & Bradstreet are used by most vendors to extend lines of credit and landlords use them to approve office leases.

Experian is used by many credit card companies and none traditional business lenders.

Equifax is most important for cash lenders such as banks.

Fact: Dunn & Bradstreet™ Controls the Majority of the Business Credit Reporting Market in the USA and Experian Business™ along with Equifax Business to a lesser extent.

Fact: We Can Influence Our Report with Strategic Planning to Meet our Goals

Fact: We must follow D&B's Rules ... Plus a few of Our Own!

Dunn and Bradstreet™ - Paydex, Rating & Score

So What is the D&B Paydex™ Score?
Paydex is Only Payment Timing!
The Paydex Score is not like a FICO™ score!

The PAYDEX™ is a 1 to 100 weighted numerical score of payment performance. The score is calculated by using up to 875 of the last payment experiences reported by vendors .
As you can see in the PAYDEX™ Score Key below, an 80 is considered a ideal PAYDEX™ score, however 80 is just paid on time.

You need 4 to 5 trade accounts that report on your business to generate a PAYDEX™ score.

This weighted average score gives more weight to the trade accounts that report higher amounts of credit extended and less weight to trade accounts that are reporting lower dollar amounts of credit.

So What is the key to the D&B Paydex™ Score?
Your Payment Timing!

The numbering system is as follows:
100 Anticipate – Paid Upon Invoice
90-95 Discount – Must Pay 21 -25 Days Prior to Due Date – Caution, the company with this score may be deemed not requiring credit as it pays so early!
86-89 PERFECT PLUS - Pays 15 -20 Days Prior to Due Date
83-85 PERFECT - Pays 6-10 Days Prior to Due Date
80 Prompt – Pays On Time - AVERAGE
70 - 15 Days Beyond Terms
60 - 22 Days Beyond Terms
50 - 30 Days Beyond Terms
 - *BELOW HERE - - SAY GOOD BYE TO CREDIT -*

40 - 60 Days Beyond Terms
20 - 90 Days Beyond Terms
20 - 120 Days Beyond Terms
UN Unavailable

DNB Rating
This is found at the top right-hand side of the business credit report. If you have provided D&B with financials of your business, you will have a rating from 5A to HH.

This score reflects your company's size based on the businesses stated net worth. If you have released financials that show a negative net worth, your business will not be rated. It will show a "-"where the rating belongs.

We highly suggest that you do not provide D&B™ with your financials! If you do not provide your financials then your rating will be a 1R or a 2R which is acceptable for developing credit lines under $500,000.

The number represents the size of your business with 10 or more employees. The 2 represents a business with less than 10 employees. The R represents that they have not been provided with financials.

After the R rating, your company will be assigned a composite credit appraisal score between 2 and 4.

DNB Composite Score

Since no financials have been reported, they base the ranking on payment history, public filings and time in business. 2 is the highest composite credit rating that you will receive without providing financial statements. 1R2 and a 1R3 will be fine if you are looking for financing.

With Dun & Bradstreet™ (DNB™) reporting and their guidelines they give to credit issuers is the requirement for six transactions a month from 10 or 15 creditors over a period of a year before they will qualify a company as creditworthy for a business loan.

DNB Problem - - - Do Not check your DnB credit more than once every two (2) weeks now or they will penalize you! They are under the premise that if you check your credit too often (in their controlling opinion) you are shopping credit and will default on all obligations.

Experian Business
Experian will actually check a trade reference for you and report it if they get the information from you. This is why it is important to include copies of any UCC-1 filings that can be telephone confirmed or other trade references.

Equifax Business
Equifax is the go to report for cash lenders that are banks and credit unions and some credit card companies may check them also.

Sage Stream
This is the newest entry on the block as a credit reporting agency who is owned by Symantec (who owns Norton antivirus). They have their own scoring models that are usually 300 to 400 points under the other big three credit reporting agencies. This is bad due to some lenders will re-score your loan approval to charge higher points. The

solution is to freeze your account with sage stream. You will have to mail in your ID and info to get this done. Here is the link for a security freeze https://www.sagestreamllc.com/security-freeze/

NOTE: Use link on ISG3.com for a special credit report provider that gives you all three personal and Equifax Business, Experian Business and you Dunn & Bradstreet report for only $49.99 per month.

SBFE – Small Business Financial Exchange is the newest player in the business credit reporting arena. This is a non-profit formed by the big top 5 USA Banks.

How Small Business Credit Cards Report to Commercial Credit Agencies

Issuer	Dun & Bradstreet	Equifax	Experian	SBFE
American Express			✓	✓
Bank of America				✓
Capital One	✓		✓	✓
Chase	✓	✓	✓	✓
Citi	✓	✓	✓	✓
Discover	✓	✓	✓	
Wells Fargo				✓

Free Tip: Credit Builder Loan
This is a method that works for both business and personal credit reporting enhancement. You must seek out a small bank or small credit union. Ask for a loan that is put immediately into a Certificate of Deposit for 3 to 12 months and you make monthly payments on this fully secured loan.

Credit Mastery: Developing Aged Corporations by ISG3

The true benefits of this Credit Builder Loan strategy is that:
1) You get an Instant Reporting Loan from a lending institution - This is significant for future bank loans as banks look at other bank loans as an admission to their exclusive country club and once, you're in – your in. 2) At the end of the agreed period you have a Certificate of Deposit. 3) You can do it again now for a larger amount and use this Certificate of Deposit as collateral.

For Dun and Bradstreet give a PAYDEX score you must have at least five (5) reporting accounts opened and reporting. Then they will average up to your last 750 payment reports to create the PAYDEX Score.

Later, once your scores are built, you will add full credit vendors as you may need them. You must be patient and allow time for the vendors' reporting cycles to get into the system and begin impacting your business credit scores. It typically takes three (3) cycles of "Net" accounts reporting to build credit scores. Once again keep in mind that it takes 90 to 120 days to build business credit scores.

Developing Your Initial Revolving Credit Accounts of Major Credit Card Vendors:
Step 1. Establish your business legally. Preferably these are clean shelf company, reinstated companies or a company in zero growth from a CPA that have a clean credit history or a that are 2-3 years old.

Step 2. Set up your company with all the requirements of appearing to be doing business with the exception of registering with credit reporting agencies. Do Not Apply for Any Credit! This will be done AFTER Step 4.

Optional: Contract as an employee a retired Fortune 100™ executive as CEO for your company. The Name of a Successful Fortune Company Executive will give instant credibility to your company.

Step 4. Register with credit reporting agencies and enroll in their credit programs. You want a 1R rating so you have 12 employees (contracted) and you **anticipate (be positive and enthusiastic about this number)** your first-year annual revenues at approximately $5,000,000. Write this number down and keep it for all future applications as you do not wish any conflicting information arising in future company research by lenders.

Step 5. Take company documents of formation along with a banking resolution to a bank that allows for interbank transfers and payments online.

Step 6. Start initial credit building steps with your company.

Banks, Lenders and Vendors who issue credit do so with the consideration that you have the ability to repay. The best way to demonstrate this is by having actual cash flow financials. If you are just getting started, then you may wish to consider the following line of thought:

If you have a portable product/ service that can be validated as a legitimate sale – then reselling your products as a distribution warehouse allows for products to be exchanged easily – especially if they are digital items with unlimited resell rights. There must be a contract for sale between companies and a finance agreement.

For example, if you were to sell a digital product for $123.45 wholesale, with a contract for 100 you just created $12,345.00 in gross sales revenue. If you allow for 30-day net payments, this becomes a credit extension that needs to be reported through your online credit building service(s). Pay off in 20 days to get the higher Paydex Score! Keep repeating this daily if possible! You must have cash on hand (or credit cards) in the amount you are seeking to transfer and report.

Everyday then, starting 20 days from the first contract, transfer the $12,345.00 from company to company to pay off that financed invoice. As you resold this to your other company it in turn resells back to another. So, you have a perfect circle – Company 1 sells to Company 2 who sells to Company 3 who in turn sells back to Company 1. As you can see, you have built financials of $370,371 in 30 days! Keep in mind you must report sales and income, with the possibility of taxes on these transactions (also sales tax or use of a resale number depending upon where a company is registered), but that is one of the costs of development. Do this for 9 months and you have generated $3,333,400 per company in sales revenues all banked by bank statements.

A rule of thumb for banks is that they lend 10% unsecured loans of annual revenues. $3,333,400 gross revenues x 10% = $333,334 per company in unsecured loans x 3 = $1,000,002!

Now, what if you don't have $12,345.00 available for daily transactions? What can be done to get the credit payments made? The good news is with the digital age of the internet and mobile phone apps the $12,345.00 can be broken down into 6 transactions of $2,057.50 if necessary and if you have the time!

Note: Some of you by now are saying what about taxes? This is where a good CPA comes in and saves the day. What you need to do is buy ten-year-old non-collectable credit card debt that is flowing on the internet for under ten cents on the dollar! Add debt to offset possible income taxes and have the CPA start on this in month nine to make sure the amount you require and have it on the books by fiscal year end.

Step 7. After first credit vendors from section 1 have reported, purchase 2 trade-lines from ISG3 and follow the rest of the credit sections. Do these in the amount of 15% of your forecasted revenue you told the credit reporting agencies. These will self-liquidate their payments in 4 - 6 months.

Step 8. Take out a 6-month Deposit Loan with ISG3's vendor (located on our website for registered members) in the amount of 10% of forecasted revenue. This gets an important large loan processes through a credit union that reports. The way a Deposit Loan is that it is a no cash out loan, so you make an interest payment and the provider makes the principal portion and the credit union reports the transaction.

Step 9. Follow the credit building instructions and continue into your new section as you complete the last.

Step 10. Write Business Plan for your company and these cannot go through the SBA programs.

Step 11. It's time to go business loan shopping!

Pull a credit report on your company to put with your business plan and make note to a lender that they cannot pull a credit report until they issue a pre-advice commitment or Conditional Letter of Intent to fund or Loan Approval based on information supplied. This way you can submit to 20 lenders if you wanted without have a credit inquiry showing up on your profile.

Step 12. Loan or Credit Line Approval and Funded. Approval great – just use the funds as per business plan and you will have any problems if you default in a year or two.

Misuse or misappropriation of funds can be serious charges to the officers of the company and if the majority is transferred as payroll or entertainment it could be construed as embezzlement also. Also with business loans and credit if you do not make at least 6-9 payments it appears as though there was no intent to repay and that is also a felony charge in many states as credit fraud.

The Credit Building System

As we instruct everyone at our seminars – if you have a problem or do not agree with a particular strategy that is presented – don't proceed with it as there are options given within this system.

Our presentation of this material is based upon the understanding that you are building business credit for the right reasons and used for the specific purpose that is designated in your business planning and operating a legal business. Make sure all your debts are planned so you can service your debt! After Enron and Bernie Made-Off corporate officers are held responsible for taxes and debt if the company is not run properly.

We use multiple companies within the strategy to get to $1,000,000 in credit as the fastest possible way and we suggest you get the Accelerated Business Tactics Vol 1 Systematic Credit Engineering for this amount of credit lines. This does have an overall higher cost; however, it is offset with unlimited options! You can use the extra companies as a fail-safe mechanism should one of the other companies fail, you can use them as guarantors of loans for another company or yourself and can also be sold for a profit!

Financials for Lenders

When building business credit and seeking hard money loans you must have documented financials 98% of the time. The trouble for most small businesses is that they want $500,000 to $1,000,000 in credit but can only show annual cash flow of $100,000 or less. With this poor cash flow and matched against DnB Industry Norms ™ a company will never get a loan due to the lack of ability to repay.

There is a solution however, financials can be done in a creative fashion as long as all taxes are paid and actual products and services are rendered with money moved in payment. The bonus to this plan is reported credit.

**CREDIT VENDORS AND LENDERS for Businesses
and Reporting Agencies They Use:**

ALLY FINANCIAL - Credit Card – Vehicle Loans – TRANSUNION
AMAZON – EQUIFAX BUSINESSES - CitiBank
AMERICAN EXPRESS - EXPERIAN – EXPERIAN BUSINESS
AMERICAN HONDA - EQUIFAX
AT&T BUSINESS - EQUIFAX
BANK OF AMERICA - EXPERIAN - TRANSUNION - ChexSystems
BANK OF AMERICA CREDIT CARDS - EXPERIAN
BARCLAYS BANK – TRANSUNION
BJ's CLUB – PERKS FOR BUSINESS CARD – EXPERIAN BUSINESS
BMW FINANCIAL SERVICES - EXPERIAN
CAPITAL ONE AUTO FINANCE - EXPERIAN - EQUIFAX
CAPITAL ONE BANK - EQUIFAX
CAR SMART - TRANSUNION
CARMAX - EXPERIAN - EQUIFAX- TRANSUNION
CBNA CREDIT CARDS - EXPERIAN - EQUIFAX
CHASE BANK- EXPERIAN – EQUIFAX
CITGO FLEET CARD - CitiBank
CITIBANK: THE STAPLES BUSINESS CREDIT ACCOUNT WITH REVOLVING TERMS, THE STAPLES COMMERCIAL BILLING ACCOUNT WITH NET PAY TERMS
CREDIT UNION OF TEXAS - EQUIFAX
CREDCO Auto Reseller - EXPERIAN - TRANSUNION
CHRYSLER CAPITAL – EXPERIAN BUSINESS - TRANSUNION - DOES NOT REPORT TO D&B
COMENITY BANK CREDIT CARDS – EXPERIAN BUSINESS
DISCOVER CARD – EXPERIAN BUSINESS - EQUIFAX BUSINESS
DRIVE FINANCE Auto Financing - EXPERIAN - TRANSUNION
FIFTH THIRD BANK - TRANSUNION
FIRST DATA MERCHANT SERVICES - CREDIT CARD MERCHANT ACCOUNT PROCESSOR
GOOD SAM FINANCE CENTER - BANK OF THE WEST – NO TAX RETURNS UNDER $100,000 ON RV'S & BOATS - EQUIFAX
HERTZ CORPORATION - EQUIFAX
HSBC - TRANSUNION
JP MORGAN CHASE- Business - TRANSUNION - ChexSystems
JP MORGAN CHASE BANK – EQUIFAX
NASA FEDERAL CREDIT UNION – EXPERIAN
NAVY FEDERAL CREDIT UNION - BUSINESS – TRANSUNION
NEW EGG – EQUIFAX BUSINESS – SYNCHRONY BANK
OFFICE DEPOT – NET 30 / CRDIT CARD THRU CITIBANK - REQUIRES PURCHASES OF $2,500 ANNUALLY WITH PG – EXPERIAN BUSINESS – EQUIFAX BUSINESS
ONEMAIN FINANCIAL – EQUIFAX
PNC BANK - EXPERIAN
RBS - CITIZENS BANK - EQUIFAX
RED CHECK - EQUIFAX
ROAD LOANS - EQUIFAX
SPRINT NEXTEL - EQUIFAX
SUNTRUST BANK - TRANSUNION
T-MOBILE - EQUIFAX - TRANSUNION
VERIZON WIRELESS - EXPERIAN - EQUIFAX
WELLS FARGO BANK - EXPERIAN

WELLS FARGO AUTO FINANCE - EXPERIAN - EQUIFAX
WELLS FARGO CREDIT CARDS - EQUIFAX
WESTERN UNION FINANCE -EXPERIAN
WFDS/WDS AUTO Finance - Business - TRANSUNION
USAA CREDIT UNION – EQUIFAX
US Bank - EQUIFAX BUSINESS

National Funding Sources

ACCION International - ACCION International is a private, nonprofit organization with the mission of giving people the financial tools they need – micro-enterprise loans, business training and other financial services – to work their way out of poverty.
www.accion.org/

Grants.gov - Grants.gov is your source to FIND and APPLY for federal government grants. The U.S. Department of Health and Human Services is proud to be the managing partner for
Grants.gov, an initiative that is having an unparalleled impact on the grant community.
www.Grants.gov

National Venture Capital Association - The National Venture Capital Association (NVCA) is a trade association that represents the U.S. venture capital industry. It is a member-based organization, which consists of venture capital firms that manage pools of risk equity capital designated to be invested
in high growth companies. www.nvca.org

Rockies Venture Club - RVC is the Rocky Mountain Region's premier networking organization that connects entrepreneurs, service professionals, investors, venture capitalists and other funding sources.   www.RockiesVentureClub.org

Reporting Creditors & Vendors
Amazon 800-301-5546 www.amazon.com
Amazon Corporate Credit Line is issued by Synchrony Bank
Amazon Net 55 is issued by Synchrony Bank

Amsterdam Promotional Products - www.amsterdamprinting.com

BANK OF AMERICA ALASKA AIRLINES BUSINESS CARD - EQUIFAX
Best Buy 800-811-7276 www.bestbuy.com
BJ's Club – Perks for Business MasterCard® - 844-271-2539
Chevron/Texaco Business Card - www.chevrontexacobusinesscard.com
(Chevron and Texaco Universal Business MasterCard® is issued by Regions Bank - Chevron and Texaco Business Card and Chevron and Texaco Diesel Advantage Card are issued by FleetCor Technologies Operating Company/Wex Fleet)
CITGO Fleet 800-561-4991 www.citgo.com
Conoco 866-289-5622 www.conoco.com
Dell 800-757-8434 www.dell.com
ExxonMobil Business Card 800-903-9966 www.exxon.com
FedEx Kinko's 800-488-3705 www.fedex.com
Fuelman - www.fuelman.com
Grainger 888-361-8649 www.grainger.com
Green Capital – www.greencapitalcredit.com
HP/Compaq Computers 800-888-9909 www.hp.com
Home Depot Commercial 800-685-6691 www.homedepot.com

Home Depot 877-969-9039
Kabbage www.kabbage.com for ebay sellers
Key Bank 800-254-2737 www.keybank.com
Kiva www.kiva.org
Lending Tree www.lendingtree.com
Lowes 866-232-7443 www.lowes.com
Marathon Universal Card - www.marathonuniversal.applyfleet.com
MSC Industrial Supply - www.mscdirect.com
Office Max 800-283-7674 www.officemax.com
Philips 66 866-289-5630 www.phillips.com
Quill 800-882-3400 www.quill.com
Sam's Club 800-301-5546 www.samsclub.com
Sears 800-599-9710 www.sears.com
Shell Fleet 800-223-3296 www.shell.com
Staples 800-767-1275 www.staples.com
Sunoco 800-935-3387 www.sunoco.com
Target 800-440-5317 www.target.com
Texaco 800-839-2267 www.texaco.com
Uline Packaging 800-958-5463 www.uline.com
Universal Platinum FleetCard MasterCard®- www.fleetcardsusa.com
issued by Regions Bank
Vouch Financial www.vouch.com need 1 peer loan guarantor
Valero 877-882-5376 www.valero.com
Wal-Mart 877-294-7548 www.walmart.com
Wex Fleet – Fuel Cards www.wexinc.com/product-recommendations
Accepted at more than 180,000 WEX Network locations nationwide.
(Wex is the issuer for Conoco Universal / Stripes / Exxon Mobil Fleet / ALON Universal / Phillips66 Universal / CITGO Fleet Universal / 7-Eleven Universal Fleet / RaceTrac Universal Fleet / QuickTrip Fleetmaster Plus / Circle K Universal Card / Gulf Universal Fleet / 76 Universal Card Union76
Wright Express 888-743-3893 www.wrightexpress.com

Additional Business Credit Cards by Bank

Brex Mastercard® Corporate Credit Card
Brex Mastercard® Corporate Credit Card, issued by Emigrant Bank or Fifth Third Bank, NA.

Chase Bank Cards
Chase Ink Business Cash card
IHG One Rewards Premier Business Credit Card
Ink Business Unlimited Credit Card - Good Credit
Ink Business Unlimited Credit Card
Ink Business Cash Credit Card
Southwest Rapid Rewards Performance Business Credit Card
Southwest Rapid Rewards Premier Business Credit Card
United Business Card
United Club Business Card
World of Hyatt Business Credit Card

Citibank
CitiBusiness® / AAdvantage® Platinum Select® Mastercard® Credit Card

Costco Anywhere Visa® Business Credit Card

Emburse Corporate Card
Emburse B2B Payment Systems
issued by Celtic Bank, a Utah-Chartered Industrial Bank

FNBO Credit Cards
Evergreen by FNBO Business Edition Credit Card
Ever ready for where your business takes you.
Earn Unlimited 2% CASH BACK2 on every purchase. Every day. Everywhere.
$200 cash bonus (20,000 points equivalent) when you spend $3,000 within the first 3 billing cycles after account is opened.2
No Annual Fee
No Category Restrictions.
No Rewards expiration
Earn 10,000 Bonus Points every Anniversary with $10,000 annual spend.
First National Bank pulls reports from both Experian and Equifax and reports to these and Transunion.

Huntington Voice Business Credit Card℠ - 4% cash-back on 1 bonus category, up to $7,000 in purchases per quarter; categories include office supply stores, computer, electronics, and camera stores, 1% cash back on all other purchases.

Sutton Bank
Ramp Visa Commercial Card and the Ramp Visa Corporate Card are issued by Sutton Bank and Celtic Bank
Airbase card is issued by Sutton Bank

U.S. Bank
U.S. BANK BUSINESS ALTITUDETM CONNECT WORLD ELITE MASTERCARD®
U.S. BANK TRIPLE CASH REWARDS VISA® BUSINESS CARD
U.S. BANK BUSINESS LEVERAGE® VISA SIGNATURE® CARD
U.S. BANK BUSINESS PLATINUM CARD

The following resources are of private funding options to help small businesses. Visit www.sba.gov for all federal programs.

Program: AC Agribusiness Partners

Advantage Capital Community Development Fund, LLC www.advantagecap.com (504) 522-4850

Equity Fund providing funding from $2,000,000 to $15,000,000

Since 1992, they have invested more than $4.1 billion in over 900 companies, spanning a diverse array of industry sectors and covering the entire risk spectrum. For-profit businesses, small agricultural businesses in rural areas, firms that focus on sustainable and organic agriculture, better-for-you branded food, indoor agriculture and vertical farming, and the reduction of food waste throughout the supply chain. Working capital, equipment, acquisition and/or improvement of owner-occupied real estate, expansion, ownership transitions, buyouts and acquisitions.

Program: Debt Fund and Equity Fund

Advantage Capital Community Development Fund, LLC

www.advantagecap.com (504) 522-4850

Contact this provider for current loan amounts. For-profit businesses, growing or growth potential firms, strategic growth initiatives. Working capital, equipment, acquisition and/or improvement of owner-occupied real estate, expansion, ownership transitions, buyouts and acquisitions.

Program: Small Business Guaranteed Loan

Advantage Capital Community Development Fund, LLC

www.advantagecap.com (504) 522-4850

Guaranteed Loans from $750,000 to $10,000,000. For-profit businesses, government entities, early stage to mature firms, growth projects: Working capital, equipment, acquisition and/or improvement of owner-occupied real estate, expansion, ownership transitions, buyouts and acquisitions.

Program: Small Business Loan

BrightBridge Inc. - www.brightbridgeinc.org (423) 424-4220

BrightBridge is a Community Development Financial Institution (CDFI) that maintains a portfolio of commercial loan programs that aim to meet the unmet capital needs of startup and existing businesses in our service area. The loan programs are distinctive in their purpose, borrowers, and terms. For-profit and nonprofit businesses located in designated low-income census tracts or owned by members of a targeted population, which includes low-income persons and eligible minorities. Also does SBA loan programs.

Program: Small Business Capital Fund

Greenline Ventures

www.greenlineventures.com (303) 586-8000

Providing loans from $250,000 to $2,000,000

Greenline's pricing and terms are generally more favorable compared to market rate capital. Borrowers headquartered or with significant operations in a low-income census tract. Providing growth capital and general working capital, acquisitions or expansion into new markets, equipment, refinancings

Program: New Markets Tax Credit Financing

Hope Credit Union Enterprise Corporation

www.hopecu.org (866) 321-4673

Since 1994, Hope Credit Union has empowered individuals, families, and business owners with access to affordable financial services. Contact provider for current lending amounts.

Grocery stores, manufacturers, commercial developers, and operating businesses in New Markets Tax Credit-designated areas of higher distress as defined by the CDFI Fund and varies with needs of the community.

Program: Kiva Crowdfunded Microloans

Kiva - www.kiva.org (828) 479-5482

Funding up to $15,000 for small businesses including start-up capital or expansion capital

Program: Kiva Crowdfunded Loans

Local Initiative Support Corporation (LISC) - www.lisc.org (212) 455-9800

Funding up to $10,000 for Startup and existing businesses working with a LISC Trustee. Providing working capital, equipment, inventory funding.

Program: Leasehold Improvement/FF&E Loans

Local Initiative Support Corporation (LISC)

www.lisc.org (212) 455-9800

Providing loans from $100,000 to $500,000

Existing businesses in LISC communities

Leasehold improvements, remodeling and expansion, furniture, fixtures, equipment

Program: Maker Space Loans

Local Initiative Support Corporation (LISC)

www.lisc.org (212) 455-9800

Providing loans from $500,000 to $3,000,000

Owners of multi-tenant maker spaces

Adaptive reuse of old industrial buildings, warehouses, and large commercial spaces to a multi-tenant facility

Program: Commercial Real Estate Loans

Local Initiative Support Corporation (LISC)

www.lisc.org (212) 455-9800

Providing loans from $500,000 to $5,000,000

Owners of commercial and mixed-use projects, acquisition and construction

Program: Permanent Working Capital

Local Initiative Support Corporation (LISC)

www.lisc.org (212) 455-9800

Providing loans from $100,000 to $500,000

Commercial and small business working capital

Program: Secured Term Loans

Native American Bank

www.nativeamericanbank.com (720) 963-6002

Contact provider for current loan amounts

Tribes, Tribal owned enterprises, Alaska Native Village Corporations, and businesses owned by individual Native Americans and Alaska Natives

Program: Secured Revolving Lines of Credit

Native American Bank

www.nativeamericanbank.com (720) 963-6002

Contact provider amounts of lines of credit

Tribes, Tribal owned enterprises, Alaska Native Village Corporations, and businesses owned by individual Native Americans and Alaska Natives

Program: Secured Term Loans

Native American Bank

www.nativeamericanbank.com (406) 338-7000

Contact provider for current loan amounts

Tribes, Tribal owned enterprises, Alaska Native Village Corporations, and businesses owned by individual Native Americans and Alaska Natives.

Program: Secured Revolving Lines of Credit

Native American Bank

www.nativeamericanbank.com (406) 338-7000

Contact provider for current lines of credit amounts

Tribes, Tribal owned enterprises, Alaska Native Village Corporations, and businesses owned by individual Native Americans and Alaska Natives

Program: Transformation Loan Fund

Primary Care Development Corporation

www.pcdc.org (212) 437-3900

Providing loans from $100,000 to $2,000,000

Federally Qualified Health Centers (FQHCs) and other community health centers; behavioral health institutions including mental health centers and substance use treatment facilities; AIDS Service Organizations (ASOs); PACE (Program of All-inclusive Care for the Elderly) programs; and safety net hospitals including ambulatory care and outpatient centers. Upgrading electronic health record systems (EHRs) to the newest generation, which includes outcomes-oriented programming and allows for real-time information exchange between organizations and outcomes measurement; implementing patient-centered service integration efforts to provide comprehensive care, including services historically provided by mental health organizations, substance-use disorder treatment programs, and others; expanding the workforce, hiring varied staff who can extend clinical capacity, engage patients in consistent care, and perform analysis of costs and outcomes data; and diversifying delivery to include emerging treatment modalities that improve patients' access to care, ex. Telehealth.

American Express Cards
AMEX American Express ® - AMEX Green Card ® - AMEX Gold Card ®
AMEX Centurion Card ® (incorrectly often call AMEX Black Card) are all great cards to have when you have credit.

Lowest Score 680 - Ave Score 720 (with the exception of the Centurion Card) PG required in most cases.

Business Green Rewards Card from American Express OPEN
APR N/A. Annual Fee $0 introductory for the first year, then $95
Gold Delta SkyMiles® Business Credit Card from American Express
APR 15.24% – 19.24% variable. Annual Fee $0 introductory for the first year, then $95.

SimplyCash® Business Credit Card from American Express – Cash Back Card for business. Introductory APR 0% for the first 9 months After that, your APR will be 12.24% – 19.24% variable. Annual Fee $0

Blue for Business® Credit Card from American Express
Introductory APR 0% for the first 9 months. After that, your APR will be 11.24% – 19.24% variable. Annual Fee $0

Business Platinum Card® from American Express OPEN
APR N/A. Annual Fee $450. or a fully secured AMEX Platinum Card ® with $50,000 secured account Use this card to maximum every month and payoff balance.

AMEX Centurion Card ® – AKA "AMEX BLACK CARD"
American Express created the Centurion Card ® in 1999 in response to an urban legend of a "black" charge card that had no limit, made of anodized titanium, and was only given to the wealthiest people.

The card is offered by invitation only to existing American Express customers who spend and pay off $250,000 per year on their other AMEX cards or using a bank that offers a fully secured Centurion Card. (see www.isg3.com website for more information on a fully secured card – this normally requires a deposit of $300,000 plus our fees). The exact criteria for issuance are not advertised, but an annual income of over $1 million and a net worth of $10 million seems to be the common ground.

You will pay a one-time $7,500 card initiation fee with annual fee of $2,500 per card. Only $10,000 per year for the perks!

BlueHub Loan Fund -BlueHub Capital - www.bluehubcapital.org (617) 427-8600

Contact provider for loan amounts for targeted economically disadvantaged small businesses. $2.6 billion Invested in low-income communities and $13.6 billion in additional capital leveraged by projects.

There have been well-publicized reports of purchases using the Centurion card for exotic cars, yachts, and even million-dollar pieces of art for the Rewards points!!!

The advantage to building massive credit using a fully secured Centurion Card ® is that once you have the card you are automatically put on a very high value marketing list sold by American Express. One you have the Centurion Card ® your will get fully pre-approved offers that require very little to complete – some just require a signature and an EIN or SSN!

Important Note 1: With American Express if you have ever had a delinquent account, they will have it in their records and will either deny you a card or require a secured card thorough an affiliate bank.

Important Note 2: With American Express you must use the card to its maximum in the first two months to establish a spending pattern. If you ignore this, you will have to call in to get your account re-approved on purchases that seem outside your normal spending patterns. You must max out this card at least 3 times a year!

Balboa Capital - www.balboacapital.com
Balboa Capital is a technology-driven direct lender that specializes in working capital loans. Easy Application /Quick Credit Decisions. Get up to $250,000 with Basic Information. Get up to $2 Million with a Full Financial Package. Absolutely No Hidden Fees! No Restrictions on How You Can Use Your Loan! **Perfect Credit Isn't Required!**

BlueHub Capital - www.bluehubcapital.org (617) 427-8600 Contact provider for loan amounts for targeted economically disadvantaged small businesses. $2.6 billion Invested in low-income communities and $13.6 billion in additional capital leveraged by projects in 2023.

Blue Vine - Invoice Financing - www.bluevine.com - 1-888-452-7805
85% of the invoice amount upfront and the rest, minus fees, when your client pays. Their standard rate is 1% per week with a minimum of 3 weeks. There are no hidden fees: No origination fees, No Termination Fees, No monthly minimums, No long-term contracts, No daily/weekly payments, No pre-payment penalties. 20-30% discount on the standard rate as you build history with Blue Vine. Here are the details one deal they completed for our client: $20,000 Invoice Amount – Repayment Due in 4 weeks – Client was issued a $17,000 advance fee and was given a $2,200 success fee when their customer paid invoice. Total cost was $800 to Blue Vine. Requirements: 530 personal credit score. Blue Vine has helped with many of the Covid-19 programs PPP and EIDL, etc.

CAN Capital - www.cancapital.com
CAN Capital can help fund business related expenses that your company may need quickly. The Business Term Loan product has a set maturity date when the business must pay off the loan. Business Loans through CAN Capital offer anywhere from $2,500 to $150,000** in financing with a range of 4 to 24 months in maturity making them ideal for any small business. No personal collateral is needed and funds can be transferred in as little as 2 business days. Business must have at least a monthly gross revenue of $4,500 or more.

Your business's monthly revenue is relatively stable. Your business has been in operation for at least 4 months. No checks! A small, fixed amount is automatically deducted from your business bank account each weekday via ACH. No personal collateral needed. Approval is based on your business's strength.

CAN Capital TrakLoan™ is the newest concept in flexible loan financing and can help small businesses smartly manage their cash flow. Ideal for businesses with credit card processing. With TrakLoan, your daily payments are tied to your payment card sales so you remit more when your sales are high and less when sales are low. Funds are available from $2,500 to $150,000. No personal collateral is needed. Learn more about TrakLoan. Instead of sending a large amount once a month, a flat percentage of your business's credit and debit card sales are automatically remitted daily. ‡ A larger amount is sent on busy sales days than on slow days. The process stops automatically when your loan is repaid.

No personal collateral is needed. A stellar credit history is not required to qualify. There are no checks to write all ACH. On a slow day your business remits less; on a busy day it remits more.
Remittances are made through processing credit and debit card sales—you can remain 100% focused on growing the business. There is no maturity date and there are no fixed payment amounts. It is quick and easy when compared to other options such as a traditional loan.

CAPITAL ONE SPARK BUSINESS Card – www.isg3.com This can be either a secured or conventional credit card – see Credit Mastery Personal Section for ideas and preparations for this card.

Celtic Bank - www.celticbank.com – Small Business Loans – Equipment Financing – SBA Approved Lender - Minimal requirements for non SBA funding – requires personal credit check and personal guarantee. 2Yr companies with $100,000 annual revenues have received $250,000 to $350,000 based on guarantor.

Celtic Bank Express Loans – $50K – $150K – Get pre-approved today and funded in as little as 5 business days - Celtic Bank is a nationwide small business lender specializing in SBA loans. The Celtic Bank Express Loan was specifically designed with small business owners in mind. Our streamlined loan program offers working capital loans with lower interest rates and extended repayment terms. Celtic Bank is the 6th largest SBA lender in the nation for FY 2015.
Requirements: at least 2 years in business.

Commerce Bank - www.commercebank.com
Small business and personal loans and auto financing. No acccount needed and not state specific.

Credibly - www.credibly.com
Credibly offers small business loans ranging from $5k up to $200k with no spending restrictions. Loans funded within 48 hours. All loans through Credibly are originated by WebBank of Utah. Requirements: Business FICO greater than 500, 6 months in business, $15k average monthly bank deposits, and U.S. – based business

DealStruck - www.dealstruck.com
Combines traditional business loans, asset-based lined of credit, inventory lines of credit, and many other revenue-based loan products .
Requires past two years tax returns along with past years bank statements. Pre-approved for up to $500,000 in funding in a few minutes on approved credit. Requirements: 600 personal credit score and at least 1 year in business

Business Loan: Business owner term loans up to $250,000 with a fixed monthly payment along with terms up to 48 months in length.

Inventory Line of Credit: Ideal for inventory-based companies that want to take grow their business by securing more inventory while keeping control of their cash flow.

Asset Based Line of Credit: Perfect for businesses that depend on steady revenue to support their business operations, this option allows small business owners to borrow against unpaid customer invoices.

Expansion Capital Group - www.ecg.com
Financing from ECG of up to $500,000 with only a simple application + 3 months bank and/or credit card statements are needed, not the business plans banks require. Tax liens up to $175,000 or open bankruptcies in the last year will not disqualify your business. Businesses with strong performance, even owners with poor credit histories can be approved. Pay back your loan with small daily payments unlike the larger monthly payments required by banks. Quote within 24 hours and money in your account as fast as 2 business days. Banks require 4–6 weeks on average. Pledge of only business assets in certain cases.

Funding Circle - www.fundingcircle.com
Borrow $25,000 to $500,000 over 1 to 5 years; Borrow for almost any business goal. Funding Circle has funded 12,000 businesses globally for a total over $1.5 billion using their private investors (almost peer to peer lending as investors choose what they wish in their portfolio).
Requirements: 620 personal credit score and at least 2 years in business
Affordable: term business loans starting at 5.49%, no hidden fees
Fast: apply in 10 minutes, 72 hour decision time and funding within 10 days upon approval.

Fundation - www.fundation.com
Fundation Group LLC is a technology-empowered direct lender that delivers small balance commercial loans. They offer fixed rate loans up to $500,000 using their own capital. Fundation fills a void in the small balance commercial loan market by offering loans to businesses that banks reject with a simplified process and capital with terms that will enable them to grow. Fundation's technology uses a streamlined the loan application process by collecting third party data and automating the majority of the credit review process. Requirements: 630 personal credit score and at least 5 years in business.

Green Capital – Receivable Financing -   www.greencapitalcredit.com
$10K+ per month minimum revenue and 6+ months in business.
Approvals within 24 hours and same day instant funding upon approval.

Headway Capital - www.headwaycapital.com
Up to $35,000 that funds next day upon approval. Headway Capital states they are simpler and quicker than working with a bank or merchant cash advance provider. Situation based lending overrides credit score. Chicago-based Headway Capital is part of Enova International (NYSE: ENVA), an online lender that advertises servicing over $15 billion in loans to more than 3 million consumers since 2004.

Huntington Bank (acquired TCF Equipment Financing) www.huntington.com
Products Include: Tax Leases; TRAC Leases; Operating Leases; Lease Purchases/Finance Leases; $1 Purchase Option Leases or Equipment Loans; Vendor Leasing/Financing; Interim Funding/Progress Funding; Equipment Finance Agreement.

Huntington Bank offers funding for:
Agriculture - Agri Equipment Finance (Grow Operations for Hemp :))
Capital Markets - Customer exposure management and asset acquisition.
Commercial Marine - Vessel loans and leases
Commercial Trucking – loans and leases
Construction - Financing for the construction & environmental industries
Franchise Finance - National Lender to Franchises
Franchise Acquisition
Golf - Golf carts, turf equipment, and most other needs
Healthcare - 18 years providing financing to the healthcare industry
Homecare - Financing the Homecare market for nearly two decades
Manufacturing - Financing a variety of manufacturing industries
Municipal - Special solutions for municipality funding needs
Specialty Markets - Funeral Vehicles, Motorcoach, and more...
Towing & Recovery Industry Equipment Financing for over 10 years.

Revolving Lines of Credit - Used to finance the ongoing originations of specialty finance companies based on agreed-upon underwriting standards.

Term Loans - Used to finance an existing pool of assets originated by an issuer, that will liquidate over time, or to finance the purchase of a pool of assets by a buyer.

Recourse and Non-Recourse - The ability and flexibility to include recourse to help mitigate risks and achieve efficient financing, where appropriate.

Huntington Commitments $50 million - $250 million (with syndication capability to $1 billion+).

Target Industries - **Commercial specialty finance companies**, including:

Small to Large Ticket Equipment
Commercial Real Estate
Private Credit/CLOs
Mortgage Warehousing/Residential
ABL
Rail
Accounts Receivable
Aircraft

Kabbage – www.kabbage.com
Kabbage claims to have funded over $1 billion to help businesses grow. Kabbage is the industry leader in providing working capital online with much going to eBay sellers. Apply, qualify and get cash instantly. No application fee. No obligation until you take cash. Ongoing access to cash, 24/7 Minimum Requirements: One year or more in business. Over $50,000 a year in revenue. Qualify for lines from $2,000 to $100,000. Loans are repaid over 6 months. No early payment fees. Fees are 1% - 12%* of your selected loan amount the first two months and 1% for each of the remaining four months. No early payment fees. Every month, for six months, you pay back 1/6 of the total loan amount plus the monthly fee. You can pay early and save.

Each draw is treated as an agreement between you and Kabbage. Draw against your line as often as once a day. Pay only for what you take.
Kabbage's maximum rate for months 1 and 2 is 12%. Third party partners may occasionally charge an additional 1.5% for months 1 and 2.
Requirements: 550 personal credit score and at least 1 year in business.

Key Bank Equipment Finance –www.keyequipmentfinance.com
Key Equipment Finance has been helping our clients with equipment, vehicles, aircraft and software financing for over 44 years. As a division of KeyBank, they offer clients direct and convenient access to a full suite of banking, lending and investment solutions.

Kiva Zip 0% Interest Loans - zip.kiva.org/borrow
Kiva Zip is a non profit that provides entrepreneurs with 0% interest loans up to $5,000. Kiva Zip loans are crowdfunded by a global community of over one million people who can be potential customers and brand

ambassadors to your business. They have a 94% funding success rate and you can apply online.

Lending Club - Google Adwords – PPC resellers – CPA ventures
Google Adwords loan offers up to $25,000 strictly for google adwords financed by Lending Club. 12 month term with 6 months is 0% interest with no prepayment penalties, then next 6 months is at 9.9% interest. Loan payment for first 6 months is just 2% of the outstanding loan amount. Last 6 months, the remaining principle and interest are paid until the full amount is paid off in the 12th payment.

They request a current business bank statement and personal guarantee using a soft inquiry via Experian Personal.

LiftForward - www.liftforward.com
LiftForward specializes in small business lending with Working Capital Loans of $10,000 to $250,000. Clients are given the opportunity to increase the size of their loan as they grow and create history with LiftForward. Many of their Clients started with a $50,000 loan and now have $1,000,000 loans as per their website. They will also refinance your MCA loan into a monthly product. Requirements: 650 personal credit score and at least 1 year in business.

LiftForward Asset Backed Loans of 50,000 to $500,000
LiftForward specializes in small business lending. LiftForward will structure the right loan product for you. Requirements: 620 personal credit score and at least 2 years in business.

LiftForward Purchase Order Financing of $50,000 to $500,000
LiftForward specializes in small business lending with a Purchase Order Financing product. Lending on reciept of purchase order opposed to invoice financing. Requirements: 620 personal credit score and at least 2 years in business.

Live Oak Bank - www.liveoakbank.com 877-890-5867
Specializes in industry focused lending from $25,000 to $5,000,000.
This Bank Likes Certificate of Deposit - prime for Certificate of Deposit Funding in this book and Credit Mastery Advanced Funding Tools.

Investment Advisory Loans - means commercial real estate funding! Also select commercial construction such as Hotels and Self Storage, etc.
Succession Financing – Live Oak can help with partner buyout lending solutions, eliminating the need for a seller note. 25% of their portfolio.
Acquisition Financing – The process of buying other businesses and providing the role of financing in structuring a transaction. 40% of their portfolio.

Extensive financing options: competitive rates, no financial covenants and no prepayment penalty. Term: 10 years for business purposes and 25 years for real estate. Loan amounts: Live Oak can fund loans starting at $25,000 up to $5 million, with an expedited process for amounts up to $350,000. Industry focused team handles your loan from application to approval in as few as 10 days and funding within 40 days many times as little as 3 days.

Marlin Finance Company – www.marlinfinance.com
Offering a comprehensive set of vendor, manufacturer and distributor finance solutions including private label programs. True business loans from $5,000 to $150,000 with flexible 6-24 month terms. Apply online in 10 minutes or less and receive funds in as little as 1 day.

Menards Contractor Card /Menards Commercial Account – issued by Capital One - EQUIFAX or EQUIFAX Business.
PG Required for all Sole Proprietorships, Partnerships and required for Corporations and LLCs in business less than 2 years.
If credit line requested is greater than $25,000 you will be required to submit your most recent two years of financial statements or tax returns. If business entity is a tax-exempt organization, please provide tax-exempt documentation. Menards Commercial Account appears as it can be a net 30-55 or credit line. 2% - 7% cash back and up to 50 free rountrip airline tickets!!! (as of Jan 2016 and can end at anytime).

National Funding - www.nationalfunding.com - Small business loans nationwide with a range of financial services and solutions, including business loans, equipment financing, merchant cash advance, and other merchant services. Business financing available from $5,000 to $500,000 with same day approvals, and funding delivered in as few as 24 hours. Requirements: 600 personal credit score and at least 2 years in business.

Navitas Equipment Financing - www.navitascredit.com
Once the equipment buying decision is made, without the capital needed to acquire it…everything comes to a stop. When your customers are looking to finance your equipment, Navitas delivers the capital solutions they need right at the point of sale.

For the Equipment Seller - Navitas works with thousands of dealers nationwide to help them provide their customers with affordable financing options to increase their sales closing rates dramatically.

For the Business Owner - Navitas provides extended payment plans to match your exact budgeting needs to acquire new or used equipment.

Finance Almost Any Type of Commercial Equipment
Approvals In Minutes
Lower Rates for Quality Credits
Support Challenging Credit Histories and Start-Ups

Newtek - www.newtekone.com
As a full-service, non-bank/bank lender, Newtek Small Business Finance is able to provide a flexible, low-cost lending option that offers longer periods than conventional loans with financing from $50,000 to $10 million. Newtek claims to have lent over half-a-billion dollars to over 800 U.S. based small businesses. Newtek will look for a minimum monthly volume of at least $10,000 with merchant account advances and been in business for over a year and process at least $3,500 in credit card sales each month. Conventional loan requirements: 620 personal credit score and at least 2 years in business.

Newtek Commercial Real Estate Loans from $500,000 to $10 Million with terms up to 25 years along with possibly 90% LTV. Fully amortizing with no balloon payments. Purchase or refinance owner-occupied real estate with funding for renovation and expansion of owner-occupied real estate. U.S domiciled for profit companies only with an average net income over the last 2 years must not exceed $2.5 million. Owners must be U.S. citizens or can be resident aliens in good standing. Owner operated businesses must occupy 51% or greater of the building.

On Deck Capital -
Offers both Business Term Loans and Lines of Credit.

On Deck Capital Lines of Credit up to $100,000 and APRs as low as 13.99% - Requirements: Companies in business at least one year with $200,000+ in gross annual revenue along with a majority owner with a 600+ personal credit score.

They base the line amount and rate based on their assessment of your business along with your business and personal credit with rates from 13.99% – 36.00% APR. Fixed weekly payments that are automatically deducted from your business bank account. A $20 monthly maintenance fee, however there are no fees charged when you draw money.

On Deck Capital Business Term Loans up to $500,000 and annual interest rates as low as 5.99% OAC. Requirements: Companies in business at least one year with $100,000+ in gross annual revenue along with at least one owner with a 500+ personal credit score. Fixed daily or weekly payments automatically deducted from your business bank account.

On Deck Capital Short Term Loans of 3-12 month terms as low as 9% Total Interest Percentage OAC with average rates of 19%+ Total Interest Percentage (Total Interest Percentage calculates the total amount of interest paid as a percentage of the loan amount). Example: On a 6-month, $10,000 loan with 9% Total Interest Percentage and weekly payments, the interest cost is $900, for a total payback amount of $10,900.

On Deck Capital Long Term Loans of 15-36 month terms as low as 5.99% Annual Interest Rate OAC - Average rates of 30% Annual Interest Rate. This rate excludes any additional fees. Example : On a 24 month, $100,000 loan with 5.99% Annual Interest Rate and weekly payments, the interest cost is $6,167, for a total loan payback amount of $106,167.

On Deck Capital Additional Term Loan Fees: One-time fee to cover cost of servicing and processing the loan. 1st loan: 2.5% of loan amount; 2nd loan: 1.25% of loan amount; 3rd+ loan: 0-1.25% of loan amount.

One United Bank – www.oneunited.com
Multi Family Housing Lender for loans of $500,000 to $7,000,000 with terms up to 40 years and closings in 45 days. Max 75% LTV.
Commercial Real Estate Loans to $7,000,000 also!

OrangeFi - www.orangefi.com
START UP Funding! Up to $250,000 with 0% for 24 months as of Mar 2019. No front fees – No prepayment penalty! This is a revolving credit line with cash advances. Based on personal credit score.

PayPal – www.paypal.com No credit check lending – based on cashflow thru your business PayPal account. Based upon a minimum of $20,000 of annual revenue accepted into your account. Flexible repay and low interest rates. The loan is underwritten by Web Bank of Utah.

Quote 2 Fund - www.quote2fund.com
Quote 2 Fund connects you to a nationwide network of over 5,000 banks and lenders with a single (free) application. Quote 2 Fund for alternative financing programs to SBA loans. Poor Credit O.K. - Bankruptcies O.K. - Tax Liens O.K. - Start-ups O.K. - No Collateral O.K. Requirements: 600 personal credit score and at least 2 years in business.

RapidFinance — Small Business Loan - www.rapidfinance.com
Low-cost loan options with terms up to 18 months. Receive up to $500,000 funding in just 3 days to use for any business purpose. Supplement existing traditional financing or alternative working capital. Requirements: Average personal FICO score of 600 and at least 2 years in business

Regents Capital Corporation –www.regentscapital.com
Whether secured or unsecured, Regents' Working Capital Loans offers affordable rates, flexible terms and rapid funding advantages. Regents' clients often incorporate these short term structures into their larger funding portfolios to cover both everyday and unexpected business expenses. With unsecured loans, how you use the cash is up to you; approval of the loan is not conditional upon the uses for the loan. Plus Equipment financing and leasing.

New Market Tax Credit - Rural Development Partners, LLC - www.rdpimpact.com (641) 585-1000. Businesses, nonprofit organizations, communities, government entities for job growth in rural America using Tax Credits.

SmartBiz. - www.smartbizloans.com
Streamlined SBA loan process for a loan from $5,000 to $350,000. SBA loans offering low rates from 6% to 8%*, 10 year terms. Pre-qualify in minutes, and get funds as fast as 7 days after application is complete. * Loans have a variable rate of Prime Rate plus 2.75% to 4.75%. Requirements: 600 personal credit score and at least 2 years in business

Stearns Bank - www.stearnsbank.com
Stearns Bank is a $2 billion, top-performing bank specializing in nationwide equipment financing with more than $600 million in equipment sales annually. The Equipment Finance Division finances new or used commercial equipment in various industries including healthcare, construction, agricultural, paving, machine tools, and vocational vehicles. The average ticket size is $50,000, however as a Preferred SBA Lender, Stearns can provide financing up to $5 million.

The Wells Fargo Business Secured Credit Card is an essential tool for businesses looking to establish or rebuild their business credit with Wells Fargo. We have had clients convert these cards in 12 months to a $10,000+ credit card. Secured credit line from $500 up to $25,000 depending on your starting deposit to fund the card. $25 annual fee. Choose between rewards points or cash back.

Wells Fargo Business Platinum Credit Card with credit lines up to $50,000, it's tailored for businesses with annual sales of up to $2 million.
Credit line up to $50,000 with No Annual fee. Optional rewards program. Choose between rewards points or cash back.

Wells Fargo Business Elite Card provides credit lines up to $100,000 for businesses with annual sales above $1 million. No annual fee. Up to $100,000 credit line and choose between rewards points or cash back.

Credit Mastery: Developing Aged Corporations by ISG3

U.S. Bank - Equifax Business
U.S. Bank FlexPerks® Business Edge™ Travel Rewards - Lowest Score 720 and easiest approval. APR 11.99% – 17.99% variable. Annual Fee $0 introductory for the first year, then $55.

U.S. Bank Business Edge™ Platinum - Lowest Score 720 – 750. Introductory APR 0% for the first 12 months After that, your APR will be 9.99% – 17.99% variable. Annual Fee $0

U.S. Bank Business Edge™ Cash Rewards - Lowest Score 720- 750. Introductory APR 0% for the first 9 billing cycles on purchases. After that, your APR will be 11.99% – 17.99% variable. Annual Fee $0

U.S. Bank Business Edge™ Select Rewards - Lowest Score 720 -750. Introductory APR 0% for the first 9 months After that, your APR will be 11.99% – 17.99% variable. Annual Fee $0

If Loan or Credit Line Is Not Funded:

Time to Use Advanced Business Credit Tactics

OK, try a leased CD (Certificate of Deposit). These can be arranged as a non-liened non-encumbered deposit.

This is the least expensive way to go. The bank can't use these funds as a guarantee in this case, however the bank will get a multiplier from the Federal Reserve for these deposits that can offset some of the lending risk.

Make sure your loan officer knows this! These can be processed in 14 days upon approval in most cases! Provider will need to verify your lease funds and have them escrowed prior to transfers.

An example is a loan was being considered by a bank that did not have adequate reserves for the loan. $2M dollars of CD's were placed in bank at a lease cost of 7.5% or $150,000. The client did not have the $150,000 and made arrangements for a flash funding source to provide the funds that were escrow secured. The bank did 500,000 per day in concert with the escrow company.

The flash funding for the $150,000 cost the client 20% or $30,000 and had to place those funds in a separate escrow arrangement. All in all the cost for the $2M loan was $180,000 or 9%.

OK, we turn to our advanced business credit tactics for a Collateral CD (Certificate of Deposit). These can be arranged as a full collateral guaranteed deposit. This is the most expensive way to go and slowest of this method as it takes 60 days sometimes. Also, the LTV on these are 70% so plan accordingly.

Options

Option: Sell account receivables and their contracts - use caution when taking this route to ensure that these funds can be repaid on time.

Option: Use another company to guarantee your loan. It eliminates a personal guarantee and the lender will want a loan package on both companies along with formal documentation from executives as to the transaction – also be prepared for telephone calls from bankers on this strategy. This is another reason for a multiple company strategy!

Option: Perform a Merger or Acquisition if not publicly traded, this is not that complicated as it is done at a state level then notify the IRS on the changes. When you fold another company into another it can blend the financials to make the primary company look larger. This may have tax implications and you need to consult a CPA regarding tax matters. Once Loan is approved and issued the process can be reversed if desired.

Business Trust Deposit Loans - Currently on Hold – check www.isg3.com for updates

Incredible Reporting with No Credit Check or Personal Guarantee!
Go as Big as You Can Afford!
Deposit Loans are one of the most fantastic tools used for enhancing your corporate or personal credit profile!

Business Trust Deposit Loans are structured as to have no cash out to the borrower – in other words you obtain a loan through a service that retains the loan funds and you pay interest only on the loan for a period of 3 to 12 months.

This is great credit building tool and now is the time to obtain a Deposit Loan in the amount of $50,000 to $150,000. This will have an associated cost of 2.99 to 7.99 % APR. So, make sure you can service your debt costs and keep positive reporting on this loan.

You can pay this loan off early, but to get your corporation the maximum credit you will want to go 6 months on this plan.

This loan is processed through a reporting credit union with loan amounts from $25,000 to $1,000,000.

After repaying this loan you can take a business plan into a bank and normally get a loan in the amount of $25,000 to $50,000. The reason is you now have a proven track record of paid credit history. Your only weak spot can be your cash flow for your ability to repay, but this is your company's objective to service your debt obligations.

Obtain a Verify on Demand – Proof of Funds account to show blocked funds – see our Credit Mastery Advanced Tools for the entire process.

Leasing a Certificate of Deposit (CD) * Strategy for over $1 Million

Leasing a CD is fairly simple process where you can simply place fees in escrow and released as per agreement.

The CDs are also available and we have placed these several times at banks and credit unions to show financial strength of you the Client. This is used when the bank will do a loan if they had the extra funds. So you are in essence providing your loan funds by leasing a bank instrument on an annual basis.

This is done at a far lower cost and for amounts as low as $500,000 to $50M USD. Fees historically ranged from 4.5% to 7.5%.

1) Provide proof of funds in the amount of the placement fee based and submit along with CIS (Client Information Sheet) and Passport.

2) After due diligence, you will enter into contract that stipulates the terms and conditions along with the name of the bank or credit union you wish the CDs to be placed.

3) After contract, CD-NC's will be placed at bank or credit union as per contract and escrow agreement.
We have placed $5M in one week via escrow providing $1M per day with a 7.5% fee.
see our Credit Mastery Advanced Tools for the entire process.

Private Investor Funds – SEC Reg D Exemption
For capitalization without personal guarantees or credit checks we recommend using an exempted Registered Security with a Form D – Reg D offering. This consists of writing a private placement memorandum and contacting broker dealers to fund with project from private investors and hedge funds. These are usually high interest vehicles around 12% - 16% and this interest is paid quarterly to the investors. So $1,000,000 will have a

debt service cost of $120,000 to $160,000 annually – make sure your companies business can support this before starting.

This is not a difficult process and is faster to obtain capital than conventional credit building.

This is an entirely different process than building business. see our Credit Mastery Advanced Tools for the entire process.

SBA LOANS - <u>BRING A BANKABLE BUSINESS PLAN</u>!
– without this they will not help you obtain any type of loan.

Small businesses are the foundation and driving force behind our country's entrepreneurial spirit. The Small Business Administration (SBA) can help you start or expand your business if you meet their qualifications.

SBA Loans can offer greater flexibility with lower interest rates and longer terms for more affordable payments. They are designed to support the growth of start-ups and other existing businesses that might not benefit from normal lending channels.

Start your business.
Purchase machinery, equipment, furniture or fixtures.
Acquire inventory or working capital.
Purchase an existing business.
Purchase, construct, expand or improve a building.
Refinance existing business related debt.
With an SBA Loan:

7(a) – Existing Business can obtain Term Loans up to $2,000,000
Express Lines of Credit up to $350,000
504 CDC Real Estate Loans up to $4,000,000
SBA encourages Minority and Women start up and ongoing businesses

SBA Loan Guarantee Programs
From SBA.gov: SBA provides a number of financial assistance programs for small businesses including 7(a), 504 and disaster assistance loans. Within this section, we'll review eligibility requirements, SBA's loan programs, surety bonds and the role of SBA, equity capital topics, special purpose loans, SBA partner topics and 7(a) lender programs. Though the SBA does not provide grants to help you start a business, included is information on organizations and sites that can assist you in locating special purpose grants. US Small Business Administration (SBA.gov).

Bank Loans

Bank Loans
When you go to a bank for a loan what is the first thing a lender normally asks for? A Well Written Business Plan with 3 year Financials and 2 year Personal Financial Statements (past financials or future forecasts)! Plus, a credit application to check both the business credit rating and the principals credit rating.

--- NEVER GIVE FALSE PAST FINANCIAL STATEMENTS OR TAX RETURNS!
(if you give false financials or false tax returns you just committed credit fraud! It is common and acceptable to give lenders enthusiastic future financial forecasts!)

Some people still think there are big advantages to using an older shelf corporation and this is true for building credibility as a marketing tool, but without annual tax returns or tax returns without any substantial operating figures... to a lender it is a pink elephant!

It gets even worse when you show $100,000 to $5,000,000 in credit lines in the current year on a 10-year-old aged or shelf corporation without 3 years tax returns!

Speaking of tax returns, some people think you can falsify 1120 corporate tax returns.... Guess What? When the lender gives this information over to the IRS, The IRS wants the tax money you stated!!! Trying to send in an amended tax return after doing that is asking for a full audit and endless headaches.

Lender's want Financials they can validate it's called Due Diligence!

What are the two most important points to a Lender for issuing credit or loans?

1. Your Credit History! A Verifiable History with a Corporation with Financials!

2. Your Ability to Repay! Financial Proof of your ability to repay a Loan!

What is another financial tool a lender wants to see for a Loan?

A well written business plan with actual figures!

Who do you think a lender going to issue a loan to?

A startup company without a credit history or a company with at least a six-month history of credit with verifiable financials!

It's the lender's money so you have to give them what they require for acquiring loans and lines of credit.

Credit Mastery: Developing Aged Corporations by ISG3

Credit Building Plan to $1,000,000 in a Capsule with Multiple Companies!

Step 1. Begin with 3 – corporations or LLC's or mix of thereof. Preferably these are shelf companies, reinstated companies or from a CPA that have a clean credit history and are 2-3 years old. Another key point that helps in credit / financial development is that each of these companies would have a reason to do business with each other and report any credit transactions.

Step 2. Set up each company as per Section 1 with the exception of registering with credit reporting agencies. Do Not Apply for Any Credit! This will be done after Step 4.

Step 3. Contract as employees a retired Fortune 100™ executive as CEO for each company if your budget allows for this.

Step 4. Register with credit reporting agencies and enroll in their credit programs. You want a 1R rating so you have 12 employees (contracted) and you anticipate your first-year annual revenues at approximately $5,000,000

Step 5. Take company documents of formation along with a banking resolution to a bank that allows for inter-bank transfers and payments online. This is a bank you will never seek a loan from, period!

Step 6. Start initial credit building steps with each company.

Step 7. Start selling products and services between companies. Make sure you have a portable product/service that can be validated as a legitimate sale. Reselling products as distribution warehouses allows for products to be exchanged easily – especially if they are digital items with unlimited resell rights. There must be a contract for sale between companies and also a finance agreement. These can be further backed by filing a UCC-1 on the agreement.

Now if you sell a digital product for $123.45 wholesale, with a contract for 100 you just created $12,345.00 in gross sales revenue. If you allow for 30-day Net payments this is a credit extension that needs to be reported through your online credit building service(s). Pay off in 20 days so as to get the higher Paydex Score! Keep repeating this daily!

Everyday then, starting 20 days from the first contract, transfer the $12,345.00 from company to company to pay off that particular financed invoice. As you resold this to your other company it in turn resells back to another. So, you have a perfect circle – Company 1 sells to Company 2 who sells to Company 3 who in turn sells to Company 1.

As you can see you have built financials of $370,371 in 30 days! Keep in mind you must report sales and income and possibly pay taxes on these transactions (also sales tax or use of a resale number depending upon where a company is registered), but that is one of the costs of development. Do this for 9 months and you have generated $3,333,400 per company in sales revenues all banked by bank statements. A rule of thumb for banks is that they lend 10% unsecured loans of annual revenues. $3,333,400 gross revenues x 10% = $333,334 per company in unsecured loans x 3 = $1,000,002!

Now, What if you don't have $12,345.00 available for daily transactions? What can be done to get the credit

Credit Mastery: Developing Aged Corporations by ISG3

payments made? The good news is with the digital age of the internet and mobile phone apps the $12,345.00 can be broken down into 6 transactions of $2,057.50 if necessary and if you have the time!

Note: Some of you by now are saying what about taxes? This is where a good CPA comes in and saves the day. What you need to do is buy ten-year-old non-collectible credit card debt that is flowing on the internet for under ten cents on the dollar! Add debt to offset possible income taxes and have the CPA start on this in month nine to make sure the amount you require and have it on the books by fiscal year end.

Step 7. After first credit vendors from section 1 have reported, purchase 2 trade-lines from ISG and follow the rest of the credit sections. Do these in the amount of 15% of your forecasted revenue you told credit reporting agencies. These will self-liquidate their payments in 4 - 6 months.

Step 8. Take out a 6-month Deposit Loan with ISG's vendor (located on our website for registered members) in the amount of 10% of forecasted revenue. This gets an important large loan processes through a credit union that reports. The way a Deposit Loan is that it is a no cash out loan, so you make an interest payment and the provider makes the principal portion and the credit union reports the transaction.

Step 9. Follow the credit building instructions and continue into each new section as you complete the last.

Step 10. Write Business Plan for each company and these cannot go through the SBA programs.

Step 11. It's time to go business loan shopping!

Pull a credit report on each company to put with your business plan and make note to a lender that they cannot pull a credit report until they issue a pre-advice commitment or Conditional Letter of Intent to fund or Loan Approval based on information supplied. This way you can submit to 20 lenders if you wanted without have a credit inquiry showing up on your profile.

Step 12. Loan or Credit Line Approval and Funded. Approval great – just use the funds as per business plan and you will have any problems if you default in a year or two.

Misuse or misappropriation of funds can be serious charges to the officers of the company and if the majority is transferred as payroll or entertainment it could be construed as embezzlement also. Also with business loans and credit if you do not make at least 6-9 payments it appears as though there was no intent to repay and that is also a felony charge in many states as credit fraud.

At the Credit Mastery Seminar we give you the exact money transfer formula we use for building multiple corporations for their fincials andbank statements! www.isg3.com

BUSINESS PLAN – without this they will not help you obtain any type of loan.

Small businesses are the foundation and driving force behind our country's entrepreneurial spirit. The Small Business Administration (SBA) can help you start or expand your business if you meet their qualifications.

SBA Loans can offer greater flexibility with lower interest rates and longer terms for more affordable payments. They are designed to support the growth of start-up's and other existing businesses that might not benefit from normal lending channels.

Start your business.
Purchase machinery, equipment, furniture or fixtures.
Acquire inventory or working capital.
Purchase an existing business.
Purchase, construct, expand or improve a building.
Refinance existing business related debt.
With an SBA Loan:

7(a) – Existing Business can obtain Term Loans up to $2,000,000
Express Lines of Credit up to $350,000
504 CDC Real Estate Loans up to $4,000,000
SBA encourages Minority and Women start up and ongoing businesses

SBA Loan Guarantee Programs

From SBA.gov: SBA provides several financial assistance programs for small businesses including 7(a), 504 and disaster assistance loans. Within this section, we'll review eligibility requirements, SBA's loan programs, surety bonds and the role of SBA, equity capital topics, special purpose loans, SBA partner topics and 7(a) lender programs. Though the SBA does not provide grants to help you start a business, included is information on organizations and sites that can assist you in locating special purpose grants. US Small Business Administration (SBA.gov).

Business Plans

Business plans must be easy to read, easy to understand and make common sense to an average person not in business. Your plan must include accurate information and especially your financials and financial forecasts.

A well written business plan is not only for financing it is also comparable to a road-map to your business success. After you have completed a plan go back and read it every three months to see if you are on track for your projected goals. This can help you keep with your sales and marketing objectives if you have gotten distracted by day to day business operations.

Your Financial Forecast must meet D&B Industry Norms figures within 5 per cent of their figures. Look up you SIC code related to your business, take a photo copy and then go to work on making your business plan meet the industry norms or companies that are financially sound and successful.

Another method for gaining numbers is to go to the D & B website and purchase a full report on a competitive company, this will give you exact operating cost, profits and losses and every figure you need to prepare your financial forecast for your business plan.

Use D&B INDUSTRY NORMS for Writing A Business Plan:
ALWAYS USE FIGURES THAT ARE IN THESE PUBLICATIONS ADJUSTED TO YOUR PROJECTED ANNUAL SALES!

Suggestions for your Business Plan:

Buy the Expanded Business Report on at least one of your Top 5 Competitors at Dunn and Bradstreet. Yes, this will cost you a few hundred dollars per report, however you have the best operational financial figures you need for a business plan. This will give you the figures you need for submitting a business plan to a banker or an investor - They will obtain a report on your company and possibly your competitors and many times the Dunn & Bradstreet Industry Norms Report.

This report uses a business's SIC code and employee size for a financial picture of a company. These are extremely important to mirror the industry norms in your financials, if your financial forecasts are more than 10% different the lender or investor may feel you are a dreamer and the business will not succeed.

Another method for obtaining comparable operations figures is to get franchise packages from at least 2 franchisors. They will give you certain figures, but not all and for some a franchise is a viable option for starting a business.

Investors want a return. They can appreciate a great sales job and a motivating description of how it will be done along with how much they stand to gain – so write a separate business plan for investors. This is the plan you will also incorporate into a private placement memorandum if seeking private investor funds.

Bankers want to be repaid. Bankers want to see figures they can validate with a reporting service like Dunn & Bradstreet and compare to Industry Norms Reports. So keep the word count and sales pitch low and rich with realistic figures for the Bankers and Lenders – this is why a Lender/Bank Loan Business Plan should be different than an Investor Business Plan.

The Operating Business Plan is your business plan that is written as a road map for your business.

No sales pitches to the bank – just realistic forecasts and benchmarks. Read your plan every quarter for your quarterly evaluation.

This can be a life saver if you see you are not achieving your goals and gives you the opportunity to ask this important question: If you are not achieving your forecasted goals ... is it due to your initial figures were not accurate or is it that you have not followed my business plan?

Note: We have included pages for 12 months in this workbook so you can continue and grow your credit. Also, this will help for determining your needs with a CPA for acquiring debt to offset taxes.

Corporate Guarantees

Corporate Guarantees are a powerful tool for those with multiple companies with credit having been built out to equal or twice the amount of funding you are seeking.

Using one company as a guarantor for another company's debt is a well-kept financing secret that we wish to use for obtaining funding when necessary. The key of this is to build out multiple companies and when required you can use one company as a guarantor for another. One important note is that you cannot be the officer/director/shareholder/member of both companies as this would apper strange to a lender.

This has been done by large corporations such as General Motors for both their wholly owned subsidiaries and independent companies who manufacture parts for them. This is done many times when a smaller company obtains a contract and is short on operational cash and cannot obtain a loan to fulfill their contract. This is a win – win situation for both companies and should be explored prior to doing a merger! If a bank or lender accepts a third-party guarantee, it will be less paperwork and faster to engage.

Why are guarantees and indemnities important?
Guarantees and indemnities are a common method that a creditor can protect themselves from the risk of default on an obligation by a borrower or credit recipient.

The following is a sample guarantee :

Sample - CORPORATE GUARANTEE

This GUARANTEE dated this _____ day of _____, 20__.

From: _____
(hereafter known The "Guarantor")

To: _____
(hereafter known The "Lender")

Re: _____
(hereafter known as The "Debtor")

IN CONSIDERATION OF the Lender extending future credit from time to time to the Debtor, and other valuable consideration, the receipt and sufficiency of which is hereby acknowledged, the Guarantor, guarantees the prompt, full and complete performance of any and all present and future duties, obligations and indebtedness (the "Debt") due to the Lender by the Debtor, under the terms of certain debt agreements (the "Agreement") and under the following terms and conditions:

1. The Guarantor guarantees that the Debtor will promptly pay the full amount of principal and interest of the Debt as and when the same will in any manner be or become due, either according to the terms and conditions provided by the Agreement or upon acceleration of the payment under the Agreement by reason of a default.
2. The Guarantor agrees not to pledge, hypothecate, mortgage, sell or otherwise transfer any of the Guarantors assets without the prior written consent of the Lender.
3. To the extent permitted by law, the Guarantor waives all defenses, counterclaims or offsets that are legally available to the Guarantor with respect to the payment of the Debt of the Debtor.
4. The Lender is hereby authorized at any time, in its sole discretion and without notice, to take, change, release or in any way deal with any security securing the Debt without in any way impairing the obligation of the Guarantor.
5. The Lender will be under no obligation to collect or to protect any such security or the Debt, and its neglect or failure to collect or protect the security or the Debt is excused. Acceptance of the Guarantee is waived.
6. The Lender may grant extensions of time or other indulgences and otherwise deal with the Debtor and with other parties and securities as the Lender may see fit without in any way limiting or lessening the liability of the Guarantor under this Agreement.
7. Any impairment of the security, which the Lender may from time to time hold as security for the Debt, will in no way operate to discharge the Guarantor in whole or in part, it being specifically agreed that the Lender is not required to exercise diligence to enforce its rights against the Debtor.
8. The Lender may release, surrender, exchange, modify, impair or extend the periods of duration or the time for performance or payment of any collateral securing the obligations of the Debtor to the Lender, and may also settle or compromise any claim of the Lender against the Debtor or against any other person or corporation whose obligation is held by the Lender as collateral security for any obligation of the Debtor or the Lender.

9. This Guarantee is for the use and benefit of the Lender, and will also be for the use and benefit of any subsequent Lender to whom the Lender may assign this Guarantee.
10. The liability of the Guarantor will continue until payment is made of every obligation of the Debtor now or later incurred in connection with the Debt and until payment is made of any loss or damage incurred by the Lender with respect to any matter covered by this Guarantee or any of the Agreement.
11. The Guarantor further waives all rights, by statute or otherwise, to require the Lender to institute suit against the Debtor, and to exercise diligence in enforcing this Guarantee or any other instrument.
12. All present and future indebtedness of the Debtor to the Guarantor is hereby assigned to the Lender. All monies received by the Guarantor from the Debtor will be received in trust for the Lender and upon receipt are to be paid over to the Lender until such time as the Debt owed by the Debtor has been fully paid and satisfied.
13. The Guarantor represents that at the time of the execution and delivery of this Guarantee nothing exists to impair the effectiveness of this Guarantee.
14. All of the Lender's rights, powers and remedies available under this Guarantee and under any other agreement in force now or anytime later between the Lender and the Guarantor will be cumulative and not alternative, and will be in addition to all rights, powers and remedies given to the Lender by law or in equity.
15. The Lender may, at its option, proceed in the first instance against the Guarantor to collect the obligations covered by this Guarantee without first proceeding against any other person, firm or corporation and without resorting to any property held by the Lender as collateral security.
16. All pronouns will include masculine, feminine and/or neuter gender, single or plural number, as the context of this Guarantee may require.
17. This Guarantee is made pursuant to the laws of the State of Wisconsin. In the event that this Guarantee must be enforced by the Lender, all reasonable costs and expenses, including attorney's fees, incurred by the Lender will be paid by the Guarantor.
18. The invalidity or unenforceability of any one or more phrases, sentences, clauses or sections in this Guarantee will not affect the validity or enforceability of the remaining portions of this Guarantee or any part of this Guarantee.
19. No alteration or waiver of this Guarantee or of any of its terms, provisions or conditions will be binding upon the Lender unless made in writing over the signature of the Lender or its representative.
20. Words of "Guarantee" contained in this Guarantee in no way diminish or impair the absolute liability created in this Guarantee.
21. Any notice to be given to the Guarantor may be sent by mail, telephone, fax, email or otherwise delivered to the address provided below.

Signed by Guarantor _____ Date _____

Signed by Debtor _____ Date _____

Corporate seal

Notary Seal

Notary Information and statement

Credit Mastery: Developing Aged Corporations

Mergers and Acquisitions for Multiplying Credit

Perform a Merger or Acquisition, when not a publicly traded entity, is not that complicated as it is done at a state level with filings and then notify the IRS on the changes. Check with your state's secretary of state office for more information and filing forms.

When you fold another company into another it can blend the financials to make the target company look larger.

This may have tax implications and you need to consult a CPA regarding tax matters.

Once a loan is approved and issued the process can be reversed if desired (reverse merger or reverse acquisition).

We are going to assume that you have two companies with credit lines already posted to the credit reporting agencies at this point. These will be your two highest credit level companies (those with a history of high limits). This stage may take place in the 9 month of the multiple company strategy, unless you have accelerated these entities by using trade-lines, UCC-1 filings on a shelf or aged corporation and thereby can be done in month 4-5 if the tow companies have strong financial merit. First, you will need to do a corporate resolution stating that the Board of Directors, Shareholders and Officers have agreed to a merger with _____, Company.

Here are following examples of the merger form used by the State of Colorado and these vary from state to state, so visit your Secretary of States website and download the forms appropriate to the state your legal entity in formed within.

Enter the Information on the first company involved in the merger. Next fill in the information on the second company:

ID Number	0000000001 *(Colorado Secretary of State ID number)*
Entity name or true name	DEF Company
Form of entity	Corporation
Jurisdiction	YYY County

Credit Mastery: Developing Aged Corporations

Along with company two's address (form shows an extra section for a third company within a single merger filing):

The surviving entity is the company that will be used for financing!

ID Number _____
(Colorado Secretary of State ID number)

Entity name or true name _____

Form of entity _____

Jurisdiction _____

Street address _____
(Street number and name)

_____
(City) (State) (ZIP/Postal Code)

_____
(Province – if applicable) (Country)

Mailing address
(**leave blank** if same as street address)
_____
(Street number and name or Post Office Box information)

_____
(City) (State) (ZIP/Postal Code)

_____
(Province – if applicable) (Country)

(If the following statement applies, adopt the statement by marking the box and include an attachment.)
☐ There are more than three merging entities and the ID number (if applicable), entity name or true name, form of entity, jurisdiction under the law of which it is formed, and the principal address of each additional merging entity is stated in an attachment.

2. For the surviving entity, its entity ID number (if applicable), entity name or true name, form of entity, jurisdiction under the law of which it is formed, and principal address are

Credit Mastery: Developing Aged Corporations

ID Number   0000000001
Entity name or true name   **DEF Company**

Credit Mastery: Developing Aged Corporations

Notice:

Causing this document to be delivered to the Secretary of State for filing shall constitute the affirmation or acknowledgment of each individual causing such delivery, under penalties of perjury, that such document is such individual's act and deed, or that such individual in good faith believes such document is the act and deed of the person on whose behalf such individual is causing such document to be delivered for filing, taken in conformity with the requirements of part 3 of article 90 of title 7, C.R.S. and, if applicable, the constituent documents and the organic statutes, and that such individual in good faith believes the facts stated in such document are true and such document complies with the requirements of that Part, the constituent documents, and the organic statutes.

This perjury notice applies to each individual who causes this document to be delivered to the Secretary of State, whether or not such individual is identified in this document as one who has caused it to be delivered.

8. The true name and mailing address of the individual causing this document to be delivered for filing are

_____ _____ _____ _____ (Last)
                     (First)   (Middle)   (Suffix)
_____ (Street
         number and name or Post Office Box information)
_____
_____ _____ _____ (City)
         (State)   (ZIP/Postal Code)
_____ _____.
    (Province – if applicable)   (Country)

(If applicable, adopt the following statement by marking the box and include an attachment.)
☒ This document contains the true name and mailing address of one or more additional individuals causing the document to be delivered for filing.

Disclaimer:

This form/cover sheet, and any related instructions, are not intended to provide legal, business or tax advice, and are furnished without representation or warranty. While this form/cover sheet is believed to satisfy minimum legal requirements as of its revision date, compliance with applicable law, as the same may be amended from time to time, remains the responsibility of the user of this form/cover sheet. Questions should be addressed to the user's legal, business or tax advisor(s).

Just fill in the information in box 8 and file! Make sure both companies have completed the resolution to merger below

At the Credit Mastery Seminar we give you all the forms from our mergers and acquisitions along with all of our ancillary documentation!

Credit Mastery: Developing Aged Corporations

BOARD OF DIRECTORS' RESOLUTION APPROVING
MERGER WITH WHOLLY OWNED SUBSIDIARY

WHEREAS, the Board of Directors of _____ Corporation (hereinafter referred to as Corporation) determined said Corporation owns all stock of _____, Inc., which is a Corporation organized under the laws of the State of _____, and

WHEREAS, by merging _____, Inc., into said Corporation, it will be possible to gain operating efficiencies, it is hereby

RESOLVED, that said Corporation hereby merge with _____ Inc., and that after the merger is effected said Corporation shall be the Surviving Corporation and shall assume all of the debts and liabilities of both former Corporations and it is

FURTHER RESOLVED, that a special meeting of this Corporation's shareholders shall be called and held at the following time, date and place:

Time: _____

Date: _____

Location: _____

and it is hereby

FURTHER RESOLVED that the purpose of such special meeting shall be as follows:

(1) To vote upon the recommendation presented by the Board of Directors that the two Corporate entities be merged; and

(2) To approve a merger agreement between _____, Inc., and this Corporation.

The undersigned, _____, certifies that he or she is the duly appointed Secretary of _____ Corporation and that the above is a true and correct copy of a resolution duly adopted at a meeting of the directors thereof, convened and held in accordance with law and the Bylaws of said Corporation on _____, and that such resolution is now in full force and effect.

IN WITNESS THEREOF, I have affixed my name as Secretary of _____ Corporation and have attached the seal of _____ Corporation to this resolution.

Dated: _____   _____

_____ Secretary   Seal

Credit Mastery: Developing Aged Corporations

Trademarks and Servicemarks

Each of your companies should have either a Trademark or Servicemark registration for use in funding as an asset.

Application for Registration of Trademark or Service Mark

1. Provide a written description of the trademark or service mark. Your description must include all words, names, symbols, devices and designs which the applicant wishes to be included within the mark. You may attach a separate sheet if needed; however, you must describe the trademark completely:

2. Name of applicant: _____

3. Business address of applicant: _____

4. Mailing address of applicant: _____

5. Applicant is (check only one):

individual;

limited partnership;

unincorporated association;

corporation;

limited liability company;

other:

general partnership;

statutory trust;

6. a. If the applicant is a corporation, limited partnership, limited liability company or statutory trust, list:

The state of incorporation or organization: _____

The date incorporated or organized: _____
(Date – mm/dd/yyyy)

b. If a general partnership or limited partnership, list the names of the general partners or partners:

c. If a limited liability company or statutory trust, list the names of the managers, members or trustees:
d. If other, explain:

84

7. Provide the class number and title of the goods or services (see attachment). Use only one class code per registration:

Class number: _____   Title: _____

8. Provide a brief description of the goods or services within the class (i.e., what your product is, or what service you provide): _____

9. List the mode or manner in which the mark is used to identify the goods or services (e.g.: goods - labels on cans, bags, wrappers, etc.; tags, nameplates affixed directly to product; services - labels on laundry bags, advertising, window signs, etc.):

10. An application to register the mark or portions or a composite has been filed by the applicant or a predecessor in interest in the U.S. Patent and Trademark office: Yes   No

If yes, provide filing date, serial number of each application, the status and, if any application was finally refused registration or has not otherwise resulted in registration, the reasons therefore:

11. Date of first use by applicant or predecessor (the mark must be in use before it can be registered):

 a. Anywhere:

 b. In this state:

(Date – mm/dd/yyyy)

12. One photocopy or facsimile of the mark as it is actually used must accompany this application.

13. The applicant is the owner of the mark. The mark is in use and to the knowledge of the person verifying this application, no other person has registered, either federally or in this state, or has the right to use such mark either in the identical form thereof or in such near resemblance as to be likely, when applied to the goods or services of such other person, to cause confusion or to cause mistake or to deceive.

Signature: _____   Date:
(mm/dd/yyyy)

Print Name:
Title:
Email:
 Contact Person:
Daytime Phone Number:
(Email provided will receive filing evidence) *May list multiple email addresses
Important Information:
 •Registration is effective for a term of five years and is renewable for like term upon application filed within six months prior to expiration of such term.

Credit Mastery: Developing Aged Corporations

•Renewal forms are mailed by the office of the Secretary of State to registrants whose trademark or service mark is up for renewal.

•A trademark or service mark may be canceled at any time upon written request to the Secretary of State and payment of a $10.00 filing fee. •Assignment forms are available on the internet or from the office of the Secretary of State upon request. The filing fee to assign a trademark or service mark is $25.00.

The following general classes of goods and services are established for convenience of administration of this Act, but not to limit or extend the applicant's or registrant's rights. A single application for registration of a mark may include any and all goods upon which, or service with which, the mark is actually being used in a single class. IF GOODS OR SERVICES FALL WITHIN TWO SEPARATE CLASS CODES, A SEPARATE REGISTRATION MUST BE SUBMITTED FOR EACH CLASS.

Class Number and Title

Goods
1. Raw or partly prepared materials 2. Receptacles
3. Baggage, animal equipment, portfolios, and pocketbooks 4. Abrasives and polishing materials
5. Adhesives
6. Chemicals and chemical compositions 7. Cordage
8. Smokers' articles, not including tobacco products 9. Explosives, firearms, equipment's, and projectiles 10. Fertilizers
11. Inks and inking materials 12. Construction materials
13. Hardware and plumbing and steam-fitting supplies 14. Metals and metal castings and forgings
15. Oils and greases
16. Paints and painters' materials 17. Tobacco products
18. Medicines and pharmaceutical preparations 19. Vehicles
20. Linoleum and oiled cloth
21. Electrical apparatus, machines, and supplies 22. Games, toys, and sporting goods
23. Cutlery, machinery, and tools, and parts thereof 24. Laundry appliances and machines
25. Locks and safes
26. Measuring and scientific appliances 27. Horological instruments
28. Jewelry and precious-metal ware 29. Brooms, brushes and dusters
30. Crockery, earthenware, and porcelain 31. Filters and refrigerators

TM-Registration Application - Revised January 2015 32. Furniture and upholstery
33. Glassware
34. Heating, lighting and ventilating apparatus
35. Belting, hose, machinery packing, non-metallic tires 36. Musical instruments and supplies
37. Paper and stationery 38. Prints and publications 39. Clothing
40. Fancy goods, furnishings and notions 41. Canes, parasols, and umbrellas
42. Knitted, netted and textile fabrics and substitutes therefor 43. Thread and yarn
44. Dental, medical, and surgical appliances 45. Soft drinks and carbonated waters
46. Foods and ingredients of foods 47. Wines
48. Malt beverages and liquors 49. Distilled alcoholic liquors
50. Merchandise not otherwise classified 51. Cosmetics and toilet preparations 52. Detergents and soaps
Services

100. Miscellaneous

101. Advertising and business 102. Insurance and financial 103. Construction and repair 104. Communications

105. Transportation and storage 106. Material treatment

107. Education and entertainment

Credit Mastery: Developing Aged Corporations

Company 1 Information

Company Name_____
Address_____
Telephone: _____ Fax: _____
email: _____ _____
President / CEO / Director: _____
Telephone: _____ Fax: _____
email: _____ _____
Secretary: _____
Telephone: _____ Fax: _____
email: _____ _____
Treasurer: _____
Telephone: _____ Fax: _____
email: _____ _____

Secretary of State Registration Number: _____ Date: _____
Foreign Company Registration
Secretary of State Registration Number: _____ Date: _____

Office Leasing Company or Mortgage Holder: _____
Occupied on Date: _____

Office Telephone Provider: _____ Account #: _____
411 Directory Assistance Listed with: _____

Internal Revenue Service EIN: _____
Fiscal Year Ending Date: _____ State Tax ID : _____
Business License Registration #: _____ SIC Code: _____
Dunn and Bradstreet DUNNS #: _____ Date: _____
CCR #: _____ Date: _____
Experian Business #: _____ Date: _____

Bank: _____
Bank Address: _____
Phone Number: _____ Branch # : _____
Bank Account Representative: _____ Ext: ____
Account Number: _____
ABA Routing Number: _____
Wire Account #: _____
Debit Card # _____ Exp: _____
Code: _____
Website(s): _____ Website Host(s): _____
User: _____ Password: _____
Website Interface Address : _____
Admin User: _____ Password: _____

Credit Mastery: Developing Aged Corporations

Company 2 Information

Company Name_____
Address_____
Telephone: _____ Fax: _____
email: _____ _____
President / CEO / Director: _____
Telephone: _____ Fax: _____
email: _____ _____
Secretary: _____
Telephone: _____ Fax: _____
email: _____ _____
Treasurer: _____
Telephone: _____ Fax: _____
email: _____ _____

Secretary of State Registration Number: _____ Date: _____
Foreign Company Registration
Secretary of State Registration Number: _____ Date: _____

Office Leasing Company or Mortgage Holder: _____
Occupied on Date: _____

Office Telephone Provider: _____ Account #: _____
411 Directory Assistance Listed with: _____

Internal Revenue Service EIN: _____
Fiscal Year Ending Date: _____ State Tax ID : _____
Business License Registration #: _____ SIC Code: _____
Dunn and Bradstreet DUNNS #: _____ Date: _____
CCR #: _____ Date: _____
Experian Business #: _____ Date: _____

Bank: _____
Bank Address: _____
Phone Number: _____ Branch # : _____
Bank Account Representative: _____ Ext: ____
Account Number: _____
ABA Routing Number: _____
Wire Account #: _____
Debit Card # _____ Exp: _____
Code: _____
Website(s): _____ Website Host(s): _____
User: _____ Password: _____
Website Interface Address : _____
Admin User: _____ Password: _____

Company 3 Information

Company Name_____
Address_____
Telephone: _____ Fax: _____
email: _____ _____
President / CEO / Director: _____
Telephone: _____ Fax: _____
email: _____ _____
Secretary: _____
Telephone: _____ Fax: _____
email: _____ _____
Treasurer: _____
Telephone: _____ Fax: _____
email: _____ _____

Secretary of State Registration Number: _____ Date: _____
Foreign Company Registration
Secretary of State Registration Number: _____ Date: _____

Office Leasing Company or Mortgage Holder: _____
Occupied on Date: _____

Office Telephone Provider: _____ Account #: _____
411 Directory Assistance Listed with: _____

Internal Revenue Service EIN: _____
Fiscal Year Ending Date: _____ State Tax ID : _____
Business License Registration #: _____ SIC Code: _____
Dunn and Bradstreet DUNNS #: _____ Date: _____
CCR #: _____ Date: _____
Experian Business #: _____ Date: _____

Bank: _____
Bank Address: _____
Phone Number: _____ Branch # : _____
Bank Account Representative: _____ Ext: ____
Account Number: _____
ABA Routing Number: _____
Wire Account #: _____
Debit Card # _____ Exp: _____
Code: _____
Website(s): _____ Website Host(s): _____
User: _____ Password: _____
Website Interface Address : _____
Admin User: _____ Password: _____

Credit Mastery: Developing Aged Corporations

Credit Submission & Usage Report – Month 1

Credit Building Core Accounts for each Company

The first phase of business credit building is the basic core accounts that are net 30-day payment accounts. These accounts are the basic core for creating any business credit profile(s). These validate your payment history for other credit issuers that you will be applying for in the future. These always work best when using a 2-3-year-old company.

Credit Building Core Accounts for your Company

The first phase of business credit building is the basic core accounts that are net 30-day payment accounts. These accounts are the basic core for creating any business credit profile(s). These validate your payment history for other credit issuers that you will be applying for in the future. These always work best when using a 2-3-year-old company.

If you have an existing profile, make sure you have these accounts reporting on your company's profile.

DO NOT APPLY FOR CREDIT ACCOUNTS WITHOUT D&B DUNS # www.dnb.com

If you already have a D&B profile make certain that the core building accounts are shown your company's report (reapply if necessary).

Sign up with NAV.com for business credit reports plus get a Business Reporting Trade Line!

Order at least $50 worth of merchandise at your vendor every month for 3 months

To generate the fastest trade line, we will do online orders with Office Depot, Sears and Staples.

Do these in the business name and pay with the company debit card from your business bank account. You can always use PayPal services and under a business name using a personal account (however we do not recommend using personal accounts as it can break the veil of a legal entity, thereby making you personally liable for future debts).

These online purchases may not show immediately, and we recommend that you offer to submit invoices to D&B showing the purchase and payment.

Continue using your account until it shows up on the DUNS report.

Pitney Bowes 800-322-8000 - Postage Meter is $25 per month – Low Cost - High Value Reporting! Plus, they have offered lines of credit after a year up to $25,000 in the past!

Quill Net 30 - 800-982-3400 (Owned by Staples) - Net 30 Reports to DNB & Experian

MSC Industrial Supply 800-645-7270
Create this account online -then submit your EIN for $1,000 line of credit that reports very quickly.

Uline: 800-958-5463
Veripak: 800-225-8155
Gemplers - Net 30 Reports to DNB
Grainger: 888-361-8649 - Net 30 Reports to DNB
4Imprint - Net 30 Reports to DNB & Experian
AT&T Business Accounts - Monthly Reporting to DNB
FEDEX - Net 15 Reports to DNB & Experian
Marathon Petroleum - www.marathonbrand.com - Net 30 Reports to DNB & Experian

After the above accounts have been opened:

File a UCC-1 for $10,000 to $50,000 on company from another company (or yourself as a loan to company as last resort). Make sure this is relevant to your annual revenues.

Keep it Real!!! make sure that whatever amount you use to repay is justified by the monthly income of your business otherwise it is not going to fly, however in saying that does not mean that you could not return merchandise or product for a full refund. Mail a copy of this filing to all business credit reporting agencies. We want to make sure this debt is shown in the legal section of the credit report.

The Wells Fargo Business Secured Credit Card is an essential tool for businesses looking to establish or rebuild their business credit with Wells Fargo. We have had clients convert these cards in 12 months to a $10,000+ credit card. Secured credit line from $500 up to $25,000 depending on your starting deposit to fund the card. $25 annual fee. Choose between rewards points or cash back.

CAPITAL ONE SPARK BUSINESS Card – This can be either a fully secured or conventional credit card – Buying our Business Trade Line package will get fast and early results! Also see Credit Mastery Personal Section for ideas and preparations for this card.

Check Your D&B Report every two weeks
Pay off every account 10-15 days early

Need Cash to get started? There are companies who specialize in charging your credit cards as a regular transaction and not a cash advance and advance those funds into your checking account! Plastiq is a leader in this business. Www.plastiq.com

Do You Want Maximum Credit Really Fast?
Get $25,000 to $100,000 in business credit cards in under 60 days!

Adding Primary Business Trade-lines to start or add to your Equifax or Experian Business Credit file. Credit card issuers and many cash lenders rarely look and the D&B report for issuing lines of credit or loans and the more files on your report the more likely you are to get new cards issued. If you have 3 – 5 primary trade-lines added with a total of $30,000 to $50,000 it is very likely you will be granted a minimum of $15,000 to $25,000 in your first round of applications with other credit card vendors. Asking for line increases can take these cards to $25,000 each if managed properly within a 3-to-6-month time frame.

We give you our trusted business trade-line source at the Credit Mastery seminar. Get $50,000 In Experian

Business Reporting Lines and $150,000 in SBFE Reporting Lines with active accounts and depreciating balances – Current price is $5,500. This means over $100,000 in credit cards immediately when added to our system! Trade Line Packages to $300,000 Experian and $500,000 SBFE – great for $250,000+ bank funding fast when added to our system!

Should any of the processes become confusing or you have problems you should attend a seminar.

Alternative Fast Funding: Start a Crowdfunding or Patreon account for non-loan type funding. This is fully covered in the Credit Mastery seminars.

A Seminar Plug: *At the Credit Mastery seminars, we teach you how to use multiple companies within the strategy to get to $1,000,000 in credit as the fastest possible way. It is far easier to get $250,000 on 4 companies (in the shortest period) opposed to $1,000,000 on a single company. The seminar gives the exact information on how to build usable real financials for funding. You get our corporation transaction flow chart and movements. This does have an overall higher cost; however, it is offset with unlimited options! You can use the extra companies as a fail-safe mechanism should one of the other companies fail, you can use them as guarantors of loans for another company or for yourself, plus these can be sold for a profit! Plus, we give you direct access to our trade line vendors.*

Note: For Best Results - Make Sure Each Company Revenues are $10,000 per Day!
This can be sales between your group of companies – multinationals due this all the time!

Remember that in the magic month 7 our aged company will normally get 10% of total revenues in unsecured credit lines or loans! So, Generate Those Revenues!

$10,000 x 30 Days = $300,000 per month x 7 months = $2,100,000 x 10% = $210,000 in unsecured funds if only having basic trade-lines on a 1 to 3-year-old company you can get $250,000. If you transfer $100,000 per day it becomes $2,500,000! This is Per Company!

What if You Only Have $1,000?
Then Use it 10 Times a Day making online transfers!

Remember banks lend on history and the ability to repay an obligation.
Trade Lines Show History! Cash Flow Shows Ability!

This strategy requires an ongoing process for at least 9 months after funding is received. You could gradually decrease the transfer amounts over this ending period of 9 months.

Credit Mastery: Developing Aged Corporations

	Company 1	Company 2	Company 3
Applications Submitted			
Applications Approved			
Total Credit Issued			
Total Credit Reported			
Total Credit Available			
Application Submitted to			
Submission Date			
Approval Date			
Credit Line			
Account Number			
1st Charge Amount			
1st Payment [1]			
Reported to DnB™ Date			
Reported to Experian Business™ Date			

Credit Mastery: Developing Aged Corporations

	Company 1	Company 2	Company 3
Item – Date Sold			
Sale Amount			
Tax Deductible Amount			

B2 B Activity Report

	Company 1	Company 2	Company 3
Account Number			
Total Credit Issued			
Total Credit Reported			
Total Credit Available			
Product Sold			
Charge Amount			
Payment			
Reported to DnB™ Date			
Experian Date			
Transactions	**Company 1**	**Company 2**	**Company 3**

Credit Mastery: Developing Aged Corporations

This page area is left intentionally blank for notes:

Credit Mastery: Developing Aged Corporations

Credit Submission & Usage Report – Month 2

Office Supply Vendors

Office Supply Vendors

Generally, every real business has certain expenses in common and those are office supplies. Purchase at least $100 to credit line limit every month and verify the credit is reported.

Do Not Apply for Any Office Supply Vendor Accounts Without Three (3) of the Credit Core Building Accounts from section 1 Vendors Reporting On Your D&B Report!

Office Depot / OfficeMax Business Credit Account

$150 minimum purchase required. Valid only on approved applications for the Office Depot Business Credit Account. The Office Depot® Business Credit Account is issued by Citibank, N.A.

As of 8/1/2023, Business Account: non-variable: 20.80%-29.99%. These APRs will vary with the market based on the Prime Rate.

Staples – Net 30 - Staples Automated Status Line: 800-767-1275
        (note: Staples owns Quill)
Staples Net 30 requires 20+ employees to qualify

Staples Business Advantage is a free business account provides you with unlimited users at no cost, spend & budget controls, and everyday low prices. Accounts created through online enrollment accept credit card purchases only. Invoicing is available for eligible accounts. Contact a Staples Business Advantage representative to discuss account (844) 243-8645 M-F, 8 am - 5 pm ET

(Staples credit card account, issued by Citibank, N.A., was closed on 7/31/23 with no newer card issuers presented to replace Citibank.)

New Egg – Net 55 Account (not Net 30) put in $10,000 requested credit line – Issued by Synchrony Bank Using either Experian Business or Equifax Business – not a D&B reporting account.

Sears Commercial One Account - Citibank N.A.

Sunbelt Rentals Net 15 Account – PG required, however your company may get up to $40,000 line approved on a 2 yr. shelf company that is properly set up. This is great for a trade-line that shows with a high limit over actual usage. Reports to D&B.

eCredable.com - eCredable Lift is a paid service you can use to add your company's bill payments to its business credit reports.

Once you sign up, you can link up to eight types of utility accounts, including your electric, gas, mobile phone, and internet accounts. They can be automatically connected and reported to the business credit bureaus.

You can also manually add other types of common business expenses, such as vendor accounts, rent, insurance, leases, and legal services. eCredable will manually review the accounts before reporting them.

In either case, you can add up to 24 months of payment history from each account. They can all be reported to the Equifax, Creditsafe, and Ansonia business credit bureaus. Your eCredable subscription also gets reported to Dun & Bradstreet (D&B).

Amend UCC-1 Filing from Month 1
Now is the time to file a UCC-3 to amend the original UCC-1 filed in month 1. You will reduce the debt and collateral by 33% (66% balance). Again, mail a copy of this filing to all business credit reporting agencies. We want to make sure this debt is shown in the legal section of the credit report. (see Credit Mastery Seminars for in-depth UCC-1 information and sample filings) Do Not Continue to next section until the above approved accounts are reporting.

Make Sure Each Company Revenues are at Least $10,000 per Day! This can be sales between your group of companies – multi-nationals due this all the time!

	Company 1	Company 2	Company 3
Applications Submitted			
Applications Approved			
Total Credit Issued			
Total Credit Reported			
Total Credit Available			
Application Submitted to			
Submission Date			
Approval Date			
Credit Line			
Account Number			
1st Charge Amount			
1st Payment [1]			

Credit Mastery: Developing Aged Corporations

Reported to DnB™ Date			
Reported to Experian Business™ Date			
	Company 1	Company 2	Company 3
Item – Date Sold			
Sale Amount			
Tax Deductible Amount			

B2 B Activity Report

	Company 1	Company 2	Company 3
Account Number			
Total Credit Issued			
Total Credit Reported			
Total Credit Available			
Product Sold			
Charge Amount			
Payment			
Reported to DnB™ Date			
Experian Date			

Credit Mastery: Developing Aged Corporations

Transactions	Company 1	Company 2	Company 3

Credit Submission & Usage Report – Month 3

Fuel Cards

Fuel Cards

After verifying that your D&B Report contains at least 3 of the section 1 vendors and at least 1 of the section 2 vendors, you are ready to apply for the fuel cards. Fuel cards are generally necessary for almost every business – It's hard to find a business that does not use fuel cards period! Certain businesses may not and these are generally in major dense metropolitan areas – for example a jewelry store or restaurant in Manhattan, the center of New York City odds are doesn't have or use a fuel credit card, but if you are in the suburban Midwest with a distribution warehouse you most likely will. These are essential for building a solid credit report! These cards validate your company's existence as a real operating business entity.

Shell
BP
Fuel Man - www.fuelman.com
WEX Fuel Card - www.wex.com

To achieve a successful round of financing in the next round it is recommended to target a minimum of $5,000 in total credit lines.

FNBO Business Edition Secured Mastercard® Credit Card
Take control of your credit history and help build your credit.
Request your own credit limit between $2,000 and $100,000 (multiples of $50), when you apply, subject to credit approval and a security deposit. Earns interest on your security deposit. $39 annual fee

Amend UCC-1 Filing from Month 1

Now is the time to file a UCC-3 to amend the original UCC-1 filed in month 1. You will reduce the debt and collateral by another 33%. Now your balance will be down to only a third of the original amount and will be retired in the next month. Again, mail a copy of this filing to all business credit reporting agencies. We want to make sure this debt is shown in the legal section of the credit report.

Commercial Credit Line Vendors
These are the hardest to get approvals with and the most desirable for Company Credit.

DO NOT apply for any of these unless the previous sections have been completed and credit issued.

If your D&B Profile was just created as a start-up company it may be 4 months before section 3 can be completed!

Once again, Do Not Rush the Process! Even if an existing D&B Profile is used it may still require several months before section 3 can be completed!

Credit can be accelerated using purchased trade lines, however if the provider is red flagged by the credit reporting agency you may well have destroyed the company's credit building potential. This is a double-edged

Credit Mastery: Developing Aged Corporations

sword because when done correctly by a qualified credit donor it will raise your ranking faster than any other method or equally destroy it.

Do not apply for any of the accounts below unless the D&B Report shows at least 6 vendors with credit lines around $5,000 in total lines.

Apply to Only 1 or 2 Accounts from the selected companies below PER MONTH!

Leave Personal Guarantee Section BLANK!

Amazon - Convert your Amazon Net 30 to revolving after about 3 months. This will be a Citibank Card
Best Buy
Exmark
Home Depot
Pep Boys
Sam's Club
Tractor Supply Company

Remember banks lend on history and the ability to repay an obligation. Trade Lines Show History! Cash Flow Shows Ability!

Add another UCC-1 for $10,000 or more that can be justified and clear with UCC-3 in 3 months paid satisfactory. This is a legal state held record by the Secretary of State where filed.

	Company 1	Company 2	Company 3
Applications Submitted			
Applications Approved			
Total Credit Issued			
Total Credit Reported			
Total Credit Available			
Application Submitted to			
Submission Date			
Approval Date			
Credit Line			
Account Number			

Credit Mastery: Developing Aged Corporations

1st Charge Amount			
1st Payment [1]			
Reported to DnB™ Date			
Reported to Experian Business™ Date			
	Company 1	Company 2	Company 3
Item – Date Sold			
Sale Amount			
Tax Deductible Amount			

B2 B Activity Report

	Company 1	Company 2	Company 3
Account Number			
Total Credit Issued			
Total Credit Reported			
Total Credit Available			
Product Sold			
Charge Amount			
Payment			
Reported to DnB™ Date			
Experian Date			

Credit Mastery: Developing Aged Corporations

Transactions	Company 1	Company 2	Company 3

Credit Submission & Usage Report – Month 4

Credit Cards

Business credit cards are the validation of a company's credit prior to applying for bank loans.

Citibank
Key Bank
Capital One Spark Business Card

Revenued Business Card Visa - issued by Sutton Bank
Applying for Revenued is simple. Revenued doesn't perform a hard pull on an applicant's personal credit score, instead basing Flex Line limits on revenue – and not FICO alone. Once you apply, you'll receive a funding decision in as little as an hour and have access to your funds within 24 hours.

One drawback with Revenued is the ability to build credit. Using the card will not build credit. Instead, the Flex Line needs to be used (and repaid) to boost business credit. Still, for those planning to access even more capital, that should be a fairly easy task.

Here are the minimum requirements for getting Revenued:

Businesses must operate in the U.S., must not be a start-up, and MUST have been **in operation for at least six months**

Businesses must have a separate bank account with $10,000 or more in deposits and no more than three negative balance days each month
Business must not be a sole proprietorship and must have employees.
Business cannot be a financial services or law services company.

Flex Line limits are up to $100,000 and, as mentioned, are available within 24 hours of account opening. Keep in mind that Revenued does have purchasing limits on your card, however. For example, companies can spend a maximum of $10,000 per day and $50,000 per month. The maximum allowable single purchase on a card is $10,000.

Because approvals are based on your business revenue and banking activity, the Revenued Flex Line makes capital available to business owners even if they have less-than-ideal personal or business credit scores - this is ideal for the Credit Mastery multiple corporations strategy.

BJ's Perks for Business MasterCard® - 844-271-2539
Must be a BJ's Club Member to apply. This card is issued by Comenity Bank and pulls from Experian Business. You must apply over the phone you can request No Personal Guarantee and they are happy to assist! They will call you back if they need more information or a Personal Guarantee. We have seen $20,000 credit lines on these with 3 reporting trade-lines of $500 each!

Bank Loans – Do this for each company! Some have done this step in month one with a fully secured or using personal guarantee for the entire loan.

Make sure you have completed the section on Business Plans and have your written business plan ready in order to proceed. After getting at least $5,000 in cumulative Credit Lines from sections 1 – 5 it is time to apply for your first business loan. This loan should be relative to your business income to provide for repayment. (Business income can always be from loans from you to the business).

A starter Loan of $2,500 - $50,000 with your local bank is ideal. Take in your business plan (if required – most likely not on this small amount) to your local bank loan officer to obtain a small loan in any amount they counter offer and let them know this loan is strictly for building a credit history. You may have to post a security deposit against the loan, but is well worth it as these are high scoring credit points with D&B.

With the funds from the first loan go to 2 other banks and get additional secured loans for at least $1,000 and pay them off in 3 months.

Pay the loans off in 45-60 days, wait 30 days and do again for 2x the amount.

Pay off loan in 45-60 days, wait 30 days and do again for 5x the loan as you history dictates your ability to repay.

Another Source for online Loans is Kiva. They are a nonprofit organization that specializes in small business funding. www.kiva.org

For those who wish to get SBA Loans now is the time to visit the SBA and SCORE to submit your business information and start the SBA loan process. This is time consuming, and your financial projections must be on target with identical industry company's operations (more below in SBA section and Business Plan section).

Credit Mastery: Developing Aged Corporations

	Company 1	Company 2	Company 3
Applications Submitted			
Applications Approved			
Total Credit Issued			
Total Credit Reported			
Total Credit Available			
Application Submitted to			
Submission Date			
Approval Date			
Credit Line			
Account Number			
1st Charge Amount			
1st Payment [1]			
Reported to DnB™ Date			
Reported to Experian Business™ Date			
	Company 1	Company 2	Company 3
Item – Date Sold			
Sale Amount			
Tax Deductible Amount			

Credit Mastery: Developing Aged Corporations

B2 B Activity Report

	Company 1	Company 2	Company 3
Account Number			
Total Credit Issued			
Total Credit Reported			
Total Credit Available			
Product Sold			
Charge Amount			
Payment			
Reported to DnB™ Date			
Experian Date			
Transactions	**Company 1**	**Company 2**	**Company 3**

Credit Submission & Usage Report – Month 5
Almost There!

BILL Divvy Corporate Business Card is a corporate credit card that promises no fees, scalable credit lines, enforceable budgets, and more. The card is issued by Cross River Bank and, through BILL.com, it provides the ideal platform for helping small businesses (plus midsize businesses and larger commerce and retail brands) streamline the spending they make each month – without impacting their personal credit scores.

The BILL Divvy Card operates a fast application process that requires only six steps and may result in a near-instant underwriting (depending upon the business's cash supply and income). BILL also operates several different underwriting forms – the company even boasts an internal underwriting team for new applicants. Traditional and cash underwriting are offered as well, making it easy for companies to find a bespoke credit line for their unique needs.

Travel Credit Card Accounts - Apply for the following travel credit cards:
United Airlines
American Airlines

Computer Vendors
Every real business has certain expenses in common and those are computer and telecommunications equipment purchases. Purchase at least $1 000 to credit line limit every month and verify the credit is reported.

If your credit is sufficient you can apply for computer leases with a $1 buyout at end of lease. Keep in mind that you can not resell this equipment until lease is satisfied.

Dell Computers ®
CDW.com
Lenovo
HP

Do Not Apply For more than 6 credit accounts per month at anytime!

More Fuel Cards
Philips 66 ®
Conoco Corporate Account
Wex Universal Fuel Cards www.wex.com

Wex Fleet – Fuel Cards www.wexinc.com/product-recommendations
Accepted at more than 180,000 WEX Network locations nationwide.
(Wex is the issuer for Conoco Universal / Stripes / Exxon Mobil Fleet / ALON Universal / Phillips66 Universal / CITGO Fleet Universal / 7-Eleven Universal Fleet / RaceTrac Universal Fleet / QuickTrip Fleetmaster Plus / Circle K Universal Card / Gulf Universal Fleet / 76 Universal Card Union76

Fuel cards are necessary for every business! – All real businesses use fuel cards period. These are essential for building a solid credit report! These cards validate your company's existence as a real operating entity.

Credit Mastery: Developing Aged Corporations

Suggestion for Maximum Credit Faster:

File UCC-1 for $10,000 and clear with UCC-3 in 3 months paid satisfactory from one of your company to another. Make sure to show payments in your payment/invoicing for your bank statements. This is a legal state held record by the Secretary of State where filed.

Get Verify on Demand for $500,000 or more to start demonstrating credibility.

	Company 1	Company 2	Company 3
Applications Submitted			
Applications Approved			
Total Credit Issued			
Total Credit Reported			
Total Credit Available			
Application Submitted to			
Submission Date			
Approval Date			
Credit Line			
Account Number			
1st Charge Amount			
1st Payment [1]			
Reported to DnB™ Date			
Reported to Experian Business™ Date			

	Company 1	Company 2	Company 3
Item – Date Sold			
Sale Amount			

Credit Mastery: Developing Aged Corporations

Tax Deductible Amount			

B2 B Activity Report

	Company 1	Company 2	Company 3
Account Number			
Total Credit Issued			
Total Credit Reported			
Total Credit Available			
Product Sold			
Charge Amount			
Payment			
Reported to DnB™ Date			
Experian Date			
Transactions	**Company 1**	**Company 2**	**Company 3**

Credit Submission & Usage Report – Month 6

Start Writing Bank Loan Business Plan for Month 7!

Major Credit Card Accounts

Check Your D&B Report Weekly! Pay off the bills 10 days early!

The aviation fuel cards have a distinction on your credit profile that your business has an executive level of employees or owners. You must use these cards and once again you can offer a sale at the local airport to fuel someone's airplane or jet and give them a few cents a gallon discount in order to consummate a purchase. Colt Fuel or World Aviation Fuel Credit Cards. These accounts will be anywhere from $25,000 to $50,000 upon issuance, but are extremely important when going for the over $1,000,000 in credit line levels at banks.

World Fuel ® (Aviation Fuel Card)
Chevron's TotalGA ® Card (Aviation Fuel Card)
Capital One ® Business Platinum card
Advanta ® Platinum Business Card

AMEX American Express ® - -
Apply for AMEX Gold Card ® or A Fully Secured AMEX Platinum Card ® with $50,000 secured account Use this card to maximum every month and payoff balance.

This will be another card that will add to your profile and with the other credit accounts and loans we have accumulated to date this will not be hard to get issued.

Important Note 1: With American Express if you have ever had a delinquent account they will have it in their records and will either deny you a card or require a secured card thorough an affiliate bank.
Important Note 2: With American Express you must use the card to its maximum in the first two months to establish a spending pattern. If you ignore this you will have to call in to get your account re-approved on purchases that seem outside your normal spending patterns. You must max out this card at least 3 times a year!

Certificate of Deposit: Depending on Your Cash Position and the relationship you have with the lenders you are courting we can suggest it is time for a CD Courtesy Deposit or Certificate of Deposit Lease of $500,000 to $5,000,000. This is a calculated process to entice and impress a banker. It shows you have influence with others with money and have recommended they place their funds into the bank. This builds instant respect from a bank officer when they realize you were the instrumental party in having funds placed within the bank. You will be paying the fees for this process and you cannot lien nor encumber the funds. A Certificate of Deposit helps a bank with their Federal Reserve Rating and Ranking along with the FDIC. The CD Courtesy Deposit can be done at any fully insured bank or credit union. Visit www.isg3.com for current fees.

Depending on Your Cash Position and the relationship you have with the lenders you are courting we can suggest it is time for a CD Courtesy Deposit of $500,000 to $5,000,000. This is a calculated process to entice and impress a banker. It shows you have influence with others with money and have recommended they

Credit Mastery: Developing Aged Corporations

place their funds into the bank. **This builds instant respect from a bank officer when they realize you were the instrumental party in having funds placed within the bank. You will be paying the fees for this process and you cannot lien nor encumber the funds. A Certificate of Deposit helps a bank with their Federal Reserve Rating and Ranking along with the FDIC.** The CD Courtesy Deposit can be done at any fully insured bank or credit union. Visit www.isg3.com for current fees.

Should any of the process become confusing or you have problems you can contact us for coaching for as little as $50 per session online, contact our representatives for a consultation billed at an hourly rate or attend a seminar.

	Company 1	Company 2	Company 3
Applications Submitted			
Applications Approved			
Total Credit Issued			
Total Credit Reported			
Total Credit Available			
Application Submitted to			
Submission Date			
Approval Date			
Credit Line			
Account Number			
1st Charge Amount			
1st Payment [1]			
Reported to DnB™ Date			

Credit Mastery: Developing Aged Corporations

Reported to Experian Business™ Date			
	Company 1	Company 2	Company 3
Item – Date Sold			
Sale Amount			
Tax Deductible Amount			

B2 B Activity Report

	Company 1	Company 2	Company 3
Account Number			
Total Credit Issued			
Total Credit Reported			
Total Credit Available			
Product Sold			
Charge Amount			
Payment			
Reported to DnB™ Date			
Experian Date			
	Company 1	Company 2	Company 3

Transactions			

Credit Submission & Usage Report – Month 7

Hello - Loan Time!

Apply for a Business Loan at a small local lender
and/or Equipment Lease

Many times, it is much easier to get equipment your business needs via a leasing company opposed to a hard money loan. We have structured millions of dollars in equipment leases based simply on cash flow. This ranges from commercial trucks to computers to restaurant equipment.

CD Loan
Lease CD for Deposit in Bank for Unsecured Loan
- Minimum Amount $500,000

Leased CD's in the amount of $500,000 are used to enhance your bank statement for Lenders. The cost of these instruments range from 4.5 - 7.5% and are placed in your bank within 7-10 business days after fess are placed in escrow and verified. So, $500,000 will cost approximately $37,500, but it is the cost of obtaining funds without personal guarantees.

This is critical for working with a local bank for a sizable loan.

You will discuss a loan with your bank officer regarding a loan of $300,000 - $500,000. The loan officer is going to want security and this is a way to generate pseudo security for the bank, yet has a bonus for the bank in offering you a loan.

Offer to purchase a CD at the bank in the above amount and for the period of 12 months, but the condition is that it will not be encumbered or place liens against it. This is a paradox for many bankers as it creates the funds to issue a loan, yet they cannot secure the loan with the CD instrument.

The company providing the CD retains ownership and is paid the interest, yet it is placed in your company's name and therefore goes on a bank statement in your benefit, but keep in mind and tell loan officer at the bank that CD is not to be liened nor encumbered as security as it is a demonstration of financial ability.

This requires a very well written business plan and your understanding of your business plan along with your ability to convey this transaction. We are available for a fee to perform these negotiations in person with your bank for a cost of $1,000 per day plus all related expenses (travel, lodging, etc.) and is well worth the cost.

	Company 1	Company 2	Company 3
Applications Submitted			

Credit Mastery: Developing Aged Corporations

Applications Approved			
Total Credit Issued			
Total Credit Reported			
Total Credit Available			
Application Submitted to			
Submission Date			
Approval Date			
Credit Line			
Account Number			
1st Charge Amount			
1st Payment [1]			
Reported to DnB™ Date			
Reported to Experian Business™ Date			
	Company 1	Company 2	Company 3
Item – Date Sold			
Sale Amount			
Tax Deductible Amount			

B2 B Activity Report

Credit Mastery: Developing Aged Corporations

	Company 1	Company 2	Company 3
Account Number			
Total Credit Issued			
Total Credit Reported			
Total Credit Available			
Product Sold			
Charge Amount			
Payment			
Reported to DnB™ Date			
Experian Date			
Transactions	**Company 1**	**Company 2**	**Company 3**

Loan or Credit Line Not Funded: Time to Use Advanced Business Credit Tactics

Time to Use Advanced Business Credit Tactics

OK, try a leased CD (Certificate of Deposit). These can be arranged as a non-liened non-encumbered deposit. This is the most least expensive way to go. The bank cant use these funds as a guarantee in this case, however the bank will get a multiplier from the Federal Reserve for these deposits that can offset some of the lending risk.

Make sure your loan officer knows this! These can be processed in 14 days upon approval in most cases! Provider will need to verify your lease funds and have them placed in escrow prior to transfers.

An example is a loan was being considered by a bank that did not have adequate reserves for the loan. $2M dollars of CD's were placed in bank at a lease cost of 7.5% or $150,000. The client did not have the $150,000 and made arrangements for a flash funding source to provide the funds that were escrow secured. The bank did 500,000 per day in concert with the escrow company.

The flash funding for the $150,000 cost the client 20% or $30,000 and had to place those funds in a separate escrow arrangement. All in all, the cost for the $2M loan was $180,000 or 9%.

OK, we turn to our advanced business credit tactics for a Collateral CD (Certificate of Deposit). These can be arranged as a full collateral guarantee deposit. This is the most expensive way to go and slowest of this method as it takes 60 days sometimes. Also, the LTV on these are 70% so plan accordingly.

Options:

Option 1: Sell account receivables and their contracts - use caution when going this route to ensure that these funds can be repaid on time.

Option 2: Use another company to guarantee your loan. It eliminates a personal guarantee and the lender will want a loan package on both companies along with formal documentation from executives as to the transaction – also be prepared for telephone calls from bankers on this strategy. This is another reason for a multiple company strategy from the Accelerated Business Tactics Vol 1 Systematic Credit Engineering!

Option 3: Perform a Merger or Acquisition if not publicly traded, this is not that complicated as it is done at a state level then notify the IRS on the changes. When you fold another company into another it can blend the financials to make the primary company look larger. This may have tax implications and you need to consult a CPA regarding tax matters. Once Loan is approved and issued the process can be reversed if desired. This is another reason for a multiple company strategy from the Accelerated Business Tactics Vol 1 Systematic Credit Engineering!

Suggestion for Maximum Credit Faster:

File UCC-1 for $10,000 and clear with UCC-3 in 3 months paid satisfactory. This is a legal state held record by the Secretary of State where filed. See the Credit Mastery Seminar for the exact details and how to pitch this to your bank.

Get Verify on Demand for $500,000 or more to start demonstrating credibility. This is Hard Money that is deposited into a Money Market Account in your company or your name. It is fast and affordable for showing cash to banker, however you cannot lien nor encumber these funds – See the Credit Mastery Seminar for the exact details and how to pitch this to your bank.

Private Investor Funds – SEC Reg D Exemption
For capitalization without personal guarantees or credit checks we recommend using an exempted Registered Security with a Form D – Reg D offering. This consists of writing a private placement memorandum and contacting broker dealers to fund with project from private investors and hedge funds. These are usually high interest vehicles around 12% - 16% and this interest is paid quarterly to the investors. So, $1,000,000 will have a debt service cost of $120,000 to $160,000 annually – make sure your companies business can support this before starting.

This is not a difficult process and is faster to obtain capital than conventional credit building.

This is an entirely different process than building business.

Option: Sell account receivables and their contracts - use caution when going this route to ensure that these funds can be repaid on time.

Option: <u>**Have Company 3 guarantee a loan for Company 1 or 2.**</u> It eliminates a personal guarantee and the lender will want a loan package on both companies along with formal documentation from executives as to the transaction – also be prepared for telephone calls from bankers on this strategy. ***This is another reason for a multiple company strategy! See Corporate Guarantee Section of this book!***

Option 4 : Perform a Merger or Acquisition if not publicly traded, this is not that complicated as it is done at a state level then notify the IRS on the changes. When you fold another company into another it can blend the financials to make the primary company look larger. This may have tax implications and you need to consult a CPA regarding tax matters. Once Loan is approved and issued the process can be reversed if desired. This is covered at the seminar in all details as there are many items in the process to perform this satisfactorily.

To expedite all sections past section 7 we recommend the use of a Corporation of 3 years in age to accelerate the process.

Items in italics are business credit accelerators with the CD Lease and / or Deposit Loan cuts time in half.

* Leasing a Certificate of Deposit (CD) *

We have two Options for using CD's one for using the CD as Collateral (CD-C) and the other plan for non-encumbered non-liened.

Leasing a CD is fairly simple process where you can simply place fees in escrow and released as per agreement.

The CD's are also available and we have placed these several times at banks and credit unions to show financial strength of you the Client.

This is used when the bank will do a loan - only if they had the extra funds. So you are in essence providing your bank the funds to loan you, by leasing a bank instrument on an annual basis.

This is a Tactic we have used time and again! Our Best Secret to Fast Funding! We suggest this tactic for everyone seeking funding!

<u>Non Collateral Certificates of Deposit</u> - This is done at a far lower cost and for amounts as low as $200,000 to $50M USD. Fees historically ranged from 4% to 7.5%.

1) Provide proof of funds in the amount of the placement fee based. At time of publication we have a source that will fund the placement fee of $1,000,000 in CD's and can do these multiple times.

2) After due diligence, you will enter into contract that stipulates the terms and conditions along with the name of the bank or credit union you wish the CD's to be placed.

3) After contract, CD's will be placed at bank or credit union as per contract and escrow agreement.
We have placed $5M in one week via escrow providing $1M per day with a 7.5% fee.

Use Verify on Demand – Proof of Funds
Let's get started by learning the difference between these two tools and the best use for each.

Verify on Demand is an account that has been properly setup with the clients (you) information such as your name or business name. This account is created at a bank or credit union usually with actual funds being deposited into this account. Due to actual funds being placed into an account the fees are higher than Proof of Funds letters.

Proof of Funds is a statement that you have funds somewhere available for a transaction closing. Proof of Funds letters are widely available on the internet at a variety of costs, however they are much less than Verify on Demand due to this having actual funds moved into an account. Most of the Proof of Funds providers are looking to give these are real estate deals and are subject to using their services during a closing for whatever points they add to your deal. This is where they lock you in and then charge you an additional fee (points). So Proof of Funds Letters are inexpensive and are not bank to bank verifiable in most cases and are limited in scope of use and tied to a single transaction every time.

Credit Mastery: Developing Aged Corporations

Business Plan – Data Entry Section Company

This is the executive summary. It sets out the essential facts about your business — who owns it, what it does, why it exists and where it's going. Think of it as your elevator pitch. Everything you'd want to tell a potential investor, partner, employee or customer should be here. You should do this for every company!

Short introduction:
_____
_____
_____
_____
_____
_____
_____
_____

Business name
_____

Owners
_____
_____

A single sentence summary of your main business activity.
What we do is
_____
_____
_____
_____

A brief statement of what you want your business to be.
Company vision
_____
_____
_____

Describe your competitive edge.

What will keep customers coming to you instead of a competitor?
Unique selling points
_____
_____
_____
_____

Companies Products and/or Services

Product 1 _____ Product 5 _____
Product 2 _____ Product 6 _____
Product 3 _____ Product 7 _____
Product 4 _____ Product 8 _____

A brief summary of your target market.
Target Market
_____
_____
_____
_____
_____
_____
_____

Key goals for the period covered by the plan. Make them measurable, achievable and consistent.

Company Goals

1. Year 1:
_____
_____
_____

2. Year 2:
_____
_____
_____

3. Year 3:
_____
_____
_____

Capital Requirements
If you're using your plan to apply for a loan, state how much you need and what it's going to be used for. Your figures should be supported by detailed calculations in the financial plan.

Total Amount: $ _____
Purpose:
_____
_____
_____

Amount: $ _____
Purpose:
_____

_____
_____

Amount: $ _____
Purpose:
_____
_____
_____

Amount: $ _____
Purpose:
_____
_____
_____

Business Details

History - If yours is an existing business, describe its history and current situation.
Summary of the business's background to date ...
_____
_____
_____
_____
_____

Date established ___/_____/____

Operating history
List any significant events in the operating history of the company — changes of ownership, purchase or premises or assets, and so on.

Event 1
_____
_____

Event 2
_____
_____

Event 3
_____
_____

Products / Services
This is where you describe your products and services in detail. How are they positioned in the market? What benefits do they offer you customers? What makes them unique?

Product / Service 1 _____
Description:
_____
_____
_____

Product / Service 2 _____
Description:
_____
_____
_____

Product / Service 3 _____
Description:
_____
_____
_____

Product / Service 4 _____
_____
_____
_____

Product / Service 5 _____
_____
_____
_____

Structure

Describe the structure of the business, including the owners, management and staff. You could include an organization chart if you think it would be useful.

Your Company Introduction ...
_____
_____
_____
_____
_____
_____
_____
_____
_____

_____
_____
_____
_____
_____
_____
_____
_____

Business Structure
Are you a: sole proprietor, a partnership, a trust, C-Corp, LLC, SP, LLP, LP, GP

State: _____

Location(s):
_____
_____
_____

Who are the key people — the shareholders, directors, managers and staff?

Describe their background and industry experience.

Key people

Person 1:
_____
_____
_____

Person 2:
_____
_____
_____

Person 3:
_____
_____
_____

Notes:
_____
_____
_____
_____
_____

SWOT Analysis
(SWOT stands for "Strengths, weaknesses, opportunities and threats".)

A SWOT analysis is a great way to understand where your business is today and how it could be improved.

Strengths

Strength 1
_____
_____

Strength 2
_____
_____

Strength 3
_____
_____

Strength 4
_____
_____

Strength 5
_____
_____

Weaknesses

Weakness 1
_____
_____

Weakness 2
_____
_____

Weakness 3
_____
_____

Weakness 4
_____
_____

Credit Mastery: Developing Aged Corporations

Weakness 5
_____
_____
_____

Opportunities

Opportunity._____
_____
_____

Opportunity._____
_____
_____

Opportunity._____
_____
_____

Opportunity._____
_____
_____

Opportunity._____
_____
_____

Threats

Threat._____
_____
_____

Threat._____
_____
_____

Threat._____
_____
_____

Threat._____
_____
_____

Threat._____
_____
_____

Premises, Plant and Equipment

Describe your premises (planned or existing), including the location, rental details and build out.

Premises

_____
_____
_____
_____
_____

Plant and Equipment

List the plant and equipment you need to run the business. Show the value of existing assets and the cost of assets you plan to buy or rent.

1.
_____
_____

2.
_____
_____
_____

3.
_____
_____
_____

Information Systems and Telecommunications

Describe the information systems you'll use to run the business — things like your customer database, your accounting system and your stock management system. Consider SugarCRM™ or Salesforce™ for sales and customer relations management software systems. For website administration, we recommend Joomla or WordPress software interface on Linux based servers. Both of these interfaces are easy to use, have great support and variety of applications, modules and components for any business website.

Information systems

System 1.
_____
_____
_____

System 2.
_____
_____
_____

System 3.

Telecommunications

How will customers contact you? Do you have a switchboard or messaging service?
Search google for 8bitSofware.us for business Voip PBX's or iCompro Innova PBX as they lease equipment

System 1.

System 2.

System 3.

Notes:

Intellectual property, licenses and memberships

List your registered business names, including the states where they're registered.

Registered Business Names

Domain Names - Have you registered any domain names?
_____
_____
_____
_____
_____

Trademarks and Patents
Do you have any trademarks or patents?

Item 1.
_____
_____
_____
_____

Item 2.
_____
_____
_____
_____

Item 3.
_____
_____
_____
_____
_____
_____

Licenses
Do you need any licenses or government approvals to run your business?

Item 1.
_____
_____
_____
_____

Item 2.
_____

Item 3.

Memberships
Do you belong to a business or industry association?

Insurance

List details of any insurances, including the amount insured and the annual premium.

General Liability - Public Risk Insurance

Workers' compensation

Professional Indemnity / Product Liability

Business Asset Insurance

Fire, Property and Casualty Insurance
_____
_____
_____
_____

Key Person Insurance (Important as this can be leveraged)
_____
_____
_____
_____
_____

Error and Omissions Insurance –
(Required if Using Fortune 100™ Nominee Executives)
_____
_____
_____
_____

Officer and Directors Insurance
(Required if Using Fortune 100™ Nominee Executives)
_____
_____
_____

Performance Guarantee Bond
_____
_____
_____

Liability Bond
_____
_____
_____

Letter of Credit Guarantee
_____
_____
_____

Personal or Additional Entries

_____
_____
_____
_____
_____

_____
_____
_____
_____
_____
_____

_____
_____
_____
_____
_____

Goals, Achievements & Strategies

This is the heart of your plan — the place where you set out your goals and the strategies that are going to help you achieve them. Try to put specific, measurable numbers around each goal so that you can track your progress later; those numbers will also feed into the projections in your financial plan.

Goals and Achievements

Set out your major business goals for the period covered by the plan, then set milestones for each step along the way. Try to make your goals specific and measurable; for example, rather than simply saying you want to increase turnover, say how much and by when.

Goal 1.
_____
_____
_____
_____

First date._____
Second date. _____
Note:
_____
_____
_____

Goal 2.
_____

Credit Mastery: Developing Aged Corporations

_____
_____
_____

First date. _____
Second date. _____
Note:
_____
_____
_____
_____

Goal 3.
_____
_____
_____

First date. _____
Second date. _____

Note:
_____
_____
_____
_____

Marketing

How many leads do you plan to generate with your marketing? How will you track your leads? Sugar CRM™ and Salesforce™ are two great CRM software products for tracking sales and leads.

Overall Marketing Goals
_____
_____
_____
_____
_____
_____
_____

Tracking techniques
_____
_____
_____

_____
_____

Marketing Goal 1.

_____
_____
_____
_____

Marketing Goal 2.

_____
_____
_____
_____

Marketing Goal 3.

_____
_____
_____
_____

Marketing Goal 4.

_____
_____
_____
_____

Marketing Goal 5.

_____
_____
_____
_____

Marketing Goal 6.

_____
_____
_____
_____

Marketing Goal 7.

_____
_____

Marketing Goal 8.

Marketing Goal 9.

Marketing Goal 10.

What marketing techniques do you plan to use? We've listed some examples to set you thinking.
Advertising

Online Ads

Online Forum Posts

Online Blogs

PPC – Pay Per Click Campaigns

Craig's List

Facebook

Facebook Likes

Facebook PPC

Google Plus

Google PPC (Pay Per Click)

Credit Mastery: Developing Aged Corporations

_____
_____
_____
_____

Ebay Classifieds
_____
_____
_____
_____

Ebay Auctions
_____
_____
_____
_____

Amazon
_____
_____

_____
_____
_____
_____
_____

_____
_____
_____
_____
_____

National Newspaper Advertising
_____
_____
_____
_____

Local Newspaper Advertising
_____

Yellow Pages
(A single line entry is required for credit reporting agencies)

Printed Marketing Material

Business cards.

Flyers.

Brochures.

Catalogs.

_____
_____
_____
_____

Magnetic Signs. (Auto, Refrigerator, etc.)
_____
_____
_____
_____
_____

Referral cards.
_____
_____
_____
_____

Calendars
_____
_____
_____
_____

Website

Describe your website and its features:
_____
_____
_____
_____
_____
_____
_____
_____
_____
_____
_____

Email
_____
_____
_____

Direct mail - Physical mail.

Events and Publicity
Trade shows and expos.

Seminars - Webinars.

Networking events.

Sponsorships.

Referral program.

Credit Mastery: Developing Aged Corporations

_____
_____
_____
_____

Community Events
_____
_____
_____
_____
_____
_____
_____

Mobile Apps
_____
_____
_____
_____
_____

Sales

Sales Goals
Your overall goals:
_____
_____
_____
_____

Tracking techniques: What percentage of the leads you generate through your marketing do you hope to convert to sales?
_____
_____
_____
_____

Sales Goal 1
_____
_____
_____
_____

Sales Goal 2

_____
_____
_____
_____

Sales Goal 3

_____
_____
_____
_____

Sales Goal 4

_____
_____
_____
_____

Sales Goal 5

_____
_____
_____
_____

Sales Organization

Management

_____
_____
_____
_____

Team Members

_____
_____
_____
_____

Sales Training

_____

Credit Mastery: Developing Aged Corporations

_____
_____
_____
_____

Sales Materials
   Brochures:
_____
_____
_____
_____
_____

Testimonials.
_____
_____
_____
_____
_____

   Samples and photos.
_____
_____
_____
_____

   Point-of-Purchase sales material.
_____
_____
_____
_____

   Business cards.
_____
_____
_____
_____

   Appointment Cards
_____
_____
_____

Sales Methods

Sales training.

Special offers.

Special events

Product launches.

White Papers

Trade-ins.

Bartering
___

Up Sales Products
___

Customer Management and Retention
Customer Relations Management or CRM
Having successfully sold to a customer, you need to keep them coming back. What proportion of customers do you hope to retain and how?
Your ideas:
___

Tracking techniques
___

To manage your customers effectively, you need to know as much about them as possible. How will you gather and store that information?

Management techniques
Customer database.
___

Getting customer data.

CRM Software – Customer Relations Management

Questionnaires and surveys.

Retention Techniques
How will you keep them coming back?

Frequent buyers' program.

Club Memberships - Subscriptions

Reminder system

___

Newsletters
___

Email Updates
___

Service contracts
___

Networking events
___

Related Products Upselling
___

Discounts, Coupons and other offers
___

What's your pricing strategy?

Credit Mastery: Developing Aged Corporations

Do you offer a premium product at a premium price?
Do you intend on under-cutting your competition?
How do you calculate your prices?

Pricing Strategy

Overall strategy

_____
_____
_____
_____
_____
_____
_____
_____
_____
_____
_____
_____
_____
_____
_____
_____
_____
_____
_____
_____
_____
_____
_____

Prices

List the prices for each of your main products or services and brief pricing description.

Product 1:

_____
_____
_____
_____

Product 2:

_____
_____
_____

Product 3

Credit Mastery: Developing Aged Corporations

_____
_____
_____
_____

Product 4: _____
_____
_____
_____
_____

Product 5: _____
_____
_____

Competitive Overview

The industry _____
Your SIC Code: _____

Summarize the key characteristics of your industry. How large is it? Is it a growth industry or already mature? How large is the overall market? Who do they buy from?

Your summary
_____
_____
_____
_____
_____
_____
_____
_____
_____
_____
_____
_____
_____
_____
_____
_____
_____

Target Market

Credit Mastery: Developing Aged Corporations

This is where you describe your target market and your ideal customer in detail. It's important to identify a profitable niche, then try to find out as much about your potential customers as you can. Use federal, state and local websites and their studies and statistics or talk to your industry association for demographic information.

Your market summary

_____
_____
_____
_____
_____
_____
_____
_____
_____
_____

Describe your target customer group in detail. If you intend to market your services to several audiences, copy this table and describe them separately.

Age(s)

_____
_____
_____
_____
_____

Gender(s)

_____
_____
_____
_____
_____

Occupation(s)

_____
_____
_____
_____
_____

Income(s)

_____
_____
_____
_____
_____

Location(s)

_____

Credit Mastery: Developing Aged Corporations

_____
_____
_____
_____

Key Drivers
_____
_____
_____
_____
_____
_____

Size of market
_____
_____
_____
_____
_____

Growth potential
_____
_____
_____
_____
_____
_____
_____

The Competition

Start with a competitive overview, summarizing the major players in your industry, then drill down with a detailed analysis of your top five competitors.
Who is your fiercest competitor?
How do they differentiate themselves in the marketplace?
Do they market themselves on Quality? Convenience? Or Price?
Do they have any weaknesses you can exploit?

Your competitive overview
_____
_____
_____

Credit Mastery: Developing Aged Corporations

_____
_____
_____
_____
_____
_____
_____

Competitor 1_____
Established
_____
_____
_____
_____
_____

Market share
_____
_____
_____

Value
_____
_____
_____

Strengths
_____
_____
_____
_____

Weaknesses
_____
_____
_____
_____

Competitor 2 _____
Established
_____
_____
_____

Market share
_____

Credit Mastery: Developing Aged Corporations

_____
_____

Value
_____
_____
_____

Strengths
_____
_____

Weaknesses
_____
_____
_____
_____

Competitor 3 _____

Established
_____
_____

Market share
_____
_____
_____
_____

Value
_____
_____

Strengths
_____
_____
_____

Weaknesses
_____

_____
_____
_____

Competitor 4 _____

Established
_____
_____
_____
_____

Market share
_____
_____
_____
_____

Value
_____
_____
_____

Strengths
_____
_____
_____

Weaknesses
_____
_____
_____

Competitor 5 _____

Established
_____
_____
_____

Market share
_____
_____
_____

Value
_____
_____
_____

Strengths
_____
_____
_____
_____
_____

Weaknesses
_____
_____
_____
_____
_____

Now that you have completed the data information section that you will use for your business plans that you submit to lenders. Information for financials was purposely not included within this guide as there are software spreadsheet files that are better suited for this purpose.

Reporting Creditors & Vendors

Credit Card Applications for Major Corporate Credit Cards www.isg3.com
Amazon 800-301-5546 www.amazon.com
Best Buy 800-811-7276 www.bestbuy.com
Chevron/Texaco Business Card 888-243-8358 www.chevron.com
CITGO Fleet 800-561-4991 www.citgo.com
Conoco 866-289-5622 www.conoco.com
Dell 800-757-8434 www.dell.com
ExxonMobil Business Card 800-903-9966 www.exxon.com
FedEx Kinko's 800-488-3705 www.fedex.com
Gateway Computers 800-846-2000 www.gateway.com
HP/Compaq Computers 800-888-9909 www.hp.com
Grainger 888-361-8649 www.grainger.com
Home Depot Commercial 800-685-6691 www.homedepot.com
Home Depot 877-969-9039
Key Bank 800-254-2737 www.keybank.com
Kiva www.kiva.org
Lowes 866-232-7443 www.lowes.com
Office Depot 800-767-1358 www.officedepot.com
Office Max 800-283-7674 www.officemax.com
Philips 66 866-289-5630 www.phillips.com
Quill 800-882-3400 www.quill.com
Radio Shack 800-442-7221 www.radioshack.com
Reliable 800-735-4000 www.reliable.com
Sam's Club 800-301-5546 www.samsclub.com
Sears 800-599-9710 www.sears.com
Shell Fleet 800-223-3296 www.shell.com
Staples 800-767-1275 www.staples.com
Sunoco 800-935-3387 www.sunoco.com
Target 800-440-5317 www.target.com
Texaco 800-839-2267 www.texaco.com
Uline Packaging 800-958-5463 www.uline.com
Valero 877-882-5376 www.valero.com
Wal-Mart 877-294-7548 www.walmart.com
Wright Express 888-743-3893 www.wrightexpress.com

Peak Venture Group   www.peakventure.org/
Rockies Venture Club   www.rockiesventureclub.org/
Rocky Mountain Venture Capital Association   www.rockymountainvca.com/
Colorado Venture Capital Firms 5280 Partners, LLC   www.5280partners.com/
Access Venture Partners www.accessvp.com/
Altira Group LLC www.altiragroup.com/
Appian Ventures www.appianvc.com/
Aweida Venture Partners www.aweida.com/
Boulder Ventures Ltd. www.boulderventures.com/
BusinessFinance.com www.businessfinance.com/
Capital Markets Group, Inc. www.capitalmarketsgroup.com/
Centennial Ventures   www.centennial.com/
Colorado Women www.coloradowomen.org/

CSU Ventures www.csuventures.org/
Foundry Group www.foundrygroup.com/
Gefinor Ventures www.gefinorventures.com/
Intel Capital www.intel.com/about/companyinfo/capital/index.htm
Investor Avenue www.investoravenue.com/
iSherpa Capital Group www.isherpa.com/
ITU Ventures www.itu.com/
KRG Capital Partners, LLC www.krgcapital.com/
Keiretsu Forum www.keiretsuforum.com/frontend/index.aspx
Meritage Private Equity Funds www.meritagefunds.com/
Mobius Venture Capital www.mobiusvc.com/index.php
Murphree Venture Partners www.murphreeventures.com/
NoCo Angels www.nocoangels.com/
Opus www.opuscapital.com/
Pelion Venture Partners www.pelionvp.com/
Resource Capital Funds www.resourcecapitalfunds.com/home.asp
Roser Ventures, LLC. www.roserventures.com/
SAP Ventures www.sap.com/about/company/sapventures/index.epx
Sequel Venture Partners www.sequelvc.com/
Stolberg Equity Partners, LLC www.stolbergpartners.com/www/index.html
Stonehenge Capital Company, LLC www.stonehengecapital.com/
Summit Partners www.summitpartners.com/
Sutter Hill Ventures www.shv.com/
Venture Associates www.venturea.com
Vestar Capital Partners www.vestarcapital.com/en/
vFinance, Inc. www.vfinance.com/
Vista Ventures www.vistavc.com/

Colorado Enterprise Fund, Inc. www.coloradoenterprisefund.org/
Innovative Bank (SBA Community Express Lender) www.innovativebank.com/
Roaring Fork Capital (SBIC) Licensed www.roaringforkcapital.com/
San Juan Development www.sanjuandevelopment.org/
SEEDCO Financial www.seedcofinancial.org/

SBA Lenders
Most Active SBA 7(a) Lenders

Most active SBA 7(a) lenders in the United States by lending volume through January 1, 2024.

Lender	Volume	Ave Loan	Ave Rate
Live Oak	$2,291,016,699	$1,510,229	5.3%
Newtek	$945,317,357	$698,682	6.1%
Huntington Bank	$914,412,500	$201,679	5.5%
Celtic Bank	$701,707,100	$1,420,460	5.8%
Byline Bank	$623,952,600	$1,270,779	5.9%
Readycap	$578,732,700	$1,183,502	5.4%
Wells Fargo	$565,409,200	$293,262	7.4%
Harvest Finance	$450,384,800	$1,179,018	5.6%
Enterprise Bank	$442,756,800	$1,123,748	5.1%
U.S. Bank	$438,827,900	$260,896	5.9%
KeyBank	$425,479,320	$462,478	5.7%
MUFG Union Bank	$396,324,100	$1,630,963	4.0%
Commonwealth Bank	$381,635,000	$1,590,146	4.7%
TD Bank	$359,487,569	$232,227	7.3%
Metro City Bank	$307,953,300	$1,999,697	4.4%
Wallis Bank	$305,202,300	$1,816,680	5.0%
United Midwest Bank	$304,385,700	$287,156	6.0%
Pinnacle Bank	$298,615,020	$1,270,702	5.0%
PNC Bank	$296,910,000	$472,035	6.7%
Bank of Hope	$294,203,000	$1,021,538	4.9%
Bank of the West	$285,548,600	$961,443	4.6%
Berkshire Bank	$284,237,400	$1,029,846	5.7%
Peoples Bank	$263,703,150	$991,365	5.4%
Open Bank	$262,704,800	$1,889,963	4.7%

Small Business Private Lenders and Brokers:

SBICs may provide capital in the form of loans, debt securities (mezzanine debt with equity features, such as warrants), and equity. In most cases, SBICs may charge interest rates no higher than 19% for loans and 14% for debt securities. But, most SBIC financing is below these maximum interest rates. Between 2010 and 2012, SBICs licensed since October 1, 2002, reported almost $8 billion in financing to small businesses as follows:

Metric	Loans (no equity features)	Debt with Equity features	Equity
Percent of SBIC Financing Dollars	48%	34%	18%
Typical Financing Size Over 3 Year Period	$250,000 to $10 million	$250,000 to $10 million	$100,000 to $5 million
Typical Cost of Financing	Interest 9 to 16% Maximum: 19%	Interest 10 to 14% Maximum: 14%	Equity
Median Small Business Revenue at 1st Financing	$26 million	$14 million	$10 million

SBICs can only invest in small businesses. Small businesses are generally defined as businesses with tangible net worth of less than $18 million AND an average of $6 million in net income or less over the previous two years at the time of investment. A business may also be deemed "small" based on its industry using 13 CFR §121.201.

SBICs cannot finance foreign activities. Such activities include investments to support foreign operations or businesses with more than 49% of their employees or tangible assets outside the U.S.

Although SBICs invest in many different industries, SBICs are prohibited from financing any of the following: re-lenders or re-investors; passive businesses; most real estate businesses; farmland; project financings, or businesses contrary to the public interest.

More details on SBIC financing found at the source: https://www.sba.gov/sbic/

Total Financing From the inception of the SBIC program to December 31, 2020, SBICs have invested approximately $108.3 billion in approximately 186,412 financings to small businesses. As mentioned, as of June 30, 2021, the SBA had a guarantee on an outstanding unpaid principal balance of $10.9 billion in SBIC debentures, $0 in SBIC participating securities, and $32.1 million in other, primarily SSBIC, financings.

The SBA also had outstanding commitments on $3.8 billion in SBIC debentures, none for participating securities, and $7.2 million in other, primarily SSBIC, financings.

As of June 30, 2021, the SBIC program had invested or committed about $34 billion in small businesses, with the SBA's share of capital at risk about $14.7 billion.[108]

Credit Mastery: Developing Aged Corporations

In FY2020, SBICs made 2,533 financings. The average financing amount was $1,928,504.

109 In FY2020, SBIC funds were used primarily for operating capital (43.1%) and acquiring an existing business (37.4%). Other uses include refinancing or refunding debt (5.6%), research and development (2.1%), purchasing machinery or equipment (1.5%), marketing activities (1.3%), a new building or plant construction (0.6%), plant modernization (0.4%), and other uses (8%).

The total SBIC financing declined during the recession (December 2007- June 2009), reached prerecession levels in FY2011, and has generally increased since then. In FY2020, the SBICs drew nearly $2 billion in SBA leverage and invested another $2.889 billion from private capital for a total of $4.885 billion in financing for 1,063 small businesses.

SBIC Lenders (Alphabetical by State)

Name	City	State	Average Funding	Type	Contact	email	phone

Alabama
Harbert Mezzanine Partners II SBIC, L.P. Birmingham AL $759147 Mezzanine Amanda Brown abrown@harbert.net 205-987-5535

Arkansas
Diamond State Ventures III, L.P. Little Rock AR 457908 Mezzanine Joe T. Hays, Managing Director jhays@dsvlp.com 501-374-9247

Arizona
Convergent Capital Partners III, L.P. Scottsdale AZ 1552509 Mezzanine Keith Bares kbares@cvcap.com 763-432-4081
Grayhawk Ventures Fund III, L.P. Scottsdale AZ 2799998 Venture Sherman I. Chu schu@grayhawkcapital.us 602-615-2489

California
Avante Capital Partners SBIC III, L.P. 11150 Santa Monica Blvd. Suite 1470 Los Angeles 90025 CA Cliff Lyon cliff@avantecap.com 310-667-9242 investing
Avante Capital Partners SBIC III-A, L.P. 11150 Santa Monica Blvd. Suite 1470 Los Angeles 90025 CA Cliff Lyon cliff@avantecap.com 310-667-9242 investing
Avante Mezzanine Partners SBIC II, L.P. 11150 Santa Monica Blvd. Suite 1470 Los Angeles 90025 CA Jeri Harman jharman@avantemezzanine.com 310-667-9242 investing
Caltius Partners V (SBIC), L.P. 11766 Wilshire Blvd., Suite 850 Los Angeles 90025 CA James B. Upchurch jupchurch@caltius.com 310-996-9572 investing
Central Valley Fund II (SBIC), LP (The) 1590 Drew Avenue, Suite 110 Davis 95618 CA Edward F. McNulty emcnulty@cvfcapitalpartners.com 530-757-7004 investing
Central Valley Fund III (SBIC), L.P. (The) 1590 Drew Avenue, Suite 110 Davis 95618 CA Edward F. McNulty emcnulty@cvfcapitalpartners.com 530-757-7004 investing
Champlain Capital Partners II, L.P. One Post Street, Suite 925 San Francisco 94104 CA Dennis M. Leary dleary@champlaincapital.com 415-281-4181 investing
Champlain Capital Partners III, L.P. One Post Street, Suite 925 San Francisco 94104 CA Dennis M. Leary dleary@champlaincapital.com 415-281-4181 investing
Corbel Capital Partners SBIC, L.P. 11777 San Vicente Blvd., Suite 777 Los Angeles 90049 CA Jeffrey Schwartz jeff@corbelcap.com 310-442-7011 investing
DCA Capital Partners II, L.P. 3712 Douglas Blvd., Suite 350 Roseville 95661 CA

Company	Contact	Email	Address	City	Zip	State	Phone	Type
	Steven Mills	smills@dcacapital.com					916-650-5352	investing
Enhanced SBIC II, L.P.			101 California Street, Suite 1700	San Francisco	94111	CA		
	Michael Korengold	mkorengold@enhancedcap.com						investing
HCAP Partners IV, L.P.			3636 Nobel Drive, Suite 401	San Diego	92122	CA		
	Frank Mora Crespo	frank@hcapllc.com					858-259-7654	investing
Hercules Capital IV, L.P.			400 Hamilton Avenue, Suite 310	Palo Alto	94301	CA		
	Seth H. Meyer	smeyer@htgc.com					857-206-8966	investing
MV Fund II SBIC, L.P.			785 Orchard Drive, Suite 150	Folsom	95630	CA		
	Eli Wolfson	Eli@moneta.vc					818-635-4087	investing
Norwest Strategic Capital, L.P.			525 University Avenue, Suite 800	Palo Alto	94301	CA		
	Promod Haque	phaque@nvp.com					650-289-2229	investing
Pivotal Capital Fund, LP			2882 Sand Hill Road, Suite 100	Menlo Park	94025	CA		
	Renee Baker	renee@pivotalcp.com					650-233-5402	investing
SBJ Fund, LP			2001 North Main St, Suite 650	Walnut Creek	94596	CA		
	Gus Spanos	gus@sbjcap.com					415-848-1990	investing
Silver Lake Waterman Fund II, L.P.			2775 Sand Hill Road, Suite 100	Menlo Park	94025	CA		
	Thomas Conneely	tom.conneely@silverlake.com					415-525-8705	investing
St. Cloud Capital Partners III SBIC, LP			10866 Wilshire Boulevard, Suite 1450	Los Angeles	90024	CA		
	Kacy Rozelle	jhays@stcloudcapital.com					310-475-2700	investing
TCPC SBIC, LP			2951 28th Street, Suite 1000	Santa Monica	90405	CA		
	Rajneesh Vig	Raj.Vig@TennenbaumCapital.com					310-566-1041	investing
Tregaron Opportunity Fund II, L.P.			300 Hamilton Avenue, 4th Floor	Palo Alto	94301	CA		
	Todd Collins	collins@tregaroncapital.com					650-403-2084	investing
Walden Venture Capital VIII SBIC, L.P.			750 Battery Street, 7th Floor	San Francisco	94111	CA		
	Art Berliner	matt@waldenvc.com					415-273-4242	investing

Connecticut

Company	Contact	Email	Address	City	Zip	State	Phone	Type
Balance Point Capital Partners II, L.P.			285 Riverside Avenue, Suite 200	Westport	6880	CT		
	Adam Sauerteig	asauerteig@balancepointcapital.com					203-652-8555	investing
Balance Point Capital Partners IV, L.P.			285 Riverside Avenue, Suite 200	Westport	6880	CT		
	Adam Sauerteig	asauerteig@balancepointcapital.com					203-652-8255	investing
Brookside Mezzanine Fund III, L.P.			201 Tresser Boulevard, Suite 330	Stamford	6901	CT		
	David D. Buttolph	csclar@brooksidemp.com					203-595-4530	investing
Brookside Mezzanine Fund IV, L.P.			201 Tresser Boulevard, Suite 330	Stamford	6901	CT		
	Corey Sclar	csclar@brooksidemp.com					203-595-4530	investing
GarMark SBIC Fund II, L.P.			One Landmark Square, 6th Floor	Stamford	6901	CT		
	Steven C. Pickhardt	mrich@garmark.com					203-325-8500	investing
GarMark SBIC Fund, L.P.			One Landmark Square, 6th Floor	Stamford	6901	CT		
	E. Garrett Bewkes	egbewkes@garmark.com					203-325-8500	investing
Ironwood Mezzanine Fund III-A LP			45 Nod Road	Avon	6001	CT		
	Marc A. Reich	reich@ironwoodcap.com					860-409-2101	investing
Ironwood Mezzanine Fund IV-A, L.P.			45 Nod Road	Avon	6001	CT		
	Carolyn Galiette	galiette@ironwoodcap.com					860-409-2105	investing
New Canaan Funding Mezzanine VI SBIC, LP			21 Locust Avenue, Suite 1C	New Canaan	6840	CT		
	Mark Thies	mthies@newcanaanfunding.com					203-966-1071	investing
RFE Investment Partners IX, L.P.			36 Grove Street, 1st Floor	New Canaan	6840	CT		
	James Parsons	jparsons@rfeip.com					203-966-2800	investing
Small Business Community Capital II, L.P.			9W Broad Street Suite 530	Stamford	6902	CT		
	Jay Garcia	jgarcia@sbccfund.com					646-206-3284	investing
Southfield Mezzanine Capital II, L.P.			140 Greenwich Avenue, 4th Floor	Greenwich	6830	CT		
	Steven Axel	saxel@southfieldmezz.com					203-813-4100	investing

Southfield Mezzanine Capital LP   53 Greenwich Avenue, 2nd Floor   Greenwich   6830   CT
　　Steven   Axel   saxel@southfieldmezz.com   203-813-4100   investing

District of Columbia
Canapi Ventures SBIC Fund, L.P.   801 17th Street NW, Suite 1050   Washington   20006   DC
　　Walker   Forehand   walker@canapi.com   202-315-1818   investing
Farragut Mezzanine Partners III, L.P.   5301 Wisconsin Avenue NW, Suite 410   Washington   20015   DC
　　Philip   McNeill   pmcneill@farragutcapitalpartners.com   301-913-5293   investing
Farragut SBIC Fund II, L.P.   5301 Wisconsin Avenue NW, Suite 410   Washington   20015   DC
　　Philip   McNeill   pmcneill@farragutcapitalpartners.com   301-913-5293   investing
McLarty Capital Partners SBIC, L.P.   900 Seventeenth Street, NW, Suite 800   Washington   20006   DC   Chris
　　Smith   csmith@mclartycapital.com   202-419-7098   investing
Multiplier Capital II, L.P.   1920 L Street NW, Suite 550   Washington   20036   DC
　　Kevin P.   Sheehan   sheehan@multipliercapital.com   917-783-3223   investing

Florida
Anagenesis Capital Partners SBIC Fund, L.P.   575 Fifth Avenue, 14th Floor   West Palm Beach 33401   FL   Melanie
　　Brensinger   mbrensinger@anagenesiscp.com   646-661-2343   investing
Ballast Point Ventures III, L.P.   401 East Jackson Street Suite 2300   Tampa   33602   FL
　　Paul C.   Johan   info@ballastpointventures.com   813-906-8500   investing
Ballast Point Ventures IV, L.P.   401 East Jackson Street Suite 2300   Tampa   33602   FL
　　Paul   Johan   pjohan@ballastpointventures.com   investing
KLH Capital Fund III, L.P.   601 Bayshore Boulevard, Suite 850   Tampa   33606   FL
　　James B. Darnell   james@klhcapital.com   813-222-0160   investing
LFE Growth Fund III, LP   649 Fifth Avenue South, Suite 226   Naples   34102   FL
　　Leslie   Frecon   lfrecon@lfecapital.com   612-752-1801   investing
New Canaan Funding Mezzanine VII SBIC, L.P.   365 Fifth Avenue South, Suite 209   Naples   34102   FL   Mark
　　Thies   mthies@newcanaanfunding.com   203-966-1071   investing
Penta Mezzanine SBIC Fund I, L.P.   20 N. Orange Avenue, Suite 1550   Orlando   32801   FL
　　Leo   Koo   lkoo@pentamezz.com   407-648-5097   investing
Stonehenge Growth Equity Fund, L.P.   707 West Azeele Street   Tampa   33606   FL   investing
TGEF III, L.P.   707 West Azeele Street   Tampa   33606   FL
　　Steven   Lux   sflux@stonehengegep.com   813-221-8302   investing

Georgia
Source Capital Credit Opportunities IV, L.P.   75 14th Street, Suite 2700   Atlanta   30309   GA
　　Tom   Harbin   tomharbin@source-cap.com   404-249-9330   investing

Iowa
AAVIN Mezzanine Fund, LP   1245 1st Avenue SE   Cedar Rapids   52402   IA
　　James D. Thorp   jthorp@aavin.com   319-247-1072   investing

Illinois
Aldine Capital Fund II, L.P.   444 West Lake Street, Suite 4550   Chicago   60606   IL
　　Albert L. Brahm   bbrahm@aldinecapital.com   312-346-1004   investing
Aldine Capital Fund III, L.P.   444 West Lake Street, Suite 4550   Chicago   60606   IL
　　Albert L. Brahm   bbrahm@aldinecapital.com   312-346-1004   investing
Fidus Mezzanine Capital II, L.P.   1603 Orrington Avenue, Suite 1005   Evanston   60201   IL
　　Shelby   Sherard   ssherard@fidusinv.com   847-859-3938   investing
Fidus Mezzanine Capital III, L.P.   1603 Orrington Avenue, Suite 1005   Evanston   60201   IL
　　Shelby   Sherard   ssherard@fidusinv.com   847-859-3938   investing

Freeport Financial SBIC Fund LP   200 South Wacker Drive Suite 750   Chicago 60606   IL
　　Joseph V.　　Walker   JFroemming@Freeportfinancial.com   312-281-4609   investing
Granite Creek FlexCap II, L.P.   222 West Adams Street, Suite 3125   Chicago 60606   IL
　　Mark A. Radzik   mark@granitecreek.com   312-895-4503   investing
High Street Capital V SBIC, L.P.   150 North Wacker Drive, Suite 2420   Chicago 60606   IL
　　Joseph R.   Katcha   chris@highstreetcapital.com   312-267-2861   investing
Invision Capital II, L.P.   155 N. Wacker Drive, Suite 4480   Chicago 60606   IL   Robert J. Castillo
　　rcastillo@invcg.com   312-543-3363   investing
Maranon Mezzanine Fund III-B, L.P.   303 W. Madison Street, Suite 2500   Chicago 60606   IL
　　Michael Parilla   MSP@MaranonCapital.com   312-646-1205   investing
MidWest Mezzanine Fund V SBIC, L.P.   55 W. Monroe Avenue, Suite 3650 Chicago 60603   IL
　　Paul   Kreie   pkreie@mmfcapital.com   312-291-7303   investing
Midwest Mezzanine Fund VI SBIC, L.P.   55 W. Monroe Avenue, Suite 3650 Chicago 60603   IL
　　Paul   Kreie   pkreie@mmfcapital.com   312-291-7303   investing
Monroe Capital Corporation SBIC, LP   311 S. Wacker Drive, 64th Floor   Chicago 60606   IL
　　Theodore   Koenig   info@monroecap.com   312-258-8300   investing
Monroe Capital Partners Fund II, LP   312 S. Wacker Drive, 64th Floor   Chicago 60606   IL
　　Theodore   Koenig   info@monroecap.com   312-258-8300   investing
Serra Capital (SBIC) III, L.P.   2021 South First Street, Suite 206   Champaign   61821   IL
　　Dennis E.   Beard   dennis@serraventures.com   217-819-5202   investing
Svoboda Capital Fund IV (SBIC), L.P.   1 North Franklin Street, Suite 1500   Chicago 60606   IL
　　Jeffrey S.   Piper   jsp@svoco.com   312-267-8757   investing

Indianna
CCP IV-SBIC, L.P.   10 West Market Street, Suite 3000   Indianapolis   46204   IN
　　D. Scott Lutzke   scott@centerfieldcapital.com   317-237-2321   investing

Louisiana
Bluehenge Capital Secured Debt SBIC, LP   301 Main Street, Suite 920   Baton Rouge   70825   LA
　　Ari David   Kocen   adkocen@bluehenge.com 225-615-3348   investing
LongueVue Capital Partners III, L.P.   111 Veterans Boulevard, Suite 1020   Metairie 70005   LA
　　Rick   Rees   btoups@lvcpartners.com 504-293-3607   investing

Massachusetts
Crescent Direct Lending SBIC Fund, L.P.   100 Federal Street, 31st Floor   Boston 2111   MA
　　Michael Rogers   michael.rogers@crescentcap.com   617-854-1501   investing
Crystal Financial SBIC LP   Two International Place, 17th Floor   Boston 2110   MA
　　Josh   Franklin jfranklin@crystalfinco.com   617-428-8708   investing
Gemini Investors VI, L.P.   20 William Street, Suite 250   Wellesley   2481   MA
　　Matthew   Keis   mkeis@gemini-investors.com   781-237-7001   investing
Gemini Investors VII, L.P.   20 William Street, Suite 250   Wellesley   2481   MA
　　Matthew   Keis   mkeis@gemini-investors.com   781-237-7001   investing
Lineage Capital II, L.P.   399 Boylston Street, Suite 450   Boston 2116   MA
　　Erik   Dykema erik@lineagecap.com   617-778-0665   investing
Long River Ventures III, L.P.   33 Arch Street, Ste. 1700 Boston   2110   MA
　　Tripp   Peake   tpeake@lrvhealth.com   413-587-2155   investing
PVP Fund I, L.P.   One Bank Street, 2nd Floor   Williamstown   1267   MA
　　Brad   Svrluga   brad@primary.vc 518-720-3090   investing
Seacoast Capital Partners IV, L.P.   55 Ferncroft Road, Suite 110   Danvers 1923   MA
　　Thomas Gorman   tgorman@seacoastcapital.com   978-750-1300   investing

Maryland

Enlightenment Capital Solutions SBIC Fund, L.P.   4445 Willard Avenue, Suite 950   Chevy Chase   20815   MD
Jason   Rigoli   jfrigoli@enlightenment-cap.com   240-752-9618   investing

Patriot Capital III SBIC, L.P.   509 South Exeter Street Suite 210   Baltimore   21202   MD
Thomas O.   Holl, Jr.   tholland@patriot-capital.com   443-573-3024   investing

Patriot Capital IV (A), L.P.   509 South Exeter Street Suite 210   Baltimore   21202   MD
Thomas O.   Holl, Jr.   tholland@patriot-capital.com   443-573-3024   investing

PCI II, L.P.   6300 Blair Hill Lane, 4th Floor   Lutherville   21093   MD
Christopher   Pope   cpope@cscp.com   443-573-3714   investing

Spring Capital Partners III, L.P.   2330 W. Joppa Road, Suite 340   Lutherville   21093   MD
Robert M.   Stewart   rms@springcap.com   410-685-8000   investing

Spring Capital Partners IV, L.P.   The Foxleigh Building, 2330 W. Joppa Road   Lutherville   21093   MD
John C.   Acker   jca@springcap.com   410-685-8019   investing

Maine

North Atlantic Venture Fund V, L.P.   Two City Center, 5th Floor   Portland   4101   ME
Mark   Morrissette   mark@northatlanticcapital.com   207-772-4470   investing

Minnesota

Bayview Capital Partners IV LP   301 Carlson Parkway, Suite 325   Minnetonka   55305   MN
Steven   Soderling   ssorderling@tonkabayequity.com   952-345-2031   investing

Convergent Capital Partners IV, L.P.   505 N. Highway 169, Suite 175   Minneapolis   55441   MN
Matthew   Grossman   mgrossman@cvcap.com   763-432-4083   investing

GMB Mezzanine Capital III, L.P.   50 South Sixth Street, Suite 1460   Minneapolis   55402   MN
Tom   Kreimer   tkreimer@gmbmezz.com   612-243-4415   investing

GMB Mezzanine Capital IV, L.P.   50 South Sixth Street, Suite 1460   Minneapolis   55402   MN
Tom   Kreimer   tkreimer@gmbmezz.com   612-243-4415   investing

Lake Country Capital SBIC, L.P.   7701 France Avenue, Suite 240   Edina   55435   MN
Andrew P. Leonard   andrew@lakecountrycapital.com   612-800-9947   investing

Lightspring Capital I, L.P.   5775 Wayzata Blvd., Suite 700   Minneapolis   55416   MN
Susan   Gohman   sgohman@lightspringcapital.com   612-289-6614   investing

Northstar Mezzanine Partners SBIC, L.P.   2310 PWC Plaza 45 South 7th Street   Minneapolis   55402   MN
Christopher   Kocourek   ckocourek@northstarcapital.com   612-371-5718   investing

Spell Capital Mezzanine Partners SBIC II, L.P.   222 South Ninth Street, Suite 2880   Minneapolis   55402   MN
Andrea   Nelson   andrea@spellcapital.com   612-843-1545   investing

Missouri

C3 Capital Partners III, L.P.   1511 Baltimore Avenue Suite 500   Kansas City   64108   MO
Patrick F. Healy   phealy@C3cap.com   816-756-2225   investing

CFB Venture Fund L.P.   11 South Meramec Avenue Suite 1330   Saint Louis   63105   MO
Stephen B.   Broun   Bill.Witzofsky@capitalforbusiness.com   314-746-7427   investing

Cultivation Twain Seed Fund I, L.P.   1232 Washington Avenue, Suite 200   St. Louis   63103   MO
Brian   Matthews   bmatthews@cultivationcapital.com   314-565-8062   investing

Eagle Fund III, L.P.   1 N. Brentwood Blvd., Suite 1550   Saint Louis   63105   MO
Benjamin   Geis   bgeis@eagleprivatecapital.com   314-754-1400   investing

Eagle Fund III-A, L.P.   1 N. Brentwood Blvd., Suite 1550   Saint Louis   63105   MO
Benjamin   Geis   bgeis@eagleprivatecapital.com   314-754-1400   investing

Eagle Fund IV, L.P.   1 N. Brentwood Blvd., Suite 1550   Saint Louis   63105   MO
Benjamin   Geis   bgeis@eagleprivatecapital.com   314-754-1400   investing

Eagle Fund IV-A, L.P.   1 N. Brentwood Blvd., Suite 1550   Saint Louis   63105   MO
Benjamin   Geis   bgeis@eagleprivatecapital.com   314-754-1400   investing

Holleway IPA Fund, L.P.	190 Carondelet Plaza, Suite 1200	St. Louis 63105	MO
	Holly	Huels	hhuels@holleway.com	314-249-0496	investing

North Carolina

Barings Small Business Fund, L.P.	300 South Tryon Street, Suite 2500	Charlotte	28202	NC
	Scott	Chappell	scott.chappell@barings.com	704-805-7671	investing
CapitalSouth SBIC Fund IV, L.P.	4201 Congress Street - Suite 360	Charlotte	28209	NC
	Joseph B.	Alala	JAlala@capitalagroup.com	704-376-5502	investing
Concentric Partners I, L.P.	900 Ridgefield Drive, Suite 270	Raleigh	27609	NC
	Corbin	Graves	cgraves@concentricpartners.com	919-619-3238	investing
Five Points Capital Partners IV, L.P.	101 N. Cherry Street, Suite 700	Winston-Salem	27101	NC
	David G. Townsend	dtownsend@fivepointscapital.com	336-733-0355	investing
Five Points Credit SBIC IV, L.P.	101 N. Cherry Street, Suite 700	Winston-Salem	27101	NC
	Stewart Edwards	wedwards@fivepointscapital.com	333-733-0364	investing
Five Points Mezzanine Fund III, L.P.	101 N. Cherry Street, Suite 700	Winston-Salem	27101	NC
	David G. Townsend	dtownsend@fivepointscapital.com	336-733-0355	investing
Hatteras Venture Partners IV SBIC, LP	280 South Mangum Street, Suite 350	Durham	27701	NC
	Douglas Reed	doug@hatterasvp.com	919-484-0730	investing
Kian Mezzanine Partners II, L.P.	4201 Congress Street, Rotunda Building, Suite 440	Charlotte	28209	NC
	Charlie Edmondson	cedmondson@kiancapital.com	704-943-2503	investing
Mosaic Capital Investors I, LP	101 South Tryon Street Suite 2620	Charlotte	28280	NC
	H. Dabney	Smith	dsmith@mosaic-cp.com	919-636-6164	investing
Plexus Fund IV-A, L.P.	4242 Six Forks Road, Suite 950	Raleigh	27609	NC
Rhonda Penn	rpenn@plexuscap.com	919-256-6355	investing
Plexus Fund IV-B, L.P.	4242 Six Forks Road, Suite 950	Raleigh	27609	NC
	Rhonda	Penn	rpenn@plexuscap.com	919-256-6355	investing
Plexus Fund IV-C, L.P.	4242 Six Forks Road, Suite 950	Raleigh	27609	NC
	Rhonda	Penn	rpenn@plexuscap.com	919-256-6355	investing
Plexus Fund V-A, L.P.	4242 Six Forks Road, Suite 950	Raleigh	27609	NC
	Rhonda	Penn	rpenn@plexuscap.com	919-256-6355	investing
Plexus Fund V-B, L.P.	4242 Six Forks Road, Suite 950	Raleigh	27609	NC
	Rhonda	Penn	rpenn@plexuscap.com	919-256-6355	investing
Plexus Fund V-C, L.P.	4242 Six Forks Road, Suite 950	Raleigh	27609	NC
	Rhonda	Penn	rpenn@plexuscap.com	919-256-6355	investing
Salem Investment Partners III, Limited Partnership	7900 Triad Center Dr, Suite 333	Greensboro	27409	NC
	Philip	Martin	pmartin@salemip.com	704-578-4091	investing
Salem Investment Partners IV, Limited Partnership	7900 Triad Center Dr, Suite 333	Greensboro	27409	NC
	Philip	Martin	pmartin@salemip.com	704-578-4091	investing
Salem Investment Partners V, Limited Partnership	7900 Triad Center Dr Suite 333	Greensboro	27409	NC
	Kevin	Jessup	jhearn@salemip.com		investing
SharpVue Capital Credit Fund II, L.P.	3700 Glenwood Avenue, Suite 530	Raleigh	27612	NC
	James	Burke	James.Burke@sharpvuecap.com	919-890-0528	investing
Wells Fargo Strategic Capital SBIC, L.P.	550 S. Tryon Street, Floor 27	Charlotte	27609	NC
	Tim	Rafalovich	tim.rafal@wellsfargo.com	949-251-4321	investing

Nebraska

FCP Fund III, L.P.	1620 Dodge Street, Suite 800	Omaha 68102	NE
	Andrew Kemp	akemp@fcpcapital.com	402-718-8868	investing

New York

American Express Ventures SBIC, L.P.	200 Vesey Street	New York	10285	NY
	Julia	Huang	julia.huang@aexp.com	212-640-0326	investing

Argentum Capital Partners III, L.P.   60 Madison Avenue, Suite 701   New York   10010   NY
    Steve   Berman   sdberman@argentumgroup.com   212-949-8511   investing
Argentum Capital Partners IV, L.P.   60 Madison Avenue, Suite 701   New York   10010   NY
    Steven   Berman   sdberman@argentumgroup.com   212-949-6262   investing
Bridges Ventures U.S. Sustainable Growth Fund, L.P.   1350 Avenue of the Americas, 29th Floor   New York 10019   NY
    Brian   Trelstad   brian@bridgesventures.com   646-731-2759   investing
Cephas Capital Partners III, L.P.   11 Schoen Place, 8th Floor   Pittsford 14534   NY
    Clint W.   Campbell   ccampbell@cephascapital.com   585-383-1610   investing
Deerpath Funding Advantage IV, L.P.   405 Lexington Avenue, 53rd Floor   New York   10174   NY
    James H.   Kirby   jkirby@deerpathcapital.com   646-786-1022   investing
Deerpath Funding V, L.P.   405 Lexington Avenue, 53rd Floor   New York   10174   NY
    James H.   Kirby   jkirby@deerpathcapital.com   646-786-1022   investing
Energy Impact Credit Fund I LP   600 Third Avenue, 38th Floor   New York   10016   NY
    Hans   Kobler   sbic@energyimpactpartners.com   212-899-9700   investing
Firmament Capital Partners SBIC III, L.P.   One Rockefeller Plaza, Suite 1203   New York   10020   NY
    Christopher   Smith   csmith@thefirmamentgroup.com   212-956-1061   investing
GC SBIC VI, L.P.   666 Fifth Avenue, 18th Floor   New York   10103   NY   investing
GCM Grosvenor California Impact SBIC Fund, L.P.   767 5th Avenue, 14th Floor   New York   10153   NY
    Jason R. Howard   jhoward@gcmlp.com   310-683-2713   investing
Graycliff Mezzanine II LP   500 Fifth Avenue, 47th Floor   New York   10110   NY
    Andrew P.   Trigg   atrigg@graycliffpartners.com   212-300-2903   investing
Graycliff Mezzanine III (SBIC), L.P.   500 Fifth Avenue, 47th Floor   New York   10110   NY
    Andrew P.   Trigg   atrigg@graycliffpartners.com   212-300-2903   investing
McLarty Capital Partners SBIC II, L.P.   1 Rockefeller Plaza, Suite 1203   New York   10020   NY
    Chris   Smith   csmith@mclartycapital.com   212-314-0172   investing
Mizzen Capital, L.P.   488 Madison Avenue, 18th Floor   New York   10022   NY
    Liddy   Karter   kwolpert@mizzencapital.com   N/A   investing
Morgan Stanley Impact SBIC LP   1585 Broadway, 14th Floor   New York   10036   NY
    Chad   Hubert   Chad.Hubert@morganstanley.com   212-761-0439   investing
New Mountain Finance SBIC II, L.P.   787 Seventh Avenue, 48th Floor   New York   10019   NY
    John R.   Kline   jkline@newmountaincapital.com   212-720-0309   investing
New Mountain Finance SBIC, L.P.   787 Seventh Avenue, 48th Floor   New York   10019   NY
    John R.   Kline   jkline@newmountaincapital.com   212-720-0309   investing
Oaktree SBIC Fund, L.P.   1301 Avenue of the Americas 34th Floor   New York   10019   NY
    Peter   Change   pchang@oaktreecapital.com   investing
Pelham S2K SBIC, L.P.   777 Third Avenue 28th Floor   New York   10017   NY
    Jonathan   Terzi   jterzi@pelhams2k.com   212-603-9766   investing
PennantPark SBIC II, LP   590 Madison Avenue, 15th Floor   New York   10022   NY
    Arthur H.   Penn   penn@pennantpark.com   212-905-1010   investing
Pine Street Capital Partners III, L.P.   54 State Street, Suite 302   Albany   12207   NY
    Michael P.   Lasch   laschm@pinecap.com   518-449-9070   investing
QS Capital Strategies II, L.P.   527 Madison Avenue, 11th Floor   New York   10022   NY
    Benton   Cummings   bcummings@quilvestusa.com   212-920-3851   investing
QS Capital Strategies, L.P.   527 Madison Avenue, 11th Floor   New York   10022   NY
    Henrik   Falktoft   hfalktoft@quilvestusa.com   212-920-3800   investing
RF Investment Partners SBIC, L.P.   501 Madison Avenue, Suite 1401   New York   10022   NY
    Peter   Rothschild   prothschild@rf-partners.com   212-590-2440   investing
Saratoga Investment Corp. SBIC II, L.P.   535 Madison Avenue, 4th Floor   New York   10022   NY
    Michael Grisius   mgrisius@saratogapartners.com   212-906-7333   investing
Siguler Guff SBIC Fund, L.P.   825 Third Avenue, 10th Floor   New York   10022   NY
    Sean   J. Greene   sgreene@sigulerguff.com   617-648-2134   investing

Star Mountain SBIC Fund, L.P.	140 East 45th Street, 37th Floor	New York	10017	NY
	Brett	Hickey	brett.hickey@starmountaincapital.com	646-787-0222	investing
Willow Tree Credit Partners SBIC, L.P.	640 Fifth Avenue, 21st Floor	New York	10019	NY
		investing

Ohio
MCM Capital Partners III Parallel Fund, L.P.	25201 Chagrin Blvd., Suite 360	Beachwood	44122	OH
	Kevin	Hayes	kevin@mcmcapital.com	216-514-1846	investing
NCT Ventures Fund II, L.P.	274 Marconi Boulevard, Suite 400	Columbus	43215	OH
	William J.	Frank	bill.frank@nctventures.com	614-204-2544	investing
Northcreek Mezzanine Fund II, L.P.	312 Walnut Street, Suite 2310	Cincinnati	45202	OH
	Rodger	Davis	rdavis@northcreekmezzanine.com	513-985-6600	investing
Northcreek Mezzanine Fund III, L.P.	312 Walnut Street, Suite 2310	Cincinnati	45202	OH
	Rodger	Davis	rdavis@northcreekmezzanine.com	513-985-6600	investing
Oxer BCP Mezzanine Fund, L.P.	883 Yard Street	Columbus	43212	OH
	Dan	Phlegar	dan.phlegar@oxercapital.com	614-917-7659	investing
Oxer Mezzanine Fund II, L.P.	883 Yard Street	Columbus	43212	OH
	Dan	Phlegar	dan.phlegar@oxercapital.com	614-907-7373	investing
Stonehenge Community Impact Fund, L.P.	191 W. Nationwide Blvd., Suite 600	Columbus	43215	OH
	L'Quentus	Thomas	lthomas@stonehengecapital.com	614-545-7244	investing
Stonehenge Opportunity Fund IV, L.P.	192 West Nationwide Boulevard, Suite 600	Columbus	43215	OH
	Michael Affinito	bmaffinito@stonehengepartners.com	614-246-2476	investing
TTGA SBIC Pioneer Fund I, L.P.	201 E. Fifth Street, Suite 2310	Cincinnati	45202	OH
	David J.	Williams	david.williams@ttga.com	NA	investing

Oregon
True West Capital Partners Fund II, L.P.	1355 NW Everett Street, Suite 100	Portland	97209	OR
	Steven	Wilkins	srw@truewestcp.com	503-517-4628	investing
True West Capital Partners Fund III, L.P.	1355 NW Everett Street, Suite 100	Portland	97209	OR
	Steven R.	Wilkins	srw@truewestcp.com	503-517-4628	investing

Pennsylvania
Argosy Investment Partners SBIC VI, L.P.	950 West Valley Road, Suite 2900	Wayne	19087	PA
	Michael R.	Bailey	mbailey@argosycapital.com		investing
Argosy Investment Partners V, L.P.	950 West Valley Road, Suite 2900	Wayne	19087	PA
	Kirk	Griswold	kirk@argosycapital.com	610-971-9685	investing
Boathouse Capital II LP	353 West Lancaster Avenue, Suite 200	Wayne	19087	PA
	Kenneth E.	Jones	ken.jones@boathousecapital.com	610-977-2787	investing
Boathouse Capital III LP	353 W. Lancaster Avenue, Suite 200	Wayne	19087	PA
	Brian	Adamsky	brian.adamsky@boathousecapital.com	610-263-2818	investing
LBC Small Cap SBIC, L.P.	555 East Lancaster Avenue, Suite 450	Radnor	19087	PA
	Mark	Tyson	mtyson@lbccredit.com	215-883-7143	investing
Merion Investment Partners III, L.P.	555 E. Lancaster Avenue Suite 500	Radnor	19087	PA
	Gayle G. Hughes	ghughes@merionpartners.com	610-230-0880	investing
New York Credit SBIC Fund L.P.	One Presidential Boulevard, 4th Floor	Bala Cynwyd	19004	PA
	Anthony Donofrio	adonofrio@hamiltonlane.com	610-617-5328	investing
NewSpring Mezzanine Capital III, L.P.	555 East Lancaster Avenue, Suite 444	Radnor	19087	PA
	Jonathan	Schwartz	jschwartz@newspringventures.com	610-567-2387	investing
NewSpring Mezzanine Capital IV, L.P.	555 East Lancaster Avenue, Suite 300	Radnor	19087	PA
	Jonathan	Schwartz	jschwartz@newspringcapital.com	610-567-2387	investing
Renovus Capital Partners II, L.P.	460 E Swedesford Road, Suite 2050	Wayne	19087	PA

Atif Gilani atif.gilani@renovuscapital.com 610-848-7706 investing
Renovus Capital Partners III, L.P. 460 E Swedesford Road, Suite 2050 Wayne 19087 PA
Bradley Whitman brad.whitman@renovuscapital.com 610-848-7702 investing
Tecum Capital Partners II, L.P. 8000 Brooktree Road, Suite 310 Wexford 15090 PA
Stephen Gurgovits sgurgovits@tecum.com 724-602-4401 investing
Tecum Capital Partners III, L.P. 8000 Brooktree Road, Suite 310 Wexford 15090 PA
Stephen Gurgovits sgurgovits@tecum.com 312-750-3617 investing

Puerto Rico
Bluhaus Small Business Fund, L.P. 252 Ponce de Leon Avenue, Suite 2000 San Juan 918 PR
Eduardo Inclan einclan@bhcapllc.com 787-708-6747 investing

South Carolina
Route 2 Capital Partners SBIC, L.P. 110 East Court Street Suite 501 Greenville 29601 SC
R. Patrick Weston pweston@route2capital.com 864-484-9371 investing

Tennessee
Capital Alignment Partners III, L.P. 40 Burton Hills Boulevard, Suite 250 Nashville 37215 TN
Lee Ballew lballew@capfunds.com 615-915-1098 investing

CCSD II, L.P. 40 Burton Hills Boulevard, Suite 250 Nashville 37215 TN
R. Burton Harvey bharvey@capfunds.com 615-690-7183 investing

Petra Growth Fund III, L.P. 3825 Bedford Avenue, Suite 203 Nashville 37215 TN
Douglas B. Owen dbo@petracapital.com 615-313-5994 investing
Petra Growth Fund IV, L.P. 3825 Bedford Avenue, Suite 203 Nashville 37215 TN
Douglas B. Owen dbo@petracapital.com 615-313-5994 investing
Pharos Capital Partners III-A, L.P. 8 Cadillac Drive, Suite 180 Brentwood 37027 TN
Kneeland Youngblood jgoldberg@pharosfunds.com 615-234-5522 investing
Resolute Capital Partners Fund IV, L.P. 20 Burton Hills Boulevard, Suite 430 Nashville 37215 TN
Bill Nutter bill@resolutecap.com 615-665-3636 investing

Texas
Blue Sage Capital II, L.P. 2700 Via Fortuna, Suite 300 Austin 78746 TX
Alan Mire alan.mire@bluesage.com 512-536-1902 investing
Capital Southwest SBIC I, L.P. 5400 Lyndon B. Johnson Freeway Suite 1300 Dallas 75240 TX
Michael Sarner msarner@capitalsouthwest.com investing
Dos Rios Partners - A, L.P. 6104 Old Fredericksburg Rd Austin 78709 TX
Kevin Benoit kevin@dosriospartners.com 512-298-1280 investing
Dos Rios Partners, L.P. 6104 Old Fredericksburg Rd Austin 78709 TX
Kevin Benoit kevin@dosriospartners.com 512-298-1280 investing
Escalate Capital IV, L.P. 6011 W. Courtyard Drive, Suite 405 Austin 78730 TX
Simon James simon@escalatecapital.com 512-626-8330 investing
Escalate Capital Partners SBIC III, LP 6011 W. Courtyard Drive, Suite 405 Austin 78730 TX
Anthony Schell sbic@escalatecapital.com 512-651-2105 investing
Independent Bankers Capital Fund III, L.P. 1700 Pacific Avenue, Suite 2740 Dallas 75201 TX
Meg Taylor mtaylor@ibcfund.com 214-722-6200 investing
Independent Bankers Capital Fund IV, L.P. 1700 Pacific Avenue, Suite 3660 Dallas 75201 TX
Barry Conrad Bconrad@ibcfund.com 214-722-6203 investing
LCM Healthcare Fund I, L.P. 100 Crescent Court, Suite 200 Dallas 75201 TX
Kyle Bradford kyle.bradford@lattcap.com 214-613-0179 investing

Main Street Capital III, L.P. 1300 Post Oak Boulevard, Suite 800   Houston 77056   TX
    Kate   Silva   ksilva@mainstcapital.com 713-350-6039   investing
Stellus Capital SBIC II, L.P.   4400 Post Oak Parkway, Suite 2200   Houston 77027   TX
    Dean   D'Angelo   ddangelo@stelluscapital.com   301-634-3001   investing
Stellus Capital SBIC LP   4400 Post Oak Parkway, Suite 2200   Houston 77027   TX
    W. Todd Huskinson   Thuskinson@stelluscapital.com   713-292-5414   investing
Valesco Fund II, L.P.   325 North St. Paul, Suite 3700   Dallas   75201   TX
    Daniel   Moore   bmoore@valescoind.com   214-880-8690   investing

Utah
Pelion Ventures VII Financial Institutions Fund, L.P.   2750 E. Cottonwood Parkway, Suite 600   Salt Lake City   84121   UT   Blake   Modersitzki   blake@pelionvp.com   801-365-0262   investing
UV Partners IV Financial Institutions Fund, L.P.   2750 East Cottonwood Parkway, Suite 600   Salt Lake City   84121   UT   Blake   Modersitzki   jaquie@uvpartners.com   801-365-3262   notinvesting

Virginia
BSCP SBIC I, L.P.   204 South Union Street   Alexandria   22314   VA
    inquiries@boundarystreetcapital.com   703-837-6020   investing
Leeds Novamark Capital I, L.P.   11710 Plaza America Drive, Suite 160   Reston   20190   VA
    Mark   Raterman   raterman@lnc-partners.com   703-651-2149   investing
LNC Partners II - SBIC, L.P.   11720 Plaza America Drive, Suite 650   Reston   20190   VA
    Mark   Raterman   Raterman@lnc-partners.com   703-651-2149   investing

West Virginia
Mountain State Capital SBIC, L.P.   5000 Greystone Drive   Morgantown   26508   WV
    Matt   Harbaugh   matt@mountainstatecapital.com   412-401-2909   investing

CREDIT VENDORS AND LENDERS for Business

ALLY FINANCIAL - Credit Card – Vehicle Loans – TRANSUNION
AMAZON – EQUIFAX BUSINESSES - CitiBank
AMERICAN EXPRESS - EXPERIAN – EXPERIAN BUSINESS
AMERICAN HONDA - EQUIFAX
AT&T BUSINESS - EQUIFAX
BANK OF AMERICA - EXPERIAN - TRANSUNION - ChexSystems
BANK OF AMERICA CREDIT CARDS - EXPERIAN
BARCLAYS BANK – TRANSUNION
BJ's CLUB – PERKS FOR BUSINESS CARD – EXPERIAN BUSINESS
BMW FINANCIAL SERVICES - EXPERIAN
CAPITAL ONE AUTO FINANCE - EXPERIAN - EQUIFAX
CAPITAL ONE BANK - EQUIFAX
CAR SMART - TRANSUNION
CARMAX - EXPERIAN - EQUIFAX- TRANSUNION
CBNA CREDIT CARDS - EXPERIAN - EQUIFAX
CHASE BANK- EXPERIAN – EQUIFAX
CITGO FLEET CARD - CitiBank
CITIBANK: THE STAPLES BUSINESS CREDIT ACCOUNT WITH REVOLVING TERMS, THE STAPLES COMMERCIAL BILLING ACCOUNT WITH NET PAY TERMS
CREDIT UNION OF TEXAS - EQUIFAX
CREDCO Auto Reseller - EXPERIAN - TRANSUNION
CHRYSLER CAPITAL – EXPERIAN BUSINESS - TRANSUNION - DOES NOT REPORT TO D&B
COMENITY BANK CREDIT CARDS – EXPERIAN BUSINESS
DISCOVER CARD – EXPERIAN BUSINESS - EQUIFAX BUSINESS
DRIVE FINANCE Auto Financing - EXPERIAN - TRANSUNION
FIFTH THIRD BANK - TRANSUNION
FIRST DATA MERCHANT SERVICES - CREDIT CARD MERCHANT ACCOUNT PROCESSOR
GOOD SAM FINANCE CENTER - BANK OF THE WEST – NO TAX RETURNS UNDER $100,000 ON RV'S & BOATS - EQUIFAX
HERTZ CORPORATION - EQUIFAX
HSBC - TRANSUNION
JP MORGAN CHASE- Business - TRANSUNION - ChexSystems
JP MORGAN CHASE BANK – EQUIFAX
NASA FEDERAL CREDIT UNION – EXPERIAN
NAVY FEDERAL CREDIT UNION - BUSINESS – TRANSUNION
NEW EGG – EQUIFAX BUSINESS – SYNCHRONY BANK
OFFICE DEPOT – NET 30 / CRDIT CARD THRU CITIBANK - REQUIRES PURCHASES OF $2,500 ANNUALLY WITH PG – EXPERIAN BUSINESS – EQUIFAX BUSINESS
ONEMAIN FINANCIAL – EQUIFAX
PNC BANK - EXPERIAN
RBS - CITIZENS BANK - EQUIFAX
RED CHECK - EQUIFAX
ROAD LOANS - EQUIFAX
SPRINT NEXTEL - EQUIFAX
SUNTRUST BANK - TRANSUNION
T-MOBILE - EQUIFAX - TRANSUNION
VERIZON WIRELESS - EXPERIAN - EQUIFAX
WELLS FARGO BANK - EXPERIAN
WELLS FARGO AUTO FINANCE - EXPERIAN - EQUIFAX
WELLS FARGO CREDIT CARDS - EQUIFAX

WESTERN UNION FINANCE -EXPERIAN
WFDS/WDS AUTO Finance - Business - TRANSUNION
USAA CREDIT UNION – EQUIFAX
US Bank - EQUIFAX BUSINESS

National Funding Sources

ACCION International - ACCION International is a private, nonprofit organization with the mission of giving people the financial tools they need – micro-enterprise loans, business training and other financial services – to work their way out of poverty.
www.accion.org/

Grants.gov - Grants.gov is your source to FIND and APPLY for federal government grants. The U.S. Department of Health and Human Services is proud to be the managing partner for
Grants.gov, an initiative that is having an unparalleled impact on the grant community.
www.Grants.gov

National Venture Capital Association - The National Venture Capital Association (NVCA) is a trade association that represents the U.S. venture capital industry. It is a member-based organization, which consists of venture capital firms that manage pools of risk equity capital designated to be invested
in high growth companies. www.nvca.org

Rockies Venture Club - RVC is the Rocky Mountain Region's premier networking organization that connects entrepreneurs, service professionals, investors, venture capitalists and other funding sources. www.RockiesVentureClub.org

Reporting Creditors & Vendors
Amazon 800-301-5546 www.amazon.com
Amazon Corporate Credit Line is issued by Synchrony Bank
Amazon Net 55 is issued by Synchrony Bank

Amsterdam Promotional Products - www.amsterdamprinting.com

BANK OF AMERICA ALASKA AIRLINES BUSINESS CARD - EQUIFAX
Best Buy 800-811-7276 www.bestbuy.com
BJ's Club – Perks for Business MasterCard® - 844-271-2539
Chevron/Texaco Business Card - www.chevrontexacobusinesscard.com
(Chevron and Texaco Universal Business MasterCard® is issued by Regions Bank - Chevron and Texaco Business Card and Chevron and Texaco Diesel Advantage Card are issued by FleetCor Technologies Operating Company/Wex Fleet)
CITGO Fleet 800-561-4991 www.citgo.com
Conoco 866-289-5622 www.conoco.com
Dell 800-757-8434 www.dell.com
ExxonMobil Business Card 800-903-9966 www.exxon.com
FedEx Kinko's 800-488-3705 www.fedex.com
Fuelman - www.fuelman.com

Grainger 888-361-8649 www.grainger.com
Green Capital – www.greencapitalcredit.com
HP/Compaq Computers 800-888-9909 www.hp.com
Home Depot Commercial 800-685-6691 www.homedepot.com
Home Depot 877-969-9039
Kabbage www.kabbage.com for ebay sellers
Key Bank 800-254-2737 www.keybank.com
Kiva www.kiva.org
Lending Tree www.lendingtree.com
Lowes 866-232-7443 www.lowes.com
Marathon Universal Card - www.marathonuniversal.applyfleet.com
MSC Industrial Supply - www.mscdirect.com
Office Max 800-283-7674 www.officemax.com
Philips 66 866-289-5630 www.phillips.com
Quill 800-882-3400 www.quill.com
Sam's Club 800-301-5546 www.samsclub.com
Sears 800-599-9710 www.sears.com
Shell Fleet 800-223-3296 www.shell.com
Staples 800-767-1275 www.staples.com
Sunoco 800-935-3387 www.sunoco.com
Target 800-440-5317 www.target.com
Texaco 800-839-2267 www.texaco.com
Uline Packaging 800-958-5463 www.uline.com
Universal Platinum FleetCard MasterCard®- www.fleetcardsusa.com
issued by Regions Bank
Vouch Financial www.vouch.com need 1 peer loan guarantor
Valero 877-882-5376 www.valero.com
Wal-Mart 877-294-7548 www.walmart.com
Wex Fleet – Fuel Cards www.wexinc.com/product-recommendations
Accepted at more than 180,000 WEX Network locations nationwide.
(Wex is the issuer for Conoco Universal / Stripes / Exxon Mobil Fleet / ALON Universal / Phillips66 Universal / CITGO Fleet Universal / 7-Eleven Universal Fleet / RaceTrac Universal Fleet / QuickTrip Fleetmaster Plus / Circle K Universal Card / Gulf Universal Fleet / 76 Universal Card Union76
Wright Express 888-743-3893 www.wrightexpress.com

Additional Business Credit Cards by Bank

Brex Mastercard® Corporate Credit Card
Brex Mastercard® Corporate Credit Card, issued by Emigrant Bank or Fifth Third Bank, NA.

Chase Bank Cards
Chase Ink Business Cash card

IHG One Rewards Premier Business Credit Card
Ink Business Unlimited Credit Card - Good Credit
Ink Business Unlimited Credit Card
Ink Business Cash Credit Card
Southwest Rapid Rewards Performance Business Credit Card
Southwest Rapid Rewards Premier Business Credit Card
United Business Card
United Club Business Card
World of Hyatt Business Credit Card

Citibank
CitiBusiness® / AAdvantage® Platinum Select® Mastercard® Credit Card
Costco Anywhere Visa® Business Credit Card

Emburse Corporate Card
Emburse B2B Payment Systems
issued by Celtic Bank, a Utah-Chartered Industrial Bank

FNBO Credit Cards
Evergreen by FNBO Business Edition Credit Card
Ever ready for where your business takes you.
Earn Unlimited 2% CASH BACK2 on every purchase. Every day. Everywhere.
$200 cash bonus (20,000 points equivalent) when you spend $3,000 within the first 3 billing cycles after account is opened.2
No Annual Fee
No Category Restrictions.
No Rewards expiration
Earn 10,000 Bonus Points every Anniversary with $10,000 annual spend.
First National Bank pulls reports from both Experian and Equifax and reports to these and Transunion.

Huntington Voice Business Credit Card℠ - 4% cash-back on 1 bonus category, up to $7,000 in purchases per quarter; categories include office supply stores, computer, electronics, and camera stores, 1% cash back on all other purchases.

Sutton Bank
Ramp Visa Commercial Card and the Ramp Visa Corporate Card are issued by Sutton Bank and Celtic Bank
Airbase card is issued by Sutton Bank

U.S. Bank
U.S. BANK BUSINESS ALTITUDE™ CONNECT WORLD ELITE MASTERCARD®
U.S. BANK TRIPLE CASH REWARDS VISA® BUSINESS CARD

U.S. BANK BUSINESS LEVERAGE® VISA SIGNATURE® CARD
U.S. BANK BUSINESS PLATINUM CARD

The following resources are of private funding options to help small businesses. Visit www.sba.gov **for all federal programs.**

Program: AC Agribusiness Partners

Advantage Capital Community Development Fund, LLC www.advantagecap.com (504) 522-4850

Equity Fund providing funding from $2,000,000 to $15,000,000

Since 1992, they have invested more than $4.1 billion in over 900 companies, spanning a diverse array of industry sectors and covering the entire risk spectrum. For-profit businesses, small agricultural businesses in rural areas, firms that focus on sustainable and organic agriculture, better-for-you branded food, indoor agriculture and vertical farming, and the reduction of food waste throughout the supply chain. Working capital, equipment, acquisition and/or improvement of owner-occupied real estate, expansion, ownership transitions, buyouts and acquisitions.

Program: Debt Fund and Equity Fund

Advantage Capital Community Development Fund, LLC

www.advantagecap.com (504) 522-4850

Contact this provider for current loan amounts. For-profit businesses, growing or growth potential firms, strategic growth initiatives. Working capital, equipment, acquisition and/or improvement of owner-occupied real estate, expansion, ownership transitions, buyouts and acquisitions.

Program: Small Business Guaranteed Loan

Advantage Capital Community Development Fund, LLC

www.advantagecap.com (504) 522-4850

Guaranteed Loans from $750,000 to $10,000,000. For-profit businesses, government entities, early stage to mature firms, growth projects: Working capital, equipment, acquisition and/or improvement of owner-occupied real estate, expansion, ownership transitions, buyouts and acquisitions.

Program: Small Business Loan

BrightBridge Inc. - www.brightbridgeinc.org (423) 424-4220

BrightBridge is a Community Development Financial Institution (CDFI) that maintains a portfolio of commercial loan programs that aim to meet the unmet capital needs of startup and existing businesses in our service area. The loan programs are distinctive in their purpose, borrowers, and terms. For-profit and nonprofit businesses located in designated low-income census tracts or owned by members of a targeted population, which includes low-income persons and eligible minorities. Also does SBA loan programs.

Program: Small Business Capital Fund

Greenline Ventures

www.greenlineventures.com (303) 586-8000

Providing loans from $250,000 to $2,000,000

Greenline's pricing and terms are generally more favorable compared to market rate capital. Borrowers headquartered or with significant operations in a low-income census tract. Providing growth capital and general working capital, acquisitions or expansion into new markets, equipment, refinancings

Program: New Markets Tax Credit Financing

Hope Credit Union Enterprise Corporation

www.hopecu.org (866) 321-4673

Since 1994, Hope Credit Union has empowered individuals, families, and business owners with access to affordable financial services. Contact provider for current lending amounts.

Grocery stores, manufacturers, commercial developers, and operating businesses in New Markets Tax Credit-designated areas of higher distress as defined by the CDFI Fund and varies with needs of the community.

Program: Kiva Crowdfunded Microloans

Kiva - www.kiva.org (828) 479-5482

Funding up to $15,000 for small businesses including start-up capital or expansion capital

Program: Kiva Crowdfunded Loans

Local Initiative Support Corporation (LISC) - www.lisc.org (212) 455-9800

Funding up to $10,000 for Startup and existing businesses working with a LISC Trustee. Providing working capital, equipment, inventory funding.

Program: Leasehold Improvement/FF&E Loans

Local Initiative Support Corporation (LISC)

www.lisc.org (212) 455-9800

Providing loans from $100,000 to $500,000

Existing businesses in LISC communities

Leasehold improvements, remodeling and expansion, furniture, fixtures, equipment

Program: Maker Space Loans

Local Initiative Support Corporation (LISC)

www.lisc.org (212) 455-9800

Providing loans from $500,000 to $3,000,000

Owners of multi-tenant maker spaces

Adaptive reuse of old industrial buildings, warehouses, and large commercial spaces to a multi-tenant facility

Program: Commercial Real Estate Loans

Local Initiative Support Corporation (LISC)

www.lisc.org (212) 455-9800

Providing loans from $500,000 to $5,000,000

Owners of commercial and mixed-use projects, acquisition and construction

Program: Permanent Working Capital

Local Initiative Support Corporation (LISC)

www.lisc.org (212) 455-9800

Providing loans from $100,000 to $500,000

Commercial and small business working capital

Program: Secured Term Loans

Native American Bank

www.nativeamericanbank.com (720) 963-6002

Contact provider for current loan amounts

Tribes, Tribal owned enterprises, Alaska Native Village Corporations, and businesses owned by individual Native Americans and Alaska Natives

Program: Secured Revolving Lines of Credit

Native American Bank

www.nativeamericanbank.com (720) 963-6002

Contact provider amounts of lines of credit

Tribes, Tribal owned enterprises, Alaska Native Village Corporations, and businesses owned by individual Native Americans and Alaska Natives

Program: Secured Term Loans

Native American Bank

www.nativeamericanbank.com (406) 338-7000

Contact provider for current loan amounts

Tribes, Tribal owned enterprises, Alaska Native Village Corporations, and businesses owned by individual Native Americans and Alaska Natives.

Program: Secured Revolving Lines of Credit

Native American Bank

www.nativeamericanbank.com (406) 338-7000

Contact provider for current lines of credit amounts

Tribes, Tribal owned enterprises, Alaska Native Village Corporations, and businesses owned by individual Native Americans and Alaska Natives

Program: Transformation Loan Fund

Primary Care Development Corporation

www.pcdc.org (212) 437-3900

Providing loans from $100,000 to $2,000,000

Federally Qualified Health Centers (FQHCs) and other community health centers; behavioral health institutions including mental health centers and substance use treatment facilities; AIDS Service Organizations (ASOs); PACE (Program of All-inclusive Care for the Elderly) programs; and safety net hospitals including ambulatory care and outpatient centers. Upgrading electronic health record systems (EHRs) to the newest generation, which includes outcomes-oriented programming and allows for real-time information exchange between organizations and outcomes measurement; implementing patient-centered service integration efforts to provide comprehensive care, including services historically provided by mental health organizations, substance-use disorder treatment programs, and others; expanding the workforce, hiring varied staff who can extend clinical capacity, engage patients in consistent care, and perform analysis of costs and outcomes data; and diversifying delivery to include emerging treatment modalities that improve patients' access to care, ex. Telehealth.

American Express Cards
AMEX American Express ® - AMEX Green Card ® - AMEX Gold Card ®
AMEX Centurion Card ® (incorrectly often call AMEX Black Card) are all great cards to have when you have credit.

Lowest Score 680 - Ave Score 720 (with the exception of the Centurion Card) PG required in most cases.

Business Green Rewards Card from American Express OPEN
APR N/A. Annual Fee $0 introductory for the first year, then $95
Gold Delta SkyMiles® Business Credit Card from American Express
APR 15.24% – 19.24% variable. Annual Fee $0 introductory for the first year, then $95.

SimplyCash® Business Credit Card from American Express – Cash Back Card for business . Introductory APR 0% for the first 9 months After that, your APR will be 12.24% – 19.24% variable. Annual Fee $0

Blue for Business® Credit Card from American Express
Introductory APR 0% for the first 9 months. After that, your APR will be 11.24% – 19.24% variable. Annual Fee $0

Business Platinum Card® from American Express OPEN
APR N/A. Annual Fee $450. or a fully secured AMEX Platinum Card ® with $50,000 secured account Use this card to maximum every month and payoff balance.

AMEX Centurion Card ® – AKA "AMEX BLACK CARD"
American Express created the Centurion Card ® in 1999 in response to an urban legend of a "black" charge card that had no limit, made of anodized titanium, and was only given to the wealthiest people.

The card is offered by invitation only to existing American Express customers who spend and pay off $250,000 per year on their other AMEX cards or using a bank that offers a fully secured Centurion Card. (see www.isg3.com website for more information on a fully secured card – this normally requires a deposit of $300,000 plus our fees). The exact criteria for issuance are not advertised, but an annual income of over $1 million and a net worth of $10 million seems to be the common ground.

You will pay a one-time $7,500 card initiation fee with annual fee of $2,500 per card. Only $10,000 per year for the perks!

BlueHub Loan Fund - BlueHub Capital - www.bluehubcapital.org (617) 427-8600

Contact provider for loan amounts for targeted economically disadvantaged small businesses. $2.6 billion Invested in low-income communities and $13.6 billion in additional capital leveraged by projects.

There have been well-publicized reports of purchases using the Centurion card for exotic cars, yachts, and even million-dollar pieces of art for the Rewards points!!!

The advantage to building massive credit using a fully secured Centurion Card ® is that once you have the card you are automatically put on a very high value marketing list sold by American Express. One you have the Centurion Card ® your will get fully pre-approved offers that require very little to complete – some just require a signature and an EIN or SSN!

Important Note 1: With American Express if you have ever had a delinquent account, they will have it in their records and will either deny you a card or require a secured card thorough an affiliate bank.

Important Note 2: With American Express you must use the card to its maximum in the first two months to establish a spending pattern. If you ignore this, you will have to call in to get your account re-approved on purchases that seem outside your normal spending patterns. You must max out this card at least 3 times a year!

Balboa Capital - www.balboacapital.com
Balboa Capital is a technology-driven direct lender that specializes in working capital loans. Easy Application /Quick Credit Decisions. Get up to $250,000 with Basic Information. Get up to $2 Million with a Full Financial Package. Absolutely No Hidden Fees! No Restrictions on How You Can Use Your Loan! **Perfect Credit Isn't Required!**

BlueHub Capital - www.bluehubcapital.org (617) 427-8600 Contact provider for loan amounts for targeted economically disadvantaged small businesses. $2.6 billion Invested in low-income communities and $13.6 billion in additional capital leveraged by projects in 2023.

Blue Vine - Invoice Financing - www.bluevine.com - 1-888-452-7805

85% of the invoice amount upfront and the rest, minus fees, when your client pays. Their standard rate is 1% per week with a minimum of 3 weeks. There are no hidden fees: No origination fees, No Termination Fees, No monthly minimums, No long-term contracts, No daily/weekly payments, No pre-payment penalties. 20-30% discount on the standard rate as you build history with Blue Vine. Here are the details one deal they completed for our client: $20,000 Invoice Amount – Repayment Due in 4 weeks – Client was issued a $17,000 advance fee and was given a $2,200 success fee when their customer paid invoice. Total cost was $800 to Blue Vine. Requirements: 530 personal credit score. Blue Vine has helped with many of the Covid-19 programs PPP and EIDL, etc.

CAN Capital - www.cancapital.com
CAN Capital can help fund business related expenses that your company may need quickly. The Business Term Loan product has a set maturity date when the business must pay off the loan. Business Loans through CAN Capital offer anywhere from $2,500 to $150,000** in financing with a range of 4 to 24 months in maturity making them ideal for any small business. No personal collateral is needed and funds can be transferred in as little as 2 business days. Business must have at least a monthly gross revenue of $4,500 or more.

Your business's monthly revenue is relatively stable. Your business has been in operation for at least 4 months. No checks! A small, fixed amount is automatically deducted from your business bank account each weekday via ACH. No personal collateral needed. Approval is based on your business's strength.

CAN Capital TrakLoan™ is the newest concept in flexible loan financing and can help small businesses smartly manage their cash flow. Ideal for businesses with credit card processing. With TrakLoan, your daily payments are tied to your payment card sales so you remit more when your sales are high and less when sales are low. Funds are available from $2,500 to $150,000. No personal collateral is needed. Learn more about TrakLoan. Instead of sending a large amount once a month, a flat percentage of your business's credit and debit card sales are automatically remitted daily. ‡ A larger amount is sent on busy sales days than on slow days. The process stops automatically when your loan is repaid.

No personal collateral is needed. A stellar credit history is not required to qualify. There are no checks to write all ACH. On a slow day your business remits less; on a busy day it remits more.
Remittances are made through processing credit and debit card sales—you can remain 100% focused on growing the business. There is no maturity date and there are no fixed payment amounts. It is quick and easy when compared to other options such as a traditional loan.

CAPITAL ONE SPARK BUSINESS Card – www.isg3.com This can be either a secured or conventional credit card – see Credit Mastery Personal Section for ideas and preparations for this card.

Celtic Bank - www.celticbank.com – Small Business Loans – Equipment Financing – SBA Approved Lender - Minimal requirements for non SBA funding – requires personal credit check and personal guarantee. 2Yr companies with $100,000 annual revenues have received $250,000 to $350,000 based on guarantor.

Celtic Bank Express Loans – $50K – $150K – Get pre-approved today and funded in as little as 5 business days - Celtic Bank is a nationwide small business lender specializing in SBA loans. The Celtic Bank Express Loan was specifically designed with small business owners in mind. Our streamlined loan program offers working capital loans with lower interest rates and extended repayment terms. Celtic Bank is the 6th largest SBA lender in the nation for FY 2015.
Requirements: at least 2 years in business.

Commerce Bank - www.commercebank.com
Small business and personal loans and auto financing. No acccount needed and not state specific.

Credibly - www.credibly.com
Credibly offers small business loans ranging from $5k up to $200k with no spending restrictions. Loans funded within 48 hours. All loans through Credibly are originated by WebBank of Utah. Requirements: Business FICO greater than 500, 6 months in business, $15k average monthly bank deposits, and U.S. – based business

DealStruck - www.dealstruck.com
Combines traditional business loans, asset-based lined of credit, inventory lines of credit, and many other revenue-based loan products .
Requires past two years tax returns along with past years bank statements. Pre-approved for up to $500,000 in funding in a few minutes on approved credit. Requirements: 600 personal credit score and at least 1 year in business

Business Loan: Business owner term loans up to $250,000 with a fixed monthly payment along with terms up to 48 months in length.

Inventory Line of Credit: Ideal for inventory-based companies that want to take grow their business by securing more inventory while keeping control of their cash flow.

Asset Based Line of Credit: Perfect for businesses that depend on steady revenue to support their business operations, this option allows small business owners to borrow against unpaid customer invoices.

Expansion Capital Group - www.ecg.com
Financing from ECG of up to $500,000 with only a simple application + 3 months bank and/or credit card statements are needed, not the business plans banks require. Tax liens up to $175,000 or open bankruptcies in the last year will not disqualify your business. Businesses with strong performance, even owners with poor credit histories can be approved. Pay back your loan with small daily payments unlike the larger monthly payments required by banks. Quote within 24 hours and money in your

account as fast as 2 business days. Banks require 4–6 weeks on average. Pledge of only business assets in certain cases.

Funding Circle - www.fundingcircle.com
Borrow $25,000 to $500,000 over 1 to 5 years; Borrow for almost any business goal. Funding Circle has funded 12,000 businesses globally for a total over $1.5 billion using their private investors (almost peer to peer lending as investors choose what they wish in their portfolio).
Requirements: 620 personal credit score and at least 2 years in business
Affordable: term business loans starting at 5.49%, no hidden fees
Fast: apply in 10 minutes, 72 hour decision time and funding within 10 days upon approval.

Fundation - www.fundation.com
Fundation Group LLC is a technology-empowered direct lender that delivers small balance commercial loans. They offer fixed rate loans up to $500,000 using their own capital. Fundation fills a void in the small balance commercial loan market by offering loans to businesses that banks reject with a simplified process and capital with terms that will enable them to grow. Fundation's technology uses a streamlined the loan application process by collecting third party data and automating the majority of the credit review process. Requirements: 630 personal credit score and at least 5 years in business.

Green Capital – Receivable Financing - www.greencapitalcredit.com
$10K+ per month minimum revenue and 6+ months in business.
Approvals within 24 hours and same day instant funding upon approval.

Headway Capital - www.headwaycapital.com
Up to $35,000 that funds next day upon approval. Headway Capital states they are simpler and quicker than working with a bank or merchant cash advance provider. Situation based lending overrides credit score. Chicago-based Headway Capital is part of Enova International (NYSE: ENVA), an online lender that advertises servicing over $15 billion in loans to more than 3 million consumers since 2004.

Huntington Bank (acquired TCF Equipment Financing) www.huntington.com
Products Include: Tax Leases; TRAC Leases; Operating Leases; Lease Purchases/Finance Leases; $1 Purchase Option Leases or Equipment Loans; Vendor Leasing/Financing; Interim Funding/Progress Funding; Equipment Finance Agreement.

Huntington Bank offers funding for:
Agriculture - Agri Equipment Finance (Grow Operations for Hemp :))
Capital Markets - Customer exposure management and asset acquisition.
Commercial Marine - Vessel loans and leases
Commercial Trucking – loans and leases
Construction - Financing for the construction & environmental industries
Franchise Finance - National Lender to Franchises
Franchise Acquisition

Golf - Golf carts, turf equipment, and most other needs
Healthcare - 18 years providing financing to the healthcare industry
Homecare - Financing the Homecare market for nearly two decades
Manufacturing - Financing a variety of manufacturing industries
Municipal - Special solutions for municipality funding needs
Specialty Markets - Funeral Vehicles, Motorcoach, and more...
Towing & Recovery Industry Equipment Financing for over 10 years.

Revolving Lines of Credit - Used to finance the ongoing originations of specialty finance companies based on agreed-upon underwriting standards.

Term Loans - Used to finance an existing pool of assets originated by an issuer, that will liquidate over time, or to finance the purchase of a pool of assets by a buyer.

Recourse and Non-Recourse - The ability and flexibility to include recourse to help mitigate risks and achieve efficient financing, where appropriate.

Huntington Commitments $50 million - $250 million (with syndication capability to $1 billion+).

Target Industries - **Commercial specialty finance companies**, including:

Small to Large Ticket Equipment
Commercial Real Estate
Private Credit/CLOs
Mortgage Warehousing/Residential
ABL
Rail
Accounts Receivable
Aircraft

Kabbage – www.kabbage.com
Kabbage claims to have funded over $1 billion to help businesses grow. Kabbage is the industry leader in providing working capital online with much going to eBay sellers. Apply, qualify and get cash instantly. No application fee. No obligation until you take cash. Ongoing access to cash, 24/7 Minimum Requirements: One year or more in business. Over $50,000 a year in revenue. Qualify for lines from $2,000 to $100,000. Loans are repaid over 6 months. No early payment fees. Fees are 1% - 12%* of your selected loan amount the first two months and 1% for each of the remaining four months. No early payment fees. Every month, for six months, you pay back 1/6 of the total loan amount plus the monthly fee. You can pay early and save.

Each draw is treated as an agreement between you and Kabbage. Draw against your line as often as once a day. Pay only for what you take.

Kabbage's maximum rate for months 1 and 2 is 12%. Third party partners may occasionally charge an additional 1.5% for months 1 and 2.
Requirements: 550 personal credit score and at least 1 year in business.

Key Bank Equipment Finance –www.keyequipmentfinance.com
Key Equipment Finance has been helping our clients with equipment, vehicles, aircraft and software financing for over 44 years. As a division of KeyBank, they offer clients direct and convenient access to a full suite of banking, lending and investment solutions.

Kiva Zip 0% Interest Loans - zip.kiva.org/borrow
Kiva Zip is a non profit that provides entrepreneurs with 0% interest loans up to $5,000. Kiva Zip loans are crowdfunded by a global community of over one million people who can be potential customers and brand ambassadors to your business. They have a 94% funding success rate and you can apply online.

Lending Club - Google Adwords – PPC resellers – CPA ventures
Google Adwords loan offers up to $25,000 strictly for google adwords financed by Lending Club. 12 month term with 6 months is 0% interest with no prepayment penalties, then next 6 months is at 9.9% interest.
Loan payment for first 6 months is just 2% of the outstanding loan amount. Last 6 months, the remaining principle and interest are paid until the full amount is paid off in the 12th payment.
They request a current business bank statement and personal guarantee using a soft inquiry via Experian Personal.

LiftForward - www.liftforward.com
LiftForward specializes in small business lending with Working Capital Loans of $10,000 to $250,000. Clients are given the opportunity to increase the size of their loan as they grow and create history with LiftForward. Many of their Clients started with a $50,000 loan and now have $1,000,000 loans as per their website. They will also refinance your MCA loan into a monthly product. Requirements: 650 personal credit score and at least 1 year in business.

LiftForward Asset Backed Loans of 50,000 to $500,000
LiftForward specializes in small business lending. LiftForward will structure the right loan product for you. Requirements: 620 personal credit score and at least 2 years in business.

LiftForward Purchase Order Financing of $50,000 to $500,000
LiftForward specializes in small business lending with a Purchase Order Financing product. Lending on reciept of purchase order opposed to invoice financing. Requirements: 620 personal credit score and at least 2 years in business.

Live Oak Bank - www.liveoakbank.com 877-890-5867
Specializes in industry focused lending from $25,000 to $5,000,000.

This Bank Likes Certificate of Deposit - prime for Certificate of Deposit Funding in this book and Credit Mastery Advanced Funding Tools.

Investment Advisory Loans - means commercial real estate funding! Also select commercial construction such as Hotels and Self Storage, etc.
Succession Financing – Live Oak can help with partner buyout lending solutions, eliminating the need for a seller note. 25% of their portfolio.
Acquisition Financing – The process of buying other businesses and providing the role of financing in structuring a transaction. 40% of their portfolio.

Extensive financing options: competitive rates, no financial covenants and no prepayment penalty. Term: 10 years for business purposes and 25 years for real estate. Loan amounts: Live Oak can fund loans starting at $25,000 up to $5 million, with an expedited process for amounts up to $350,000. Industry focused team handles your loan from application to approval in as few as 10 days and funding within 40 days many times as little as 3 days.

Marlin Finance Company – www.marlinfinance.com
Offering a comprehensive set of vendor, manufacturer and distributor finance solutions including private label programs. True business loans from $5,000 to $150,000 with flexible 6-24 month terms. Apply online in 10 minutes or less and receive funds in as little as 1 day.

Menards Contractor Card /Menards Commercial Account – issued by Capital One - EQUIFAX or EQUIFAX Business.
PG Required for all Sole Proprietorships, Partnerships and required for Corporations and LLCs in business less than 2 years.
If credit line requested is greater than $25,000 you will be required to submit your most recent two years of financial statements or tax returns. If business entity is a tax-exempt organization, please provide tax-exempt documentation. Menards Commercial Account appears as it can be a net 30-55 or credit line. 2% - 7% cash back and up to 50 free rountrip airline tickets!!! (as of Jan 2016 and can end at anytime).

National Funding - www.nationalfunding.com - Small business loans nationwide with a range of financial services and solutions, including business loans, equipment financing, merchant cash advance, and other merchant services. Business financing available from $5,000 to $500,000 with same day approvals, and funding delivered in as few as 24 hours. Requirements: 600 personal credit score and at least 2 years in business.

Navitas Equipment Financing - www.navitascredit.com
Once the equipment buying decision is made, without the capital needed to acquire it…everything comes to a stop. When your customers are looking to finance your equipment, Navitas delivers the capital solutions they need right at the point of sale.

For the Equipment Seller - Navitas works with thousands of dealers nationwide to help them provide their customers with affordable financing options to increase their sales closing rates dramatically.

For the Business Owner - Navitas provides extended payment plans to match your exact budgeting needs to acquire new or used equipment.

Finance Almost Any Type of Commercial Equipment
Approvals In Minutes
Lower Rates for Quality Credits
Support Challenging Credit Histories and Start-Ups

Newtek - www.newtekone.com
As a full-service, non-bank/bank lender, Newtek Small Business Finance is able to provide a flexible, low-cost lending option that offers longer periods than conventional loans with financing from $50,000 to $10 million. Newtek claims to have lent over half-a-billion dollars to over 800 U.S. based small businesses. Newtek will look for a minimum monthly volume of at least $10,000 with merchant account advances and been in business for over a year and process at least $3,500 in credit card sales each month. Conventional loan requirements: 620 personal credit score and at least 2 years in business.

Newtek Commercial Real Estate Loans from $500,000 to $10 Million with terms up to 25 years along with possibly 90% LTV. Fully amortizing with no balloon payments. Purchase or refinance owner-occupied real estate with funding for renovation and expansion of owner-occupied real estate. U.S domiciled for profit companies only with an average net income over the last 2 years must not exceed $2.5 million. Owners must be U.S. citizens or can be resident aliens in good standing. Owner operated businesses must occupy 51% or greater of the building.

On Deck Capital -
Offers both Business Term Loans and Lines of Credit.

On Deck Capital Lines of Credit up to $100,000 and APRs as low as 13.99% - Requirements: Companies in business at least one year with $200,000+ in gross annual revenue along with a majority owner with a 600+ personal credit score.

They base the line amount and rate based on their assessment of your business along with your business and personal credit with rates from 13.99% – 36.00% APR. Fixed weekly payments that are automatically deducted from your business bank account. A $20 monthly maintenance fee, however there are no fees charged when you draw money.

On Deck Capital Business Term Loans up to $500,000 and annual interest rates as low as 5.99% OAC. Requirements: Companies in business at least one year with $100,000+ in gross annual revenue along with at least one owner with a 500+ personal credit score. Fixed daily or weekly payments automatically deducted from your business bank account.

On Deck Capital Short Term Loans of 3-12 month terms as low as 9% Total Interest Percentage OAC with average rates of 19%+ Total Interest Percentage (Total Interest Percentage calculates the total amount of interest paid as a percentage of the loan amount). Example: On a 6-month, $10,000 loan with 9% Total Interest Percentage and weekly payments, the interest cost is $900, for a total payback amount of $10,900.

On Deck Capital Long Term Loans of 15-36 month terms as low as 5.99% Annual Interest Rate OAC - Average rates of 30% Annual Interest Rate. This rate excludes any additional fees. Example : On a 24 month, $100,000 loan with 5.99% Annual Interest Rate and weekly payments, the interest cost is $6,167, for a total loan payback amount of $106,167.

On Deck Capital Additional Term Loan Fees: One-time fee to cover cost of servicing and processing the loan. 1st loan: 2.5% of loan amount; 2nd loan: 1.25% of loan amount; 3rd+ loan: 0-1.25% of loan amount.

One United Bank – www.oneunited.com
Multi Family Housing Lender for loans of $500,000 to $7,000,000 with terms up to 40 years and closings in 45 days. Max 75% LTV.
Commercial Real Estate Loans to $7,000,000 also!

OrangeFi - www.orangefi.com
START UP Funding! Up to $250,000 with 0% for 24 months as of Mar 2019. No front fees – No prepayment penalty! This is a revolving credit line with cash advances. Based on personal credit score.

PayPal – www.paypal.com No credit check lending – based on cashflow thru your business PayPal account. Based upon a minimum of $20,000 of annual revenue accepted into your account. Flexible repay and low interest rates. The loan is underwritten by Web Bank of Utah.

Quote 2 Fund - www.quote2fund.com
Quote 2 Fund connects you to a nationwide network of over 5,000 banks and lenders with a single (free) application. Quote 2 Fund for alternative financing programs to SBA loans. Poor Credit O.K. - Bankruptcies O.K. - Tax Liens O.K. - Start-ups O.K. - No Collateral O.K. Requirements: 600 personal credit score and at least 2 years in business.

RapidFinance — Small Business Loan - www.rapidfinance.com
Low-cost loan options with terms up to 18 months. Receive up to $500,000 funding in just 3 days to use for any business purpose. Supplement existing traditional financing or alternative working capital. Requirements: Average personal FICO score of 600 and at least 2 years in business

Regents Capital Corporation –www.regentscapital.com
Whether secured or unsecured, Regents' Working Capital Loans offers affordable rates, flexible terms and rapid funding advantages. Regents' clients often incorporate these short term structures into their larger funding portfolios to cover both everyday and unexpected business expenses. With unsecured

loans, how you use the cash is up to you; approval of the loan is not conditional upon the uses for the loan. Plus Equipment financing and leasing.

New Market Tax Credit - Rural Development Partners, LLC - www.rdpimpact.com (641) 585-1000. Businesses, nonprofit organizations, communities, government entities for job growth in rural America using Tax Credits.

SmartBiz. - www.smartbizloans.com
Streamlined SBA loan process for a loan from $5,000 to $350,000. SBA loans offering low rates from 6% to 8%*, 10 year terms. Pre-qualify in minutes, and get funds as fast as 7 days after application is complete. * Loans have a variable rate of Prime Rate plus 2.75% to 4.75%. Requirements: 600 personal credit score and at least 2 years in business

Stearns Bank - www.stearnsbank.com
Stearns Bank is a $2 billion, top-performing bank specializing in nationwide equipment financing with more than $600 million in equipment sales annually. The Equipment Finance Division finances new or used commercial equipment in various industries including healthcare, construction, agricultural, paving, machine tools, and vocational vehicles. The average ticket size is $50,000, however as a Preferred SBA Lender, Stearns can provide financing up to $5 million.

The Wells Fargo Business Secured Credit Card is an essential tool for businesses looking to establish or rebuild their business credit with Wells Fargo. We have had clients convert these cards in 12 months to a $10,000+ credit card. Secured credit line from $500 up to $25,000 depending on your starting deposit to fund the card. $25 annual fee. Choose between rewards points or cash back.

Wells Fargo Business Platinum Credit Card with credit lines up to $50,000, it's tailored for businesses with annual sales of up to $2 million.
Credit line up to $50,000 with No Annual fee. Optional rewards program. Choose between rewards points or cash back.

Wells Fargo Business Elite Card provides credit lines up to $100,000 for businesses with annual sales above $1 million. No annual fee. Up to $100,000 credit line and choose between rewards points or cash back.

U.S. Bank - Equifax Business
U.S. Bank FlexPerks® Business Edge™ Travel Rewards - Lowest Score 720 and easiest approval. APR 11.99% – 17.99% variable. Annual Fee $0 introductory for the first year, then $55.

U.S. Bank Business Edge™ Platinum - Lowest Score 720 – 750. Introductory APR 0% for the first 12 months After that, your APR will be 9.99% – 17.99% variable. Annual Fee $0

U.S. Bank Business Edge™ Cash Rewards - Lowest Score 720- 750. Introductory APR 0% for the first 9 billing cycles on purchases. After that, your APR will be 11.99% – 17.99% variable. Annual Fee $0

U.S. Bank Business Edge™ Select Rewards - Lowest Score 720 -750. Introductory APR 0% for the first 9 months After that, your APR will be 11.99% – 17.99% variable. Annual Fee $0

Credit Mastery: Developing Aged Corporations

Credit Unions – Join First with Checking Acct – Then Apply for Credit Cards (when not taking a secured card)

ABCO Federal Credit Union - Rancocas, NJ www.goabco.org
800-225-1859 690 Beverly Rancocas Road, Willingboro, NJ 08046

Achieva Credit Union - Dunedin, FL (online application)
www.achievacu.com 727-431-7680 1659 Virginia St, Dunedin, FL 34698

Affinity Plus Federal Credit Union - Saint Paul, MN (online application) www.affinityplus.org 651-291-3700 175 W Lafayette Frontage Rd, Saint Paul, MN 55107-1488

Agriculture Federal Credit Union - Washington, DC (online application) www.agfed.org 202-479-2270 1400 Independence Ave SW USDA Bldg Room SM 2, Washington, DC 20250

Air Force Federal Credit Union - San Antonio, TX (online application)
www.airforcefcu.com 210-673-5610 1560 Cable Ranch Rd Ste 200, San Antonio, TX 78245

Alliant Credit Union - Chicago, IL (online application) www.alliantcreditunion.org 800-328-1935 11545 W Touhy Ave, Chicago, IL 60666

Altra Federal Credit Union - Onalaska, WI (online application) www.altra.org 608-787-4500 1700 Oak Forest Dr, Onalaska, WI 54650
America's Christian Credit Union - Glendora, CA (online application) www.americaschristiancu.com 800-343-6328 2100 E Route 66 Ste 100, Glendora, CA 91740-4623

American Heritage Federal Credit Union - Philadelphia, PA (online application) www.amhfcu.org 215-969-0777 2060 Red Lion Rd, Philadelphia, PA 19115-1603

Andrews Federal Credit Union - Suitland, MD (online application) www.andrewsfcu.org 800-487-5500 5711 Allentown Rd, Suitland, MD 20746
Apple Federal Credit Union - Fairfax, VA (online application) www.applefcu.org 703-788-4800 4029 Ridge Top Rd, Fairfax, VA 22030
Aspire Federal Credit Union - Clark, NJ (online application) www.aspirefcu.org 732-388-0477 67 Walnut Ave, Clark, NJ 07066

Astera Credit Union - Lansing, MI (online application) www.asteracu.com 517-323-3644 111 S Waverly Rd, Lansing, MI 48917

Belvoir Federal Credit Union - Woodbridge, VA (online application)
www.belvoircreditunion.org 703-730-1800 14040 Central Loop, Woodbridge, VA 22193

California Credit Union - Glendale, CA (online application)
www.californiacu.org 800-334-8788 701 North Brand Boulevard, Glendale, CA

Capital Educators Federal Credit Union - Meridian, ID
www.caped.com 208-884-0150 275 Stratford Drive, Meridian, ID 83642

Chartway Federal Credit Union - Virginia Beach, VA (online application)
www.chartway.com 757-552-1000 2089 General Booth Boulevard, Virginia Beach, VA

Credit Mastery: Developing Aged Corporations

Coastal Federal Credit Union (online application)   www.coastal24.com
919-420-8000 1000 Saint Albans Drive, Suite 200, Raleigh, NC 27609

Communitywide Federal Credit Union - South Bend, IN
www.comwide.com   574-239-2700   1555 West Western Avenue, South Bend, IN 46619

Connexus Credit Union - Wausau, WI (online application) www.**connexus**cu.org 715-847-4700 2600 Pine Ridge Boulevard, Wausau, WI 54401

Consumers Credit Union - Waukegan, IL (online application)
www.myconsumers.org   877-275-2228   2750 Washington Street, Waukegan, IL 60079

Corporate America Family Credit Union - Elgin, IL (online application)
www.cafcu.org 800-359-1939 115 Perimeter Center Place, Atlanta, GA 30346

Crane Federal Credit Union - Odon, IN
www.cranecu.org 812-863-7000 1 W Gate Dr, Odon, IN 47562

Credit Union of New Jersey - Ewing, NJ
www.cunj.org   609-538-4061   1301 Parkway Avenue, Ewing Township, NJ 08628

Delta Community Credit Union - Atlanta, GA (online application)
www.deltacommunitycu.com   404-715-4725   1030 Delta Boulevard, Atlanta, GA 30320

Digital Credit Union - Marlborough, MA (online application)
www.dcu.org   508-481-7657   279 East Main Street, Marlborough, MA 01752

Dow Chemical Employees' Credit Union - Midland, MI (online application)
www.dcecu.org 989-835-7794   600 East Lyon Road, Midland, MI 48640

E-Central Credit Union - Pasadena, CA
www.ecentralcu.org 626-799-6000   990 South Fair Oaks Avenue, Pasadena, CA 91105

Eli Lilly Federal Credit Union - Indianapolis, IN (online application)
www.elfcu.org   317-524-5076   225 South East Street #140, Indianapolis, IN 46202

First Flight Federal Credit Union - Cary, NC (online application)
www.efirstflight.com 919-233-5237 1815 Kildaire Farm Road, Cary, NC 27834

First New England Federal Credit Union - East Hartford, CT (online application)   www.firstnewengland.org 860-282-0001 616 Burnside Avenue, East Hartford, CT 06108

First Technology Federal Credit Union - Palo Alto, CA (online application)
www.firsttechfed.com   855-855-8805   3000 El Camino Real, 3 Palo Alto Square, Suite 100, Palo Alto, CA 94306

Fort Knox Federal Credit Union - Radcliff, KY (online application)
www.fortknoxfcu.org 502-942-0254   713 West Lincoln Trail Boulevard, Radcliff, KY

Garden Savings Federal Credit Union - Parsippany, NJ
www.gardensavingsfcu.org 973-576-2000   129 Littleton Road, Parsippany, NJ 07054

Credit Mastery: Developing Aged Corporations

Great Lakes Credit Union - North Chicago, IL (online application)
www.glcu.org   847-578-7000   2525 Green Bay Road, North Chicago, IL 60064
GTE Financial Credit Union - Tampa, FL (online application) www.gtefinancial.org   813-414-7067   601 North Ashley Drive, #100, Tampa, FL

Hanscom Federal Credit Union - Hanscom AFB, MA (online application)
www.hfcu.org 800-656-4328   1610 Eglin Street, Hanscom Air Force Base, MA 01731

HeritageWest Credit Union (division of Chartway) - Tooele, UT (online application) www.heritagewestcu.com

Hughes Federal Credit Union - Tucson, AZ (online application)
www.hughesfcu.org 520-794-8341 3131 East Speedway Boulevard, Tucson, AZ 85716

INOVA Federal Credit Union - Elkhart, IN (online application)
www.inovafcu.org 574-294-6553   358 South Elkhart Avenue, Elkhart, IN 46516

Kinecta Federal Credit Union - Manhattan Beach, CA (online application) www.kinecta.org   310-643-5400   1440 Rosecrans Avenue, Manhattan Beach, CA 90266

Lake Michigan Credit Union - Grand Rapids, MI (online application)
www.lmcu.org 616-242-9790   5540 Glenwood Hills Pkwy Se, Grand Rapids, MI 49512
McGraw-Hill Federal Credit Union - East Windsor, NJ (online application)
www.mcgrawhillfcu.org   609-426-6500   120 Windsor Center Dr East Windsor, NJ 08520

Melrose Credit Union - Briarwood, NY (online application) 718-658-9800 www.melrosecu.org   139-30 Queens Boulevard, Briarwood, NY 11435
Michigan State University Federal Credit Union - East Lansing, MI (online application) www.msufcu.org 517-333-2424   3777 West Road, East Lansing, MI 48826

Money One Federal Credit Union - Largo, MD
www.moneyonefcu.org   301-925-4600   9800 Technology Way, Largo, MD 20774

Mountain America Credit Union - West Jordan, UT (online application)
www.macu.com 801-838-8998   9027 South 2200 West, West Jordan, UT 84084

NASA Federal Credit Union - Upper Marlboro, MD (online application)
www.nasafcu.com 301-249-1800 500 Prince Georges Boulevard, Upper Marlboro, MD 20774

Northrop Grumman Federal Credit Union - Gardena, CA (online application)
www.ngfcu.us 310-808-4000   879 West 190th Street, Gardena, CA 90248

Northwest Federal Credit Union - Herndon, VA (online application)
www.nwfcu.org 703-709-8900   200 Spring Street, Herndon, VA 20170

NuVision Credit Union - Huntington Beach, CA (online application)

Oceanside Christopher Federal Credit Union - Oceanside, NY (online application)

Pacific Community Credit Union - Fullerton, CA (online application)
www.yourcreditunion.com   714-526-2328 401   Imperial Highway, Fullerton, CA 92835

Credit Mastery: Developing Aged Corporations

Patelco Credit Union - Merced, CA (online application)
www.patelco.org 800-358-8228 3009 Stratofortress Drive, Atwater, CA 95301

Pen Air Credit Union - Pensacola, FL (online application)
www.penair.org 850-505-3200   1495 E Nine Mile Rd Pensacola, FL 32514
People's Trust Credit Union - Houston, TX
www.peoplestrustfcu.org 713-428-3200 One Shell Plaza, 910 Louisiana Street, Houston, TX 77002

Pinnacle Federal Credit Union - Edison, NJ   732-225-1505
www.pinnaclefcu.com   135 Raritan Center Parkway, Edison, NJ 08837
Premier America Credit Union - Chatsworth, CA (online application)
www.premieramerica.com 818-772-4000   19867 Prairie Street, Chatsworth, CA 91311

Provident Credit Union - Redwood City, CA (online application)
www.providentcu.org 650-591-7845 210 Redwood Shores Parkway, Redwood City, CA 94065

Quorum Federal Credit Union - Purchase, NY (online application)
www.quorumfcu.org 914-696-2420   2 Manhattanville Road #401, Purchase, NY 10577

RTN Federal Credit Union - Waltham, MA
www.rtn.org 781-736-9900   600 Main Street, Waltham, MA 02452

Sandia Laboratory Federal Credit Union - Albuquerque, NM
(online application) www.slfcu.org 505-293-0500   3707 Juan Tabo Boulevard Northeast, Albuquerque, NM 87111

San Diego County Credit Union - San Diego, CA (online application)
www.sdccu.com 877-732-2848 3180 University Avenue #100, San Diego, CA 92104

SCE Federal Credit Union - Irwindale, CA
www.scefcu.org 800-866-6474 12701 Schabarum Avenue, Irwindale, CA 91706

Sierra Point Credit Union - South San Francisco, CA
www.spcu.org 650-588-6140   365 South Spruce Avenue, South San Francisco, CA 94080

Self-Help Credit Union - Durham, NC (online application)
www.self-help.org 919-956-4400   301 West Main Street, Durham, NC 27701

Signal Financial Federal Credit Union - Kensington, MD (online application)
www.sfonline.org 301-933-9100 3015 University Blvd W Kensington, MD 20895

South Division Credit Union - Evergreen Park, IL (online application)
www.sdcu.org 708-396-2990 9122 South Kedzie Avenue, Evergreen Park, IL 60805
Southeast Financial Federal Credit Union - Nashville, TN 615-287-9820
www.southeastfinancial.org 325 Waldron Road, La Vergne, TN 37086
Stanford Federal Credit Union - Palo Alto, CA (online application)
www.sfcu.org 650-842-6000 525 University Avenue #21, Palo Alto, CA 94301

The Golden 1 Credit Union - Sacramento, CA (online application)
www.golden1.com 877-465-3361 1109 L Street, Sacramento, CA 95814

University Federal Credit Union - Austin, TX (online application) www.ufcu.org 512-467-8080 201 West 7th Street, Austin, TX 78701

U.S. New Mexico Credit Union - Albuquerque, NM (online application)
www.usnmfcu.org 505-342-8888 2608 Tennessee Street Northeast, Albuquerque, NM 87110

Velocity Credit Union - Austin, TX (online application)
www.velocitycu.com 512-469-7000 610 East 11th Street, Austin, TX 78701

Western Federal Credit Union - Manhattan Beach, CA
www.western.org 877-254-9328 1 Space Park Drive, Redondo Beach, CA 90278

Xceed Financial Credit Union - El Segundo, CA (online application)
www.xfcu.org 310-426-7400 888 North Nash Street, El Segundo, CA 90245

XCEL Credit Union - Secaucus, NJ (online application)
www.xcelfcu.org 800-284-8663 3680 John F Kennedy Boulevard West, Jersey City, NJ 07307

Second Chance Bank Accounts

Chase Bank - Chase offers customers a Chase Access Checking account for $25 for customers that have a not-so-good reputation with banks. In order to maintain the account, an unavoidable monthly fee of $17 is charged.

PNC Bank Foundation Checking - PNC Bank offers Foundation Checking to customers that are interested in re-establishing their reputation with banks. A minimum of $25 is required to open a Foundation Checking account.

Wells Fargo Opportunity Checking https://www.wellsfargo.com/checking/opportunity/

Wood Forrest National Bank - – Personal and Business
www.woodforrest.com They are in many Walmart's nationwide. For those of you with bad credit and on ChexSYSTEMS there is one answer that will give you a second chance personal checking account and a second chance business checking account. They require only $100 to open an account.

U.S. Bank Second Chance Checking Account -
Anyone can open a bank account with U.S. Bank. To open a second chance checking account you need a minimum deposit of $25. You also need to be debt-free elsewhere. The monthly fee for U.S. Bank is $6.95 a month for online statements or $8.95 for paper statements.

Multi-State Second Chance Banking Providers
APPALACHIAN COMMUNITY FEDERAL CREDIT UNION KY, TN, VA
BANK OF THE OZARKS - PATHWAY CHECKING AL, AR, CA, FL, GA, NC, NY, SC, TX
BBVA COMPASS BANK - EASY CHECKING – PERSONAL AND BUSINESS
 AL, AZ, CA, CO, FL, NM, TX
CENTENNIAL BANK OPPORTUNITY CHECKING - AL, AR, FL
CHASE BANK -
CITY NATIONAL BANK - BOUNCE BACK CHECKING KY, OH, VA, WV
COMMONWEALTH ONE FEDERAL CREDIT UNION - SECOND CHANCE CHECKING DC, MD, PA, VA
CORPORATE AMERICA FAMILY CREDIT UNION - FRESH START CHECKING
AZ, CA, CT, GA, IL, KS, NC, OH, PA, TX, VA
ENERGY ONE FEDERAL CREDIT UNION FRESH START CHECKING   CA, GA, OK, TX

FARMERS & MERCHANTS STATE BANK CLEAN START CHECKING   IN, MI, OH
FARMERS INSURANCE GROUP FEDERAL CREDIT UNION
AZ, CA, CO, ID, IL, KS, MI, OH, OK, OR, TX, WA
GENFED FEDERAL CREDIT UNION - NEW START CHECKING   IL, IN, OH
HOMESTREET BANK - BANK ON CHECKING   AZ, CA, HI, ID, OR, UT, WA
HOPE CREDIT UNION - EASY CHECKING AR, LA, MS, TN
LANDMARK BANK - REBOUND CHECKING   MO, OK, TX
MAIN SOURCE BANK - FRESH START CHECKING   IL, IN, KY, OH
ONEUNITED BANK - U2 CHECKING   CA, FL, MA
PARK COMMUNITY CREDIT UNION - FRESH START CHECKING   AL, IN, KY
PNC BANK - FOUNDATION CHECKING
AL, DC, DE, FL, GA, IL, IN, KY, MD, MI, MO, NC, NJ, NY, OH, PA, RI, SC, VA, WI
PREMIER BANK - STARTFRESH CHECKING   DC, MD, VA, WV
REPUBLIC BANK   CHECKING BUILDER   FL, IN, KY, OH, TN
STALEY CREDIT UNION - RENEW CHECKING   IL, IN, TN
WEBSTER BANK - OPPORTUNITY CHECKING   CT, RI, NY
WESTERN FEDERAL CREDIT UNION - RIGHT START CHECKING
AR, CA, CO, IN, KY, MI, MS, TN, TX, UT, VA, WV
WELLS FARGO OPPORTUNITY CHECKING
WOODFOREST NATIONAL BANK - SECOND CHANCE CHECKING
– PERSONAL AND BUSINESS
AL, FL, GA, KY, LA, IL, IN, MD, MS, NY, NC, OH, PA, SC, TX, VA, WV

SECOND CHANCE BANKING PROVIDERS BY STATE

ALABAMA
ALABAMA CREDIT UNION -	FIX IT CHECKING
AVADIAN CREDIT UNION -	E-CHECKING
AZALEA CITY CREDIT UNION -	OPPORTUNITY DRAFT
COMMUNITY BANK & TRUST	SECOND SLICE CHECKING
FAMILY SECURITY CREDIT UNION	GIVE ME A BREAK CHECKING
FIRST NATIONAL BANK	CREDIT BUILDER ACCOUNT
GUARDIAN CREDIT UNION	FRESH START CHECKING
TUSCALOOSA FEDERAL CREDIT UNION	STEP-N-2 CHECKING
UNITED BANK	GATEWAY CHECKING
WEST ALABAMA BANK	FRESH START CHECKING

ARKANSAS
BANK OF ARKANSAS	OPPORTUNITY CHECKING
DIAMOND BANK	DIAMOND ENCORE CHECKING
FAIRFIELD COMMUNITY CREDIT UNION	SECOND CHANCE CHECKING
FOCUS BANK	FRESH START CHECKING
RED RIVER CREDIT UNION	FRESH START CHECKING
RIVER VALLEY COMMUNITY CREDIT UNION	SECOND CHANCE CHECKING

ALASKA
TRUE NORTH FEDERAL CREDIT UNION	TRUE OPTIONS CHECKING

ARIZONA
ALHAMBRA CREDIT UNION	FRESH START CHECKING
BANK OF ARIZONA	OPPORTUNITY CHECKING
BANNER FEDERAL CREDIT UNION	OPPORTUNITY CHECKING
BASHAS' ASSOCIATES FEDERAL CREDIT UNION	NEW START CHECKING
CANYON STATE CREDIT UNION	SECOND CHANCE CHECKING
MARISOL FEDERAL CREDIT UNION	BASIC CHECKING
PIMA FEDERAL CREDIT UNION	FRESH START CHECKING

TRUWEST CREDIT UNION	OPPORTUNITY CHECKING ALSO IN TX
TUCSON FEDERAL CREDIT UNION	SECOND CHANCE CHECKING
TUCSON OLD PUEBLO CREDIT UNION	MISSION CHECKING

CALIFORNIA

ALLIANCE CREDIT UNION	FRESH START CHECKING
ALLIED HEALTHCARE FEDERAL CREDIT UNION	HEALTHY START CHECKING
ALTA VISTA CREDIT UNION	OPPORTUNITY CHECKING
AMERICAN UNITED FEDERAL CREDIT UNION	FRESH START CHECKING
COASTHILLS (COOP)	SECOND CHANCE CHECKING
E-CENTRAL CREDIT UNION	E-BUILDER CHECKING
FOOTHILL CREDIT UNION	REBOUND CHECKING
HERITAGE COMMUNITY CREDIT UNION -	SECOND CHANCE CHECKING
KAIPERM NORTH BAY FEDERAL CREDIT UNION	FRESH START CHECKING
KERN FEDERAL CREDIT UNION	FRESH START CHECKING
LOS ANGELES FEDERAL CREDIT UNION	SECOND CHANCE CHECKING
MID CITIES CREDIT UNION	SECOND CHANCE CHECKING
PREMIER AMERICA CREDIT UNION	FRESH START CHECKING
PRIORITY ONE CREDIT UNION	NEW LEAF CHECKING
SOUTHLAND CREDIT UNION	OPPORTUNITY CHECKING
UNITED ONE BANK - U2 CHECKING	
VENTURA COUNTY CREDIT UNION	SECOND CHANCE CHECKING

COLORADO

COLORADO STATE BANK AND TRUST	OPPORTUNITY CHECKING
LIBERTY SAVINGS BANK	CLEAN SLATE CHECKING
METRUM COMMUNITY CREDIT UNION	SECOND CHANCE CHECKING
NUVISTA FEDERAL CREDIT UNION	SECOND CHANCE CHECKING

CONNECTICUT

EASTERN SAVINGS BANK	SECOND CHANCE CHECKING
FINEX (CREDIT UNION)	RE-START CHECKING
HARTFORD FEDERAL CREDIT UNION	SECOND CHANCE CHECKING
NUTMEG STATE FINANCIAL CREDIT UNION	SECOND CHANCE CHECKING
TOBACCO VALLEY TEACHERS FEDERAL CREDIT UNION	MYCHANCE CHECKING

DELAWARE

WSFS BANK	FRESH START CHECKING

FLORIDA

1ST NATIONAL BANK OF SOUTH FLORIDA	NEW OPPORTUNITY CHECKING
ALABAMA CREDIT UNION	FIX IT CHECKING
ATLANTIC COAST BANK COAST	SECOND CHANCE CHECKING
AXIOM BANK	OPPORTUNITY CHECKING
CENTERSTATE BANK OF FLORIDA	FRESH START CHECKING
CENTRAL CREDIT UNION OF FLORIDA	FRESH START CHECKING
CENTRAL FLORIDA POSTAL CREDIT UNION	SECOND CHANCE CHECKING
CITY COUNTY EMPLOYEES CREDIT UNION	FRESH START CHECKING
COMMUNITY FIRST CREDIT UNION	FRESH START CHECKING
COMPASS FINANCIAL FEDERAL CREDIT UNION	RESTART CHECKING
FIRST AMERICAN BANK	FRESH START CHECKING
FIRST FLORIDA CREDIT UNION	SMART TRACK CHECKING
GOLD COAST FEDERAL CREDIT UNION	FRESH START CHECKING
GULF WINDS FEDERAL CREDIT UNION	MY OPPORTUNITY CHECKING
JAX FEDERAL CREDIT UNION	FRESH START CHECKING
JETSTREAM FEDERAL CREDIT UNION	SECOND CHANCE CHECKING

LIBERTY SAVINGS BANK	CLEAN SLATE CHECKING
MCCOY FEDERAL CREDIT UNION	FRESH START CHECKING
MEMBERSFIRST CREDIT UNION OF FLORIDA	SECOND CHANCE CHECKING
OKALOOSA COUNTY TEACHERS FEDERAL CREDIT UNION	FRESH START CHECKING
ONE SOUTH BANK	OPPORTUNITY CHECKING
SAN ANTONIO CITIZENS FEDERAL CREDIT UNION	SECOND CHANCE CHECKING
SOUTH FLORIDA FEDERAL CREDIT UNION	SECOND CHANCE CHECKING

GEORGIA

ATLANTA FEDERAL CREDIT UNION	SECOND CHANCE CHECKING
COMMUNITY BANK & TRUST -	SECOND CHANCE CHECKING
DOCO CREDIT UNION	FRESH START CHECKING
ENERGY ONE FEDERAL CREDIT UNION	FRESH START CHECKING
EXCEL FEDERAL CREDIT UNION	FRESH START CHECKING
FAMILY SAVINGS CREDIT UNION	FRESH START CHECKING
GEORGIA UNITED CREDIT UNION	RESTART CHECKING
GEORGIA'S OWN CREDIT UNION	RESOLUTION CHECKING
GWINNETT FEDERAL CREDIT UNION	FRESH START CHECKING
HEALTH CENTER CREDIT UNION	FRESH START CHECKING
MEMBERS UNITED CREDIT UNION	SECOND CHANCE CHECKING
PARK COMMUNITY FEDERAL CREDIT UNION	SECOND CHANCE CHECKING
PEACH STATE FEDERAL CREDIT UNION	FRESH START CHECKING
PINNACLE CREDIT UNION	FRESH START CHECKING
ROBINS FEDERAL CREDIT UNION	SECOND CHANCE CHECKING

IDAHO

SCENIC FALLS FEDERAL CREDIT UNION	SECOND CHANCE CHECKING

ILLINOIS

CATHOLIC & COMMUNITY CREDIT UNION	REBOUND CHECKING
FIRST AMERICAN BANK	FRESH START CHECKING
FIRST NATIONAL BANK AND TRUST COMPANY	RENEW CHECKING
GREAT LAKES CREDIT UNION	FRESH START CHECKING
MARQUETTE BANK RESTART CHECKING	
PRAIRIELAND FEDERAL CREDIT UNION	SECOND CHANCE CHECKING
ROCK VALLEY CREDIT UNION	BASIC CHECKING
SUBURBAN BANK & TRUST	FRESH START CHECKING

INDIANA

CENTRA CREDIT UNION	OPPORTUNITY CHECKING
DIAMOND VALLEY FEDERAL CREDIT UNION	FRESH START CHECKING
EVANSVILLE TEACHERS FEDERAL CREDIT UNION	OPPORTUNITY CHECKING
HERITAGE FEDERAL CREDIT UNION	SECOND CHANCE CHECKING
HORIZON BANK	FRESH START CHECKING
INTERRA CREDIT UNION	OPPORTUNITY CHECKING
ONE VISION FEDERAL CREDIT UNION	RISING STAR CHECKING
REGIONAL FEDERAL CREDIT UNION	FIRST STEP CHECKING
YOUR COMMUNITY BANK	NEW OPPORTUNITY CHECKING

IOWA

COLLINS CREDIT UNION	TAKE2 CHECKING
FEDERATION BANK	FRESH START CHECKING
GREATER IOWA CREDIT UNION	SECOND CHANCE CHECKING
NORTH IOWA COMMUNITY CREDIT UNION	FRESH START DEBIT

KANSAS

Bank/Credit Union	Checking Program
CENTRAL NATIONAL BANK	SECOND CHANCE CHECKING
UNITED CONSUMERS CREDIT UNION	SECOND CHANCE CHECKING
NATIONAL BANK OF KANSAS CITY	FRESH START CHECKING

KENTUCKY

Bank/Credit Union	Checking Program
THE CECILIAN BANK	CHOICE OPPORTUNITY CHECKING
CENTRAL BANK	CLEAN START CHECKING
CITIZENS UNION BANK	SECOND CHANCE CHECKING
EVANSVILLE TEACHERS FEDERAL CREDIT UNION	OPPORTUNITY CHECKING
FIRST UNITED BANK & TRUST COMPANY	FRESH START CHECKING
FNB BANK	SECOND CHANCE CHECKING
FORT KNOX FEDERAL CREDIT UNION	SECOND CHANCE CHECKING
HOME FEDERAL BANK	SQUARE ONE CHECKING
KENTUCKY TELCO FEDERAL CREDIT UNION	NEW START CHECKING
YOUR COMMUNITY BANK	NEW OPPORTUNITY CHECKING

LOUISIANA

Bank/Credit Union	Checking Program
NEIGHBORS FEDERAL CREDIT UNION	BASIC CHECKING
PELICAN STATE CREDIT UNION	SECOND CHANCE CHECKING
SOUTHWEST LOUISIANA CREDIT UNION	FRESH START CHECKING

MAINE

Bank/Credit Union	Checking Program
FIVE COUNTY CREDIT UNION	SECOND CHANCE CHECKING

MARYLAND

Bank/Credit Union	Checking Program
CENTRAL CREDIT UNION OF MARYLAND	RENEW CHECKING
CLEAR MOUNTAIN BANK	START FRESH CHECKING
SECURITY PLUS FEDERAL CREDIT UNION	REVIVE CHECKING

MASSACHUSETTS

Bank/Credit Union	Checking Program
ALDEN CREDIT UNION	NO BOUNDARIES CHECKING
TREMONT CREDIT UNION	SECOND CHANCE CHECKING
WASHINGTON SAVINGS BANK	REWARDS CARD CHECKING

MICHIGAN

Bank/Credit Union	Checking Program
CLARKSTON BRANDON COMMUNITY CREDIT UNION	FRESH START CHECKING
CREDIT UNION ONE	BASIC CHECKING
HORIZON BANK	FRESH START CHECKING
MARSHALL COMMUNITY CREDIT UNION	FRESH START CHECKING
MEMBERS FIRST CREDIT UNION	FRESH START CHECKING
MICHIGAN STATE UNIVERSITY FEDERAL CREDIT UNION	REBUILD CHECKING

MINNESOTA

Bank/Credit Union	Checking Program
MINNESOTA VALLEY FEDERAL CREDIT UNION	SECOND CHANCE CHECKING
PEOPLES COMMUNITY CREDIT UNION	SECOND CHANCE CHECKING
WESTCONSIN CREDIT UNION	FOUNDATIONS CHECKING

MISSISSIPPI

Bank/Credit Union	Checking Program
CITIZENS NATIONAL BANK	CLEAN SLATE CHECKING
GULF COAST COMMUNITY CREDIT UNION	SECOND CHANCE CHECKING
MAGNOLIA FEDERAL CREDIT UNION	OPPORTUNITY CHECKING
MUNA FEDERAL CREDIT UNION	FRESH START CHECKING

MISSOURI

Bank/Credit Union	Checking Program
ALLIANCE CREDIT UNION	FRESH START CHECKING
BANK OF KANSAS CITY	OPPORTUNITY CHECKING
CENTRAL BANK OF THE MIDWEST	FRESH START CHECKING
COLUMBIA CREDIT UNION	FRESH START CHECKING

Credit Mastery: Developing Aged Corporations

ELECTRO SAVINGS CREDIT UNION	FRESH START CHECKING
FIRST STATE COMMUNITY BANK	NEW OPPORTUNITY CHECKING
FOCUS BANK	FRESH START CHECKING
HEALTH CARE FAMILY CREDIT UNION	FRESH START CHECKING
MISSOURI CREDIT UNION	SMART START CHECKING
MONTGOMERY BANK MONTGOMERY	NEW START CHECKING
NATIONAL BANK OF KANSAS CITY	FRESH START CHECKING
ST. JOHNS BANK & TRUST	FRESH START CHECKING
ST. LOUIS COMMUNITY CREDIT UNION	SECOND CHANCE CHECKING
TOWN & COUNTRY BANK	OPPORTUNITY CHECKING
UNITED CONSUMERS CREDIT UNION	SECOND CHANCE CHECKING
UNITED CREDIT UNION	SECOND CHANCE CHECKING
VANTAGE CREDIT UNION	FRESH START CHECKING
WOOD & HUSTON BANK	START FRESH CHECKING

MONTANA

HELENA COMMUNITY CREDIT UNION	FRESH START CHECKING
VALLEY FEDERAL CREDIT UNION	OPPORTUNITY CHECKING

NEBRASKA

CENTRAL NATIONAL BANK	SECOND CHANCE CHECKING
WESTERN HERITAGE CREDIT UNION	FRESH START CHECKING

NEVADA

CLARK COUNTY CREDIT UNION	CHECK AGAIN CHECKING
ONE NEVADA CREDIT UNION	NEW START CHECKING
WESTSTAR CREDIT UNION	FRESH START CHECKING

NEW JERSEY

ATLANTIC FEDERAL CREDIT UNION	SECOND CHANCE CHECKING
CREDIT UNION OF NEW JERSEY	RIGHT TURN CHECKING
JERSEY SHORE FEDERAL CREDIT UNION	FRESH START CHECKING

NEW MEXICO

BANK OF ALBUQUERQUE	OPPORTUNITY CHECKING
LEA COUNTY STATE BANK	OPPORTUNITY CHECKING

NEW YORK

ALTERNATIVES FEDERAL CREDIT UNION	FRESH START CHECKING
FINANCIAL TRUST FEDERAL CREDIT UNION	SECOND CHANCE CHECKING
FULTON SAVINGS BANK	SECOND CHANCE CHECKING
GENESEE VALLEY FEDERAL CREDIT UNION	FRESH START CHECKING
UFIRST FEDERAL CREDIT UNION	SECOND CHANCE CHECKING

NORTH CAROLINA

AMERICAN PARTNERS FEDERAL CREDIT UNION	EZ 4 U CHECKING
CHARLOTTE METRO FEDERAL CREDIT UNION	FRESH START CHECKING

NORTH DAKOTA

CAPITAL CREDIT UNION	SECOND CHANCE CHECKING

OHIO

BUCKEYE STATE CREDIT UNION	SECOND CHANCE CHECKING
CHACO CREDIT UNION, INC.	SECOND CHANCE CHECKING
CHEVIOT SAVINGS BANK	CLEAN SLATE PERSONAL CHECKING
CINCINNATI CENTRAL CREDIT UNION	DIRECT STEP CHECKING
EATON FAMILY CREDIT UNION, INC.	SECOND CHANCE CHECKING
HOPEWELL FEDERAL CREDIT UNION	REBOUND CHECKING

INTERNATIONAL HARVESTER EMPLOYEE CREDIT UNION, INC. (IHECU) FRESH START CHECKING
KEMBA FINANCIAL CREDIT UNION   FRESH START CHECKING
KENT CREDIT UNION   FRESH START CHECKING
LORAIN NATIONAL BANK   BASIC CHECKING
MEMBERS TRUST FEDERAL CREDIT UNION   SECOND CHANCE CHECKING
SUN FEDERAL CREDIT UNION   FRESH START CHECKING
SUPERIOR FEDERAL CREDIT UNION   FRESH START CHECKING

OKLAHOMA
ALLEGIANCE CREDIT UNION   FRESH START CHECKING
BANK OF OKLAHOMA   OPPORTUNITY CHECKING
CITIZENS BANK OF EDMOND   FRESH START CHECKING
OKLAHOMA EDUCATORS CREDIT UNION   FRESH START CHECKING
OKLAHOMA EMPLOYEES CREDIT UNION   FRESH START CHECKING
TTCU THE CREDIT UNION   FRESH START CHECKING
WEOKIE (CREDIT UNION)   SECOND CHANCE CHECKING
WESTERN SUN FEDERAL CREDIT UNION   FRESH START CHECKING

OREGON
CONSOLIDATED COMMUNITY CREDIT UNION   SECOND CHANCE CHECKING
POINT WEST CREDIT UNION   FRESH START CHECKING

PENNSYLVANIA
ALLEGENT COMMUNITY FEDERAL CREDIT UNION FRESH START CHECKING
ERIE COMMUNITY CREDIT UNION   SECOND CHANCE CHECKING
MEADVILLE AREA FEDERAL CREDIT UNION   SECOND CHANCE CHECKING
SUN FEDERAL CREDIT UNION   FRESH START CHECKING
UTILITIES EMPLOYEES CREDIT UNION   GREEN LIGHT CHECKING
WEST BRANCH VALLEY FEDERAL CREDIT UNION SECOND CHANCE CHECKING

SOUTH CAROLINA
CAROLINA COLLEGIATE FEDERAL CREDIT UNION REBOUND CHECKING
CAROLINA TRUST FEDERAL CREDIT UNION   ENCORE CHECKING
GAFCU (GREATER ABBEVILLE FEDERAL CREDIT UNION)   FRESH START CHECKING
VITAL FEDERAL CREDIT UNION   FRESH START CHECKING

SOUTH DAKOTA
SENTINEL FEDERAL CREDIT UNION   RE-BUILDER CHECKING

TENNESSEE
FIRST NATIONAL BANK   CREDIT BUILDER ACCOUNT
GREATER EASTERN CREDIT UNION   NEW STAR CHECKING
HOLSTON METHODIST FEDERAL CREDIT UNION SECOND-CHANCE CHECKING
HOME FEDERAL BANK   SQUARE ONE CHECKING
SELECT SEVEN CREDIT UNION   SECOND CHANCE SHARE DRAFT
UT FEDERAL CREDIT UNION   NEW U CHECKING

TEXAS
AAFES FEDERAL CREDIT UNION   FRESH START CHECKING
ABILENE TEACHERS FEDERAL CREDIT UNION   RESTART CHECKING
ALLIED FEDERAL CREDIT UNION   FRESH START CHECKING
AMERICAN AIRLINES CREDIT UNION   ASCEND CHECKING
ASSOCIATED CREDIT UNION OF TEXAS   180 CHECKING
BANK OF TEXAS   OPPORTUNITY CHECKING
BAPTIST CREDIT UNION   SECOND CHANCE CHECKING
CHOCOLATE BAYOU COMMUNITY FEDERAL CREDIT UNION CLEAN SLATE CHECKING

FIRST SERVICE CREDIT UNION	FRESH START CHECKING
FORT WORTH CITY CREDIT UNION	INDEPENDENCE CHECKING
HOUSTON METROPOLITAN FEDERAL CREDIT UNION	FREEDOM 2ND CHANCE
KELLY COMMUNITY FEDERAL CREDIT UNION	SECOND CHANCE CHECKING
LAS COLINAS FEDERAL CREDIT UNION	SECOND CHANCE CHECKING
MEMBERS SOURCE CREDIT UNION	SELECT CHECKING
MEMBERS TRUST OF THE SOUTHWEST FEDERAL CREDIT UNION	START-UP CHECKING
MEMORIAL CREDIT UNION	NEW START CHECKING
NASCOGA FEDERAL CREDIT UNION	FRESH START CHECKING
NEIGHBORHOOD CREDIT UNION	FRESH START CHECKING
NORTH EAST TEXAS CREDIT UNION	FRESH START CHECKING
PEOPLES BANK	SECOND CHANCE CHECKING
POSTEL FAMILY CREDIT UNION	FRESH START CHECKING
PREMIER AMERICA CREDIT UNION	FRESH START CHECKING
PRESTIGE COMMUNITY CREDIT UNION	FRESH START CHECKING
RED RIVER CREDIT UNION	FRESH START CHECKING
RIO BANK	FRESH START CHECKING
SELECT FEDERAL CREDIT UNION	FRESH START CHECKING
SOUTHSIDE BANK	NEXT CHECKING
TARRANT COUNTY CREDIT UNION	FRESH START CHECKING
TEXAS BAY AREA CREDIT UNION	FRESH START CHECKING
TEXAS PEOPLE FEDERAL CREDIT UNION	OPPORTUNITY CHECKING
TRUWEST CREDIT UNION	OPPORTUNITY CHECKING
UNITED HERITAGE CREDIT UNION	CHOICE CHECKING
UNITY ONE CREDIT UNION	CLEAN START CHECKING
VELOCITY CREDIT UNION	ACCESS CHECKING

UTAH

AMERICAN UNITED FEDERAL CREDIT UNION	FRESH START CHECKING
CYPRUS CREDIT UNION	FRESH START CHECKING

VIRGINIA

FIRST NATIONAL BANK	SECOND CHANCE CHECKING
HEALTHCARE SYSTEMS FEDERAL CREDIT UNION	SECOND CHANCE CHECKING
MEMBER ONE FEDERAL CREDIT UNION	SMART CHOICE CHECKING
PORTALLIANCE FEDERAL CREDIT UNION	SMART CHOICE CHECKING
YOUR COMMUNITY CREDIT UNION	FRESH START CHECKING

WASHINGTON

MOUNTAINCREST CREDIT UNION	FRESH START CHECKING
SALAL CREDIT UNION	PATHWAY CHECKING

WEST VIRGINIA

FIRST NATIONAL BANK	SECOND CHANCE CHECKING
CLEAR MOUNTAIN BANK	START FRESH CHECKING
WEST VIRGINIA FEDERAL CREDIT UNION	FRESH START CHECKING

WISCONSIN

BREWERY CREDIT UNION	FRESH START CHECKING
DANE COUNTY CREDIT UNION	RELATIONSHIP BUILDER CHECKING
EDUCATORS CREDIT UNION	FRESH START CHECKING
FIRST NATIONAL BANK AND TRUST COMPANY	RENEW CHECKING
SCHNEIDER COMMUNITY CREDIT UNION	FRESH START CHECKING
TOMAHAWK COMMUNITY BANK	FRESH START CHECKING

WYOMING

GREATER WYOMING FEDERAL CREDIT UNION	FRESH START CHECKING
WYHY FEDERAL CREDIT UNION	SECOND CHANCE CHECKING
WYO CENTRAL FEDERAL CREDIT UNION	SECOND CHANCE CHECKING
VALLEY FEDERAL CREDIT UNION	OPPORTUNITY CHECKING

Credit Mastery: Developing Aged Corporations

MINUTES OF THE ANNUAL MEETING OF MEMBERS
OF
_____, LLC

The annual Meeting of Members of the above named Limited Liability Company was held on the date and time and at the place set forth in the written waiver of notice signed by all the members, fixing such time and place, and prefixed to the minutes of this meeting.

There were present at the meeting all of the members of the above named Limited Liability Company.

_____ _____
_____ _____
_____ _____

The meeting was called to order by _____ it was moved, seconded and unanimously carried that _____ act as Chairman and that _____ act as Secretary.

The Chairman then stated that all of the members were present.

The managing member presented his/hers annual report and, after discussion, the report was accepted and ordered filed with the Secretary.

The Chairman noted that it was in order to consider electing managing members for the ensuing year. Upon nominations duly made and seconded, the following were unanimously elected managing members of the Limited Liability Company, to serve for the ensuing year and until their successors are elected and qualified:

Managing Member:_____

Secretary: _____

Treasurer: _____

There being no further business to come before the meeting, upon duly made, seconded and unanimously carried, it was adjourned.

_____
            Secretary
Members:

_____ _____
_____ _____

CONSENT TO ACTION BY MEMBERS [MANAGERS]
of _____ , LLC WITHOUT A MEETING

By signing this document, the undersigned, who are all of the members [managers]_____ of_____, a[n]_____ limited liability company (the "Company"), consent to the taking of the following actions without a meeting of members [managers] in accordance with the terms of the Operating Agreement of the Company:

RESOLVED, that _____ is elected to serve as a manager of the Company for a term beginning on the date of this consent to action and ending at the next meeting of members of the Company called for the purpose of electing managers, or the manager's death, resignation, or removal, if earlier.

RESOLVED, that the Plan of Merger attached to this consent to action as Exhibit A is approved by the members of the Company, and the managers of the Company are authorized and directed to do all things necessary to complete the closing of the merger provided for in the Plan of Merger.

The actions taken will be effective when this Consent to Action has been signed by all members [managers] of the Company.

Date: _____   _____

Date: _____   _____

Date: _____   _____

Resolution to Authorize Sale/Leaseback transaction

WHEREAS, it is advisable for the Corporation to raise capital through a sale/leaseback of certain of its assets, be it:

RESOLVED, that the Corporation sell the following property: _____ to_____ for the price of_____, ($_____) and that concurrently the Corporation execute a lease for said property for a period of___years at a net annual rental not to exceed_____%, (percent) of the sales price, all in accord with generally prevailing sales/leaseback terms.

The undersigned hereby certifies that he/she is the duly elected and qualified Secretary and the custodian of the books and records and seal of_____ , a corporation duly formed pursuant to the laws of the state of_____ and that the foregoing is a true record of a resolution duly adopted at a meeting of the_____ and that said meeting was held in accordance with state law and the Bylaws of the above-named Corporation on , and that said resolution is now in full force and effect without modification or rescission.

IN WITNESS WHEREOF, I have executed my name as Secretary and have hereunto affixed the corporate seal of the above-named Corporation this day _____ , _____ of_____ .

Secretary

Resolution to Authorize Borrowing on a Line of Credit

WHEREAS, this Corporation desires to borrow money, be it:

RESOLVED, that the proper officers of this Corporation are hereby authorized to borrow from the_____ Bank, for and in behalf of this Corporation, a sum not to exceed_____ , (_____) on a promissory note maturing _____(____) days from the date hereof, to be signed by the proper officers of this Corporation, and to bear interest not to exceed the rate of_____ percent, (_____%) per annum, and with the additional privilege of renewing the balance of said loan at its maturity, for another period of_____(____) days, and the proper officers of this Corporation are hereby authorized and directed to sign any new or renewal note or notes required by_____Bank to carry out the provisions of this resolution, which new note or notes shall bear such rate of interest as shall be agreed upon between this Corporation and the_____ Bank at the time of such renewal or renewals.

The undersigned hereby certifies that he/she is the duly elected and qualified Secretary and the custodian of the books and records and seal of_____,a corporation duly formed pursuant to the laws of the state of_____ , and that the foregoing is a true record of a resolution duly adopted at a meeting of the_____ ,and that said meeting was held in accordance with state law and the Bylaws of the above-named Corporation on_____,and that said resolution is now in full force and effect without modification or rescission.

IN WITNESS WHEREOF, I have executed my name as Secretary and have hereunto affixed the corporate seal of the above-named Corporation this day ____,_____of_____.

Secretary

ISG3 – Credit Mastery - Aged Corporation With Credit Developers Manual

BOARD OF DIRECTORS' RESOLUTION APPROVING
MERGER WITH WHOLLY OWNED SUBSIDIARY

WHEREAS, the Board of Directors of _____ Corporation (hereinafter referred to as Corporation) determined said Corporation owns all stock of _____, Inc., which is a Corporation organized under the laws of the State of _____, and

WHEREAS, by merging _____, Inc., into said Corporation, it will be possible to gain operating efficiencies, it is hereby

RESOLVED, that said Corporation hereby merge with _____ Inc., and that after the merger is effected said Corporation shall be the Surviving Corporation and shall assume all of the debts and liabilities of both former Corporations and it is

FURTHER RESOLVED, that a special meeting of this Corporation's shareholders shall be called and held at the following time, date and place:

Time: _____

Date: _____

Location: _____

and it is hereby

FURTHER RESOLVED that the purpose of such special meeting shall be as follows:

(1) To vote upon the recommendation presented by the Board of Directors that the two Corporate entities be merged; and

(2) To approve a merger agreement between _____, Inc., and this Corporation.

The undersigned, _____, certifies that he or she is the duly appointed Secretary of _____ Corporation and that the above is a true and correct copy of a resolution duly adopted at a meeting of the directors thereof, convened and held in accordance with law and the Bylaws of said

ISG3 – Credit Mastery - Aged Corporation With Credit Developers Manual

Corporation on _____, and that such resolution is now in full force and effect.

IN WITNESS THEREOF, I have affixed my name as Secretary of _____ Corporation and have attached the seal of _____ Corporation to this resolution.

Dated: _____ _____

_____ Secretary

Seal:

ISG3 – Credit Mastery - Aged Corporation With Credit Developers Manual

AGREEMENT FOR PURCHASE AND SALE OF BUSINESS
(for Use to Sell Your Aged Corporations with Credit Lines when ready for sale)

This agreement is made on __/_____/_____, by _____, with his principal office located in _____ (address, city, state) ("Buyer"), and _____ of _____, Inc. located at _____ of (address, city, state) ("Seller").

ARTICLE I.
PURCHASE AND SALE
1.01. In consideration of the mutual promises and conditions contained in this agreement, Seller agrees to sell to Buyer, and Buyer agrees to purchase from Seller, on the terms, conditions, warranties and representations set forth in this Agreement:
(a) the business owned by Seller, being conducted, located _____, _____ ("the Business");
(b) all of the stock in trade, inventory, and merchandise of the Business as described in Exhibit "A" attached to this agreement;
(c) all of the fixtures, equipment, and other tangible assets of the Business as shown on attached Exhibit "B";
(d) any leasehold interest owned by Seller under the lease for the premises where the Business is located; and
(e) all the trade, business name, goodwill, and other tangible or intangible assets of the Business Exhibit "C".

ARTICLE II.
AMOUNT OF PURCHASE PRICE
2.01. The total purchase price to be paid by Buyer to Seller for all the properties, assets and rights of the Business described in this Agreement ("Purchase Price") shall be $_____.00.
2.02. The Purchase Price is allocated as follows:
$_____ Inventory
$_____ Fixtures & Equipment
$_____ Goodwill, Trade name & Other Tangible Assets
Total:$_____.00

ARTICLE III.
PAYMENT OF PURCHASE PRICE
3.01. The total Purchase Price of $_____.00 shall be paid as follows:

(a) $_____.00 has already been paid to Seller by Buyer;
(b) the sum of $_____.00 (from above selection for Down Payment) in cash, cashier's check

or equivalent, shall be paid when this Agreement is signed;
(c) the balance of the Purchase Price shall be paid by delivery from Buyer to Seller of a promissory note executed in favor of Seller by Buyer in the form attached as Exhibit "D". This note shall be secured by a Security interest on the assets of the Business.

ARTICLE IV.
CLOSING
4.01. The closing of the sale and purchase of the Business ("the Closing") shall take place located at _____, ___, _____, _____ , or at such other place and date as the parties may agree to in writing.
4.02. At the closing the Seller shall:
(a) deliver clear and marketable title and ownership to Buyer of all assets subject to this Agreement;
(b) execute the Bill of Sale attached as Exhibit "E" to this agreement;
(c) execute the Assignment of Assumed Name Certificate attached as Exhibit "F" to this agreement; and
(d) execute any other documents necessary to finalize this Agreement.
4.03. At the Closing the Buyer shall:
(a) pay all remaining moneys owed to Seller; and
(b) execute any other documents necessary to finalize this Agreement.

ARTICLE V.
REPRESENTATIONS, WARRANTIES, COVENANTS AND AGREEMENTS BY SELLER
5.01. Seller agrees and warrants and represents to Buyer that:
(a) the financial records for the Business, previously inspected by Buyer, contain a full and complete record and account of the financial affairs of this Business and truthfully set forth all liabilities, assets and other matters pertaining to the fiscal or financial condition of this Business through the date of inspection and furthermore, that there have been no material changes in the financial condition of this Business since that time except for transactions normal to this Business;
(b) Seller is the lawful owner of this Business and has good right and due authorization to sell it. At the time of signing this Agreement, Seller neither knows nor has reason to know of the existence of any outstanding claim or title, or interest, or lien in, to, or on this Business except as shown on the financial records of this Business inspected by Buyer;
(c) all fixtures and equipment sold pursuant to this Agreement are free and clear of any lien (including UCC financing statements) and/or debt unless otherwise set forth in a written statement from Seller to Buyer;
(d) Seller owes no obligations and has contracted no liabilities affecting this Business or which might affect the consummation of the purchase and sale described in this Agreement that are not shown on the financial records inspected by Buyer and that have not been expressly disclosed to Buyer;
(e) there are no taxes due and owing on account of Seller's operation of the Business for unemployment compensation, withholding tax, social security tax, sales tax, personal property tax, franchise tax, income tax, and other taxes of any nature, unless otherwise set forth in a written statement from Seller to Buyer;

(f) any accounts payable due and owing as of the Closing shall remain the responsibility of Seller and shall be paid promptly as they become due and payable;
(g) no litigation, actions or proceedings, legal, equitable, administrative, through arbitration or otherwise, including but not limited to lawsuits, claims or disputes with employees, customers and vendors, etc., are pending or threatened that might affect this Business, the assets being purchased, or the consummation of the purchase and sale described in this Agreement;
(h) Seller agrees to indemnify and hold Buyer harmless from any and all claims, causes of actions, damages, or debts, including legal fees, resulting from any actions, occurrences or events occurring prior to the Closing;
(i) all mechanical equipment sold pursuant to this Agreement is in good working condition; and
(j) Seller shall provide to Buyer ___ weeks of full-time training in the operations of the Business at Buyers location and expense. Each week shall be deemed consisting of __ business days and a ___ hour day. The __ week training period maybe divided into individual weeks as seen fit by Seller in order to achieve maximum results for Buyer. Seller will provide up to an additional _____ hours of telephone training over a period of ____ months.

ARTICLE VI.
REPRESENTATIONS, WARRANTIES AND AGREEMENTS BY BUYER

6.01. Buyer agrees and warrants and represents to Seller that Buyer will duly notify all authorities, suppliers, creditors, and/or other entities that Buyer is to be responsible for all liabilities associated with the operation of the Business, including without limitation withholding taxes, social security taxes, unemployment contributions, salaries, and purchases incurred after the Closing, and Buyer specifically agrees to assume such liabilities as of the Closing.

ARTICLE VII.
COMPLIANCE WITH BULK SALES LAW

7.01. At the Closing, Seller will deliver to Buyer a sworn list of all existing creditors of the Business.
7.02. By reason of this list Seller and Buyer agree that notice to creditors under the Bulk Sales law of Delaware will not be required and need not be given except in respect to any creditors named on this list.
7.03. Any such debt, unless otherwise provided for in this Agreement, is to be paid solely by Seller, and Seller does indemnify and hold Buyer harmless from any and all loss, expense, damage or liability, including counsel fees, that Buyer may incur or become subject to by reason of noncompliance with the Bulk Sales law.

ARTICLE VIII.
TRADE NAME, TELEPHONE NUMBER AND POST OFFICE BOX

8.01. Seller assigns to Buyer the exclusive right to use the trade or business name and Seller agrees not to use, or authorize others to use, this name or a similar name in the State of _____.
8.02. Seller agrees to allow Buyer to assume the Business telephone number, current advertising arrangements, including "Yellow Pages Advertising," and the Post Office Box, if any, currently used by the Business for a mailing address.

ARTICLE IX.
DELIVERY OF BOOKS AND RECORDS

9.01. All books, records, files, documents and papers, including customer lists and all records of the accounts of customers used in the operation of or relating to the Business shall be transferred and delivered to Buyer at the Closing.

9.02. All of these books, records, files, documents and papers shall be available to Seller at any reasonable time for any proper purpose, and Seller has the right to freely examine and to copy all such materials prior to closing.

ARTICLE X.
NON ASSUMPTION OF LIABILITIES

10.01. Unless otherwise expressly provided for in this agreement, the liabilities and obligations incurred by Seller prior to the Closing are not assumed by Buyer but continue as liabilities and obligations of Seller and shall be solely paid by Seller.

10.02. In the event Buyer is required to pay after the Closing any valid lien, debt, or expense incurred by Seller prior to the Closing Date, Buyer shall have the right to offset any such lien, debt, or expense actually paid by Buyer, which is the valid and legal obligation of the Seller, against any payment owed to Seller by Buyer.

ARTICLE XI.
INDEMNIFICATION OF SELLER

11.01. Buyer will indemnify and hold Seller and the property of Seller free and harmless from any and all claims, losses, damages, injuries and liabilities arising from or in connection with the operation of the Business after the Closing.

ARTICLE XII.
PRORATIONS

12.01. There shall be prorated between Seller and Buyer on the basis of 30 days per month as of 12:01 am Eastern Standard Time on the date of the Closing all property taxes, rent, insurance premiums, and utility bills, etc.

ARTICLE XIII.

13.01. After execution of this Agreement by the parties, default shall consist in the failure of either party to perform its respective obligations and duties and/or a breach of a warranty or covenant in this agreement.

13.02. In the event of default of Seller, Buyer is entitled to a refund of payments made for purchase up to closing date less Sellers administration costs.

13.03. In the event of default of Buyer, Seller is entitled to sell any and all assets including company for payment. All payments made for purchase up to closing date shall not be returned or refunded for any reason.

DEFAULT

ARTICLE XIV.
COSTS AND EXPENSES

14.01. All costs and expenses incurred in finalizing the purchase and sale described in this Agreement in the manner prescribed by this Agreement shall be paid by Buyer and Seller in the following manner:
(a) Buyer and Seller agree to jointly waive an attorney to prepare the Closing documents and be equally responsible for the attorney fees and expenses incurred in preparation of these documents. This sum shall be due and payable at Closing. Should either party retain an additional attorney to review the documents necessary for the transfer of the Business, the attorney fees so incurred shall be the responsibility of the party retaining the attorney.
(b) Any other Closing costs and expenses shall be paid at the Closing by the parties, Buyer and Seller, in equal proportions.

ARTICLE XV.
RESTRICTIVE COVENANTS

15.01. Should Seller violate any paragraph of this Article, any remaining amounts now due, or which shall become due, from Buyer to Seller shall not be considered paid in full.

ARTICLE XVI.
GENERAL AND ADMINISTRATIVE PROVISIONS

16.01. Parties Bound. This Agreement shall be binding upon and inure to the benefit of the Parties to this Agreement and their respective heirs, executors, administrators, legal representatives, successors and assigns.

16.02. Assignment. The Seller shall have the right to transfer or assign interest in this Agreement without the prior written consent of the Buyer.

16.03. Corporate Authority. If any party to this Agreement is a legal entity (partnership, corporation and/or trust), such party represents to the other that this Agreement, the transaction contemplated in this Agreement, and the execution and delivery hereof, have been duly authorized by all necessary partnership, corporate or trust proceedings and actions, including without limitation the action on the part of the directors, if the party is a corporation. Certified copies of such corporate or other resolutions authorizing this transaction shall upon request be delivered at the Closing.

16.04. Use of Pronouns. The use of the neuter singular pronoun to refer to the Parties described in this Agreement shall be deemed a proper reference even though the Parties may be an individual, a partnership, a corporation, or group of two or more individuals, partnerships or corporations. The necessary grammatical changes required to make the provisions of this Agreement apply in the plural sense where there is more then one party to this Agreement, and to either corporations, partnerships or individuals, males or females, shall in all instances be assumed as though in each case fully expressed.

16.05. _____ Law. This Agreement shall be subject to and governed by the laws of the State of _____. Any and all obligations or payments are due and payable in address given buy Seller and by Buyer.

16.06. Severability. If any provision of this Agreement should, for any reason, be held violation of any applicable law, and so much of this Agreement be held unenforceable, then the invalidity of such a specific provision in this Agreement shall not be held to invalidate any other provisions in this Agreement, which other provisions shall remain in full force and effect unless removal of the invalid provisions destroys the legitimate purposes of this Agreement, in which event this Agreement shall be canceled.

16.07. Entire Agreement. This Agreement represents the entire understanding of the Parties hereto. There are no oral agreements, understandings, or representations made by any party to this Agreement that are outside of this Agreement and are not expressly stated in it.

16.08. Notices. All notices or other communications required or permitted to be given pursuant to this Agreement shall be in writing and shall be considered as properly given if mailed from within the United States by first class mail, postage prepaid, and addressed as follows:

to Seller: _____, Inc, located at
_____

to Buyer:_____, located at
_____

Buyers EIN or SSN for transfer and assignment of Tax Payer Identification Number ____-___-_____

A party may change the address for notice by giving of such change to the other party in writing.

SIGNED, ACCEPTED, AND AGREED TO on __/___/____ by the undersigned parties, who acknowledge that they have read and understand this Agreement and the Attachments and Schedules to it and they execute this legal document voluntarily and of their own free will.

Respectfully submitted,

BY:_____
BUYER:_____
Signed: _____
BUYER:

BY:_____
SELLER:_____
Signed: _____
SELLER:

Exhibit "A"

All of the stock in trade, inventory, and merchandise of the Business

Exhibit "B"

All of the fixtures, equipment, and other tangible assets of the Business:

_____
_____
_____
_____
_____
_____
_____
_____
_____
_____
_____
_____

Computers:

_____
_____
_____
_____

Business Telephone System :

_____
_____
_____
_____

Exhibit "C"

Tangible and Intangible Assets

Credit Line: _____
Credit Line: _____
Credit Line: _____
Credit Line: _____
Credit Line: _____
Credit Line: _____
Credit Line: _____
Credit Line: _____
Credit Line: _____
Credit Line: _____
Credit Line: _____

Credit Card: _____
Credit Card: _____
Credit Card: _____
Credit Card: _____
Credit Card: _____
Credit Card: _____
Credit Card: _____
Credit Card: _____
Credit Card: _____
Credit Card: _____
Credit Card: _____

Lease: _____
Lease: _____
Lease: _____
Lease: _____
Lease: _____
Lease: _____
Lease: _____

Trademarks: _____
Patents: _____
Patents Pending: _____
Copyrights: _____

Exhibit "D".

Installment Note

$ _____.00 (Note)   _____ (Date)

For value received, the undersigned _____ ("Borrower"), _____ (Address), promises to pay to the order of _____, Inc. ("Lender"), the face value of the loan or note of $_____.00 at a monthly interest rate of ____% or annual interest rate of ___%, in monthly Installments as described further below, to a place designated by Lender, which may from time to time change per the written notice of Lender to Borrower, with the initial address being:
_____

Until the Loan or Note is due in full, for whatever reason, the unpaid principal and accrued interest shall be payable in monthly installments ("Installments"), payable on the __st (day) of each month ("Installment Due Date") of $ _____, and continuing until _____ ("Due Date"), at which time the remaining unpaid principal, interest, and other costs, if any, shall be due in full unless this Note was called earlier per the rights of the Lender under this Agreement.

Any payments on this Note shall first be applied against legal or collection costs until paid in full, as then may be due, and then against outstanding interest until paid in full, as then may be due, and finally applied to the outstanding principal balance.

1. Prepayment. The Borrower reserves the right to prepay this Note (in whole or in part) prior to the Due Date with no prepayment penalty.

2. Collection Costs, Attorney's Fees, and Late Charge. If any payment obligation under this Note is not paid when due, the Borrower promises to pay all costs of collection, including reasonable attorney fees, whether or not a lawsuit is commenced as part of the collection process, without protest of any kind, legal or otherwise. If the note remains unpaid for an additional 30 days after Lender gives demand, the Borrower shall be required to pay a ____% late charge based on the Installment amount. Each late Installment shall make another ____% due.

3. Default Events. If any of the following events of default occur, this Note and any other obligations of the Borrower to the Lender, shall become due immediately, without demand or notice:

1)   failure of the Borrower to pay the monthly installment payment on or before the Installment Due Date;

2)   death of the Borrower or Lender;

3)   filing of bankruptcy proceedings involving the Borrower as a Debtor;

4)	application for the appointment of a receiver for the Borrower;

5)	making of a general assignment for the benefit of the Borrower's creditors;

6) insolvency of the Borrower;

7) a misrepresentation by the Borrower to the Lender for the purpose of obtaining or extending credit.

4. Borrower Waivers. Borrower waives presentment for payment, protest, and notice of protest and nonpayment of this Note.

5. Additional Lender Rights. No renewal or extension of this Note, delay in enforcing any right of the Lender under this Note, or assignment by Lender of this Note shall affect the liability or the obligations of the Borrower. All rights of the Lender under this Note are cumulative and may be exercised concurrently or consecutively at the Lender's option.

6. Notices.

Any notice required by this Agreement or given in connection with it, shall be in writing and shall be given to the appropriate party by personal delivery or a recognized over night delivery service such as FedEx.

If to the Borrower: _____(name)
_____(address)
____-____-_____ Social Security Number

If to the Lender: _____(name)
_____(address)

7. No Waiver.

The waiver or failure of either party to exercise in any respect any right provided in this agreement shall not be deemed a waiver of any other right or remedy to which the party may be entitled.

8. Entirety of Agreement.

The terms and conditions set forth herein constitute the entire agreement between the parties and supersede any communications or previous agreements with respect to the subject matter of this Agreement. There are no written or oral understandings directly or indirectly related to this Agreement that are not set forth herein. No change can be made to this Agreement other than in writing and signed by both parties.

9. Governing Law.

This Agreement shall be construed and enforced according to the laws of the State of _____ and any dispute under this Agreement must be brought in this venue and no other.

10. Headings in this Agreement

The headings in this Agreement are for convenience only, confirm no rights or obligations in either party, and do not alter any terms of this Agreement.

11. Severability.

If any term of this Agreement is held by a court of competent jurisdiction to be invalid or unenforceable, then this Agreement, including all of the remaining terms, will remain in full force and effect as if such invalid or unenforceable term had never been included.

In Witness whereof, the parties have executed this Agreement as of the date first written above.

_____   _____
Borrower   Lender

Generic Investment Club Partnership Agreement

this should have a Form D filing accompanying this to be in compliance with SEC regulations.

_____, herewith form a general partnership to be known as the _____ Investment Club.

The partnership shall commence on _____ and shall continue for a period of five years, and then thereafter year for year, unless earlier terminated by this agreement.

Each partner shall on or before _____ make an initial capital contribution of $_____ (_____ & ___/100 dollars).

Partners shall be entitled to make additional capital contributions of at least $_____ (_____ & ___/100 dollars) at any regular meeting of the partnership, provided, however, that the no partners capital contribution shall at any time exceed _____ percent of the total capital of the partnership. Profits and losses shall be allocated to each partner in the same proportion as their capital account bears to the total capital of the partnership.

Books of account shall be created and maintained of all transactions of the partnership. A yearly report shall be presented to members of the results of the operation of the partnership. The books shall be open to examination by partners at all reasonable times. Upon a vote of the partners, an accounting firm may be appointed to perform bookkeeping or other services. It shall not be necessary for the affairs of the partnership to be audited; however, upon the vote of the majority of the partners an audit may be commissioned.

The partners shall by vote designate an official depository for funds. Withdrawals shall be made by the signature of partners.

The partnership shall hold regular meetings at least quarterly. The time and place for the holding of meetings shall be determined by vote of the partners. At the first regular meeting of the partners, the partners by majority vote shall elect a presiding officer who shall act as the Chairman of meetings. Meetings shall be held following Robert's Rules of Order to the extent that the same are appropriate. Thereafter, each year, a new Chairman shall be elected. Partners may appoint any other partner, and only another partner, to act as their proxy at any meeting which proxy shall be required to be in writing. Voting shall be by percentage of capital. No quorum shall be required for regular business; however, the following business shall require a quorum of the members, determined by percentage of capital at the beginning of the meeting:

(a) dissolution or other termination of the partnership;

(b) changes in the partnership agreement

All business of the partnership shall be determined by a simple majority of the partners present, except for dissolution or changes in the partnership, which shall require a 2/3 majority.

Upon the vote of a majority of the partners, a special meeting may be held upon 10 days prior notice.

Each partner shall have the right to participate in the management of the partnership including the selection of investments. No partner shall have the right or authority to bind or to obligate the partnership, except in accordance with a vote of the members.

No business shall be conducted with any brokerage, bank or other institution in which any partner has a financial interest, or is employed, except an interest as a shareholder in a publicly traded company which does not exceed 5% of the outstanding shares of the company, unless after a disclosure, the partners by majority vote assent thereto. All partners shall disclose such conflicts to the other partners.

The partnership interests herein may not be assigned or transferred without the approval of a majority of the partners. This approval shall not be unreasonably withheld.

New partners may be admitted upon a majority consent of the existing partners. The minimum initial capital contribution of a new partner shall be $_____
(_____& ___ /100 dollars). The amount necessary for such admission may be changed no more often than yearly upon motion and vote by the partners.

The total number of partners shall not exceed _____.

The partnership shall not purchase securities on margin.

The partnership may not purchase investments of the following types:
_____
_____
_____

The partners may designate a broker or brokers for trading of securities; however, the partnership may not grant discretionary trading authority to any brokerage.

A partner may withdraw by notice to the partnership. The partnership shall not be dissolved by such withdrawal unless the remaining partners determine not to continue the business of the partnership.

Upon withdrawal, a partner shall receive the value of their capital account as of the date of their withdrawal within 30 days, except that if the repayment of the capital account of any withdrawing partner shall require the liquidation of securities the repayment of the capital account may be postponed for no more than 14 additional days to allow a vote of the members to determine which securities to liquidate. Upon this withdrawal, the partner shall render a hold harmless agreement naming the Partnership and the individual partners for everyone's protection.

Upon the death, incapacity or legal disability of a partner, the same shall be deemed to be a withdrawal, and the disability of any partner, the capital account of the partner shall be repaid as is provided above.

1. Notices.

Any notice required by this Agreement or given in connection with it, shall be in writing and shall be given to the appropriate party by personal delivery or a recognized over night delivery service such as FedEx.

See Exhibit 1 for the name and addresses for each partner.

2. No Waiver.

The waiver or failure of either party to exercise in any respect any right provided in this agreement shall not be deemed a waiver of any other right or remedy to which the party may be entitled.

3. Entirety of Agreement.

The terms and conditions set forth herein constitute the entire agreement between the parties and supersede any communications or previous agreements with respect to the subject matter of this Agreement. There are no written or oral understandings directly or indirectly related to this Agreement that are not set forth herein. No change can be made to this Agreement other than in writing and signed by both parties.

4. Governing Law.

This Agreement shall be construed and enforced according to the laws of the State of _____ and any dispute under this Agreement must be brought in this venue and no other.

5. Headings in this Agreement

The headings in this Agreement are for convenience only, confirm no rights or obligations in either party, and do not alter any terms of this Agreement.

6. Severability.

ISG3 – Credit Mastery - Aged Corporation With Credit Developers Manual

If any term of this Agreement is held by a court of competent jurisdiction to be invalid or unenforceable, then this Agreement, including all of the remaining terms, will remain in full force and effect as if such invalid or unenforceable term had never been included.

In Witness whereof, the parties have executed this Agreement as of the date first written above.

_____   _____
Signature   Printed Name

_____   _____
Signature   Printed Name

_____   _____
Signature   Printed Name

_____   _____
Signature   Printed Name

If there are more partners, have them sign below as well.

_____
Date

Exhibit One:
Names & Addresses of all partners for contact purposes

_____   _____
Name   Address

_____   _____
Name   Address

_____   _____
Name   Address

_____   _____
Name   Address

Non-disclosure and Non-Circumvention Agreement, Relating to Negotiations

_____, Inc. et al, referred to as COMPANY, and _____, referred to as RECIPIENT, agree:

The parties intend to engage in substantive negotiations and discussions regarding certain new and useful business opportunities, trade secrets, economic studies, inventions and scientific information. And, furthermore, the parties intend to engage in substantive negotiations and discussions regarding the exploitation of technology related to items for which patents are pending;

The rights related to such information, generally regarding _____, shall be as follows:

COMPANY claims sole rights to the information, and COMPANY is willing to disclose the same, in consideration of the following covenants and agreements made by RECIPIENT:

RECIPIENT shall hold in confidence all of such information, and shall not directly or indirectly disclose to others such information. RECIPIENT shall protect such information from disclosure by reasonable means, including but not limited to at least the same level of security that the RECIPIENT uses for its most crucial proprietary and trade secret information.

Further, RECIPIENT agrees that it shall not use any advantages derivable from such information in its own business or affairs, unless the same is pursuant to an agreement with COMPANY.

Additionally, any improvements made as a result of the disclosure by RECIPIENT shall be disclosed to COMPANY, and, COMPANY further agrees to assign such improvements to COMPANY, and to execute any and all further documents as may be requested by COMPANY to perfect the rights of COMPANY to such information.

RECIPIENT shall be liable for the full amount of the loss by Company plus legal / collection fees from any / all transaction(s) regarding the business of _____ discussed or proposed in documentation for any violation of this agreement and will be subject to arbitration in the State of _____ by an approved party of the COMPANY.

The obligation of confidentiality shall not apply to any information which was already known to RECIPIENT at the time of disclosure; was already published at the time of disclosure, or, that was disclosed by a third party prior to the disclosure by COMPANY, provided that the third party had

authority to make such disclosure. RECIPIENT shall notify COMPANY, in writing, and at the earliest time possible, the information disclosed by RECIPIENT which RECIPIENT claims falls under the provisions of this paragraph related to earlier knowledge, publication, or prior disclosure.
The obligations of confidentiality will cease at such time when, COMPANY generally knows the information through no fault of RECIPIENT, or upon voluntary disclosure of such information to the public.

Upon request RECIPIENT shall return all tangible documents or documents disclosed by COMPANY which are subject to this agreement. Further, RECIPIENT upon such return shall destroy and all copies of the same and will, upon request of the COMPANY execute an affidavit of compliance in a form acceptable to the COMPANY verifying the destruction and full compliance with this agreement.

Dated: _____

_____ (et al)
_____ By Recipient

_____
_____, Inc. (et al)   By Company

ISG3 – Credit Mastery - Aged Corporation With Credit Developers Manual

SPECIAL SEMINAR TICKET COUPON WITH THIS BOOK!

SAVE $500 on The Credit Mastery Business Credit Seminar in FT Worth Tickets

Good 1/1/2024 thru 6/30/2025

You Must Bring this Book to Seminar!

With this page intact!

This Offer Can Not be Used with Any Other Offer(s) or Other Discounted Tickets (ie: Ticket for 2)

One Time Use Only

Coupon Approved by:

_____

Seminar and Date Attended:

_____

ISG3 – Credit Mastery - Aged Corporation With Credit Developers Manual

TERMS OF USE / PRIVACY POLICY / LEGAL YADA YADA / WE ARE PRINTING THIS SECTION WITH REMORSE – HOWEVER IN TODAY'S SOCIETY...

This section applies to ISG3, LLC, ISG3, ISG3.com website and ISG3 products et al.

Copyright 2015-2024 ISG All Rights Reserved. No part of this book / ebook may be altered in any form whatsoever, electronic or mechanical- including photocopying, recording, or by any informational storage or retrieval system without express written, dated, and signed
permission from ISG, the author.

Disclaimer and Legal Notices: This publication is for informational purposes only and the author, his agents, heirs, and assignees do not accept any responsibilities for any liabilities, actual or alleged, resulting from the use of this information. This publication is not "professional advice." The author encourages the reader to seek advice from a professional where any reasonably prudent person would do so. While every reasonable attempt has been made to verify the information contained in this publication/book /eBook, the author and his affiliates cannot assume any responsibility for errors, inaccuracies or omissions, including omissions in transmission or reproduction. Any references to people, events, organizations, or business entities are for educational and illustrative purposes only, and no intent to falsely characterize, recommend, disparage, or injure is intended or should be so construed. Any results stated or implied are consistent with general results, but this means results can and will vary. The author, author's agent(s), and assign(s), make no promises or guarantees, stated or implied. Individual results will vary and this work is supplied strictly on an "at your own risk" basis.

This content is only an expression of organization development components recommended to certain conditions and thereby is not lawful, bookkeeping nor economical advice. Please seek advice from with a CPA, Lawyer, Financial Adviser in these concerns.

The contents of this e-book/ document/ publication is for informational or entertainment purposes only. Before engaging in any actions you should consult a CPA or Attorney for accounting and legal advice.

Author, Publisher and distributors are not responsible for any profits, losses or debts incurred or accrued using the information presented within. We are not related to any credit reporting agency or lenders and give no endorsements either, the mention of FICO, DNB, Dunn & Bradstreet Trademarks are used in reference only.
This publication is strictly for use by initial purchaser and is not for redistribution or duplication in any form. By purchasing any of our products or services you are bound by these terms of use and when you access any of our sites it is the same as signing your name on the dotted line. If these terms of use are unreasonable to you then please do not purchase any of our products or services.

We do not promise, guarantee or imply that you, or that your use of our products and services will improve your operation, raise your profile or increase your revenues. As with any business, successful or unsuccessful use of our products will widely vary among our customers depending on many factors, including but not limited to, the customer's skill set, creativity, motivation, level of effort, individual expertise, capacity and talents, business experience, economic trends, banking trends, your cost structure and the market in which you compete.

We also know that many of our customers will not implement our program, much as many gym members won't go to the gym. We obviously cannot compel you to use our products. You obviously need to implement our products to find out for yourself the usefulness of what we are offering, and we sincerely hope that you do. Similarly, we provide no assurance that either improved operations or earnings in one month can be duplicated or approached in any other month.

For all these reasons, your purchase and use of our products and services should be based upon your own due diligence and judgment on how best to use our products. You should not view our company's products and services as responsible for any success or failure of your business; we provide a tool that you can use to try to improve the operation of your business.

ISG3 – Credit Mastery - Aged Corporation With Credit Developers Manual

Your decision to purchase and use our products and services should be based on your own due diligence, and not on any representation that we make to you. We will not be responsible for any success or failure of your business after you implement the products and services you receive from us.

ISG3 Offers:

    ISG3 Seminars Ft Worth, Atlanta, and Las Vegas
        Business Credit Mastery Seminar
        Open A Credit Union Seminar
        Buying Mortgage Notes and Bank Paper Seminar
        Going Offshore Seminar

    Certificate of Deposit Lease Program

ISG3 Credit Books:

    Credit Mastery Developing Aged Corporations
    Credit Mastery Business Credit – Personal Credit

Publications and seminar tickets are available through our website: www.isg3.com
ISG3, LLC

One on One Telephone Coaching Available

at 720-443-3317 with a reasonable hourly rate

We thank you again for your purchase and wish

the ultimate success for you and your company!